History of the Boilermakers' Society

Volume 2   1906–1939

History of the Boilermakers' Society

Volume 2   1906–1939

by J. E. Mortimer

London
GEORGE ALLEN & UNWIN
Boston   Sydney

George Allen & Unwin (Publishers) Ltd,
40 Museum Street, London WC1A 1LU, UK

George Allen & Unwin (Publishers) Ltd,
Park Lane, Hemel Hempstead, Herts HP2 4TE, UK

Allen & Unwin, Inc.,
9 Winchester Terrace, Winchester, Mass. 01890, USA

George Allen & Unwin Australia Pty Ltd,
8 Napier Street, North Sydney, NSW 2060, Australia

History of the Boilermakers' Society: Volume I, 1834–1906, was
published by Allen & Unwin in 1973. It is now out of print.

First published in 1982

British Library Cataloguing in Publication Data

Mortimer, J. E.
    History of the Boilermakers' Society.
2: 1906–1939
1. Boilermakers' Society – History
I. Title
331.88'12184'0941   HD6668.B6
ISBN 0-04-331085-0

Library of Congress Cataloging in Publication Data

Mortimer, J. E. (James Edward), 1921–
    History of the Boilermakers' Society.
Includes index.
CONTENTS: v. 1. 1834–1906. – v. 2. 1906–1939.
1. Amalgamated Society of Boilermakers, Shipwrights,
Blacksmiths and Structural Workers – History. I. Title.
HD6668.B6M67   331.88'121184'0941   74-168690
ISBN 0-04-906001-5 (v. 1)
ISBN 0-04-906002-3 (pbk.)

Set in 11 on 13 point Times by Grove Graphics, Tring
and printed in Great Britain
by Mackays of Chatham

Preface

This second volume covers many dramatic years in the history of the Boilermakers' Society. It was a period of boom and slump, of full employment and mass unemployment, of victory and defeat in negotiations, of strikes and lockouts, of improvements and worsened conditions and of political controversy. Earlier leaders and personalities of the trade union and labour movement, such as John Hill, Mark Hodgson, Ted Hill and Harry Pollitt, stride through its pages. At every crucial period in the history of the British labour movement the Boilermakers' Society played a significant role.

This second volume, like the first, was written primarily for the interest, information and, I hope, inspiration of the membership. For this reason it is not annotated with footnotes and source references. I set out deliberately not to let anything get in the way of the narrative. I hope the members when reading it will find the history as instructive as I did in writing it.

In writing the history I have tried to describe events objectively from a standpoint of trade union commitment. It may be argued that objectivity and commitment are incompatible. I do not think they are. Every work of recorded history is an essay in selection and every historian approaches his material with a stock of ideas. It is right, therefore, that I should state my own commitment. I am in favour of trade unionism and I believe it to be a very important force for social progress. Because of this commitment I believe I am better able to understand not only its strength but also the weaknesses which it has to overcome. I have tried to describe fairly the strengths and weaknesses which emerge in the history of the Boilermakers' Society.

I thank Hugh Clegg and John Hepplewhite for reading the manuscript and making suggestions for corrections and improvements. I remain solely responsible for the final text and for any errors of fact or judgement which it contains.

J. E. MORTIMER

Contents

Illustrations

Chapter 1

Social Reform and Industrial Struggle

By 1906 the Boilermakers' Society had become one of Britain's most influential unions. It was the main union organising the largest section of skilled workers in the shipbuilding and shiprepairing industries, and Britain was easily the world's leading shipbuilding power. Now, over three-quarters of a century later, it is useful to recall that in 1906 it was the common belief that Britain's imperial might rested on her "command of the seas". The British Empire was the largest and the most powerful in the history of the world. Shipbuilding was one of the vital industries, and some would argue *the* vital industry, that had made this possible.

The following table gives the number and gross tonnage of merchant vessels of 100 tons gross and upwards launched in various countries in 1906:

	Number	*Tons*
Great Britain and Ireland	886	1,828,343
Denmark	18	24,712
France	48	35,214
Germany	205	318,230
Holland	89	66,809
Italy	30	30,560
Japan	107	42,489
Norway	69	60,774
Sweden	23	11,579
United States – coast	192	169,358
Great Lakes	50	271,729

The world's total output was 2,919,763 tons. Thus Britain was building not far short of two-thirds of the world's output.

It was indicative of Britain's shipbuilding supremacy that in 1906 a new luxurious passenger liner was launched into the Tyne which was to become the fastest and most illustrious ship for many years to come. She was the *Mauretania*, with accommodation for 560 first class passengers, 500 second class, 1,400 third class and 800 crew. The standard of furnishing and fittings was the highest in the history of passenger liner construction. The *Mauretania* was to remain in service until the mid-1930s. She was the symbol of British shipbuilding at the peak of its power.

British supremacy was greatly aided by the development of turbine propulsion, due, above all, to the work of Charles Parsons. Turbine propulsion began to take the place of the reciprocating piston engine. The new system was developed on the Tyne. It was said of the new system that it had fewer mechanical troubles, was more economical and that ships fitted with it could travel faster.

In other fields too the skill of the members of the Boilermakers' Society was in demand. They were employed in railway workshops, on metal bridge-building and in the new developments with structural steelwork. Industry in the year 1906 was booming and all looked well for the future of the Society and its members. For the first time the total membership had exceeded 50,000 – at the end of the year the number was 52,056 – and membership contributions amounted to nearly £173,000 for the year. This also was a record figure and was not exceeded until the immediate pre-war boom year of 1913.

Profound changes were, however, already taking place to disturb the future. New competitors were emerging to challenge British supremacy, the British economy was not as sound as it appeared to many and the pattern of British politics was being reshaped.

A NEW GOVERNMENT

In 1906 a Liberal Government was elected pledged to a policy of social reform. Labour representation in Parliament was also substantially increased. Twenty-nine members of the Labour Representation Committee were elected and became the new Labour

Party. On many issues they were supported by the miners' group of
fourteen Members, who were still outside the LRC, and by a
number of Members who had been elected as 'Lib-Labs'. Trade
unionists looked to the new Government to restore their rights
following the decision of the law lords in the House of Lords in the
Taff Vale case in 1900.*

In the first volume of this history an account was given of the
campaign leading to the passing of the Trade Disputes Act 1906.
When this new legislation was first proposed in Parliament by the
newly-elected Government it fell short of the demands of the trade
union movement. Instead it followed fairly closely recommendations
made by a Royal Commission which had been established in 1903
by the previous Conservative Government. The Liberal Government's initial proposals were strongly resisted by the unions who
were able to count on the support of the newly-elected group of
Labour Members of Parliament. In face of this pressure and the
known attitude of many Liberal back-benchers the Liberal Government withdrew their proposals and accepted very largely the suggestions of the unions. A substantial number of Liberal Members
of Parliament had given pledges during the General Election
campaign that they would vote in favour of the protection of trade
union rights.

The Trade Disputes Act 1906 removed the doctrine of civil conspiracy from trade disputes. Secondly, the new Act gave a wide
definition of a 'trade dispute'. The significance of this wide definition
was that it embraced sympathetic strike action by workers not
directly involved in a dispute with their own employer. Thirdly, the
Act gave protection for peaceful picketing in a trade dispute 'at or
near a house or place where a person resides or works or carries
on business or happens to be'. Fourthly, the Act removed liability
for inducing breaches of contracts of employment in contemplation
or furtherance of a trade dispute. It also removed liability for
actions which interfered with the trade, business or employment of
some other person, providing always that the action was in contemplation or furtherance of a trade dispute. Finally, the Act
established the general immunity of trade union funds from liability
for certain unlawful acts of members, servants or agents. It was
this particular section of the Act which reversed the judgement in

* See Chapter 12 in Volume 1.

the Taff Vale case in which it had been held that a union was liable for certain acts done by its members in the course of their employment.

SOCIAL REFORM

Between 1906 and 1910 the Liberal Government introduced numerous other measures of social reform. In 1906 provision was made for the feeding of school children by local education authorities, and a Workmen's Compensation Act greatly extended the compensation rights of workers. Money was also voted for relief work for the unemployed. In the following year an Education Act introduced school medical inspection. In 1908 Parliament established the principle of old age pensions and passed an Act granting the miners' claim for an eight-hour day. This was followed in 1909 by the passing of a Housing and Town Planning Act, a Trade Boards Act to deal with wages in sweated industries, a Labour Exchanges Act to help unemployed workers in certain trades, and a new Fair Wages Clause to help trade unionists establish 'fair' wages when employed on public contracts.

In 1910 the Liberal Government was challenged on its budget by the hereditary House of Lords. Two General Elections were fought in 1910 and on both occasions the combined Liberal and Labour vote significantly exceeded the vote for the Conservatives. Nevertheless, the number of Liberal Members of Parliament was much reduced in comparison with 1906 when the Liberals had a landslide victory. After the two General Elections of 1910 the Liberal Government continued with further measures including the National Insurance Act, providing for health and unemployment insurance, a Shops Act, which granted a half holiday for employees, and, in 1912, a Coal Mining Minimum Wage Act.

There was a number of factors which contributed to this unprecedented surge of social reform. One was the pressure exerted by the trade union movement and the growing influence of the political labour movement. The 1906 General Election had seen the first significant group of successful Labour candidates. In many constituencies trade unionists had also secured pledges in favour of reform from Liberal candidates and even from a number of Conservatives. In 1906 Labour secured nearly 6 per cent of the total vote. Some four years later, despite the fall in the number of elected Liberal Members, Labour increased its share of the vote to more than 7 per cent.

The new-found political strength of the labour movement had a direct effect on the thinking of some of the ruling circles of society. Social reform was seen as an alternative to social unrest. There was already the example of Germany, where Bismarck had introduced a number of social reforms not because he was a liberal but because he was an anti-socialist. The amelioration of social conditions was seen as an antidote to revolutionary agitation. The German Bismarkian reforms had aroused considerable interest among influential people in Britain.

Some of the top people were also concerned about the efficiency of the British economy and were becoming disturbed at the indications that Britain might fall behind other leading industrial powers. During the Boer War for example it had been revealed that many of the recruits for the British Army were of a deplorably low physical standard. Signs were already beginning to accumulate that Germany was surpassing Britain in national economic strength. In these circumstances it was felt that the poor physical condition of many industrial workers, and particularly of their children, was undermining British economic strength.

Finally there was a number of influential people who felt the need for social reform because they were disturbed and indeed shocked by the deficiences of the society in which they were living. They felt it wrong that children should go without the necessary food for reasonable health or should be denied shoes and clothing. They were compassionate too about the welfare of the unemployed at a time when there was no state unemployment benefit. Similarly, they were deeply concerned about the welfare of elderly workers who finished their days in poverty because of the absence of any kind of old age pension.

All these separate but related influences helped to motivate and shape the programme of social reform initiated by the Liberal Government in the years between 1906 and the outbreak of the First World War. The Boilermakers' Society played its part in the effort of the trade union and labour movement to press for and to support the social reform programme. The opposition of the

Conservatives had to overcome, and at times elements within the Liberal Party itself threatened the progress of the programme. Unfortunately the reactionary opponents of social reform were able to take advantage of public dissatisfaction caused by unemployment. This was one of the main causes of the decline in Liberal support between 1906 and 1910.

At the beginning of 1907 nearly 5,800 members of the Boilermakers' Society out of a total membership of about 52,000 were unemployed. This number fell to slightly under 3,000 by the middle of the year but increased again towards the end of the year to more than 6,500. At the 1906 Trades Union Congress a resolution had been carried urging that in view of the large number of unemployed efforts should be made to limit the amount of overtime worked by trade unionists.

Following the Congress the Parliamentary Committee of the TUC held a conference of engineering, metal and shipbuilding trade unions to consider what might be done to limit overtime. This conference was held in London in March 1907 and was attended by representatives of twenty-five trade unions with a total membership of nearly 350,000. Resolutions were carried at the conference calling for a reduction in the normal hours of labour, the abolition of overtime wherever possible and negotiations within the engineering and shipbuilding industries with a view to achieving these objectives. At the 1907 TUC a further resolution was carried reaffirming the recommendations that a limit should be imposed on the amount of overtime worked by trade unionists. The Boilermakers' Society, however, found little response from employers to their suggestions for the control of overtime by joint agreement.

At the beginning of 1907 the TUC opened a campaign to press the Government to introduce old age pensions. The need for pensions had been confirmed by Congress for many years. In a circular to all affiliated unions the TUC said

the facts are of such a nature as should stimulate all workmen to press forward this great reform, and are also of such a nature as to constitute a blot upon the character of the nation. Half a million old people over 65 years of age are dependent on charity or Bumbledom for the ordinary necessaries of life . . . and as you know the honest poor have a horror of the workhouse.

The General Council said that if the principle of granting pensions was right for the army officer, the civil servant and the statesman, it was equally so for the soldier of labour. They urged that trade unionists should assist the efforts of Labour Members of Parliament to secure the immediate introduction of old age pensions. In March the Boilermakers' Society wrote to all branches urging that resolutions should be forwarded to their respective Members of Parliament supporting the action of the Labour Party in its demand for immediate old age pensions. Branches were also asked to send a copy of the letter to the Chancellor of the Exchequer.

In the September 1907 issue of the monthly report of the Boilermakers' Society an article was published contrasting the income of old people in Britain with the income of the rich. It pointed out that in 1901, according to the census of that year, there were more than 1,200,000 people of 70 years of age and upwards and more than 2,000,000 over 65 years of age. A pension of 5s per week would have required an annual sum of £15,000,000 if paid to all of 70 and over, or £26,000,000 if paid to all of 65 years of age and over. The article pointed out that a grant of £50,000 had recently been voted by the Government to Lord Cromer. The journal of the Boilermakers' Society said that the Government 'which declares it has no money for the workers can find heaps of money for its rich favourites'.

PARLIAMENTARY CANDIDATES

In the early part of 1907 the Boilermakers' Society decided by ballot vote to select two representatives to constitute a panel of parliamentary candidates. These candidates were then to be available for selection by constituency labour representation committees. On the first ballot John Hill was elected and on the second ballot James Conley narrowly defeated J. H. Jose. John Hill was probably the most militant and left-wing of the then full-time officials of the Boilermakers' Society. He was a district delegate in Scotland. James Conley had fought the Kirkdale division of Liverpool at the 1906 General Election.

In the early autumn of 1907 there was a by-election at Kirkdale. Local Labour opinion favoured the re-adoption of James Conley. This placed the Boilermakers' Society in some difficulty because

7

John Hill had been put at the top of the poll for the Society's panel of candidates. The Executive Council felt they had no alternative but to ask the local Labour committee in Kirkdale to adopt John Hill. The dilemma was put to James Conley and he, generously, accepted the decision of the Executive Council. This difficulty led the Society to decide that, for the future, members of the panel of candidates should be of equal standing and that constituencies should then be free to choose from the panel.

The labour movement in Kirkdale adopted John Hill as their candidate but unfortunately there were religious and political divisions within the movement which reduced the effectiveness of the ensuing election campaign. The Labour Party found it extremely difficult to find premises for a campaign headquarters and John Hill was bitterly attacked by anti-socialists in the constituency. He wrote afterwards that 'according to my opponents I was an atheist; I was going to break up the marriage tie and destroy the home life. I was going to take away the liberties of the people and reduce them all to a state of servitude . . .' The Labour Party were defeated in the by-election.

A THREATENED LOCKOUT

In August 1907 the Society was threatened with a national lockout by the Shipbuilding Employers' Federation. The threat arose from a dispute at the Walker shipyard of Armstrong Whitworth where the management had put apprentice platers to do the work of caulkers. The district delegate of the Society tried on four successive days to persuade the management to resolve the issue by negotiation but in the meanwhile to follow past practice and remove the apprentices from the work they were doing. These efforts were unsuccessful. The firm were later supported in their attitude by the Shipbuilding Employers' Federation. The caulkers then went on strike.

On 16 August the Shipbuilding Employers' Federation gave notice to the Boilermakers' Society that unless there was a return to work at the Walker yard of Armstrong Whitworth all members of the Society employed in federated shipyards would be discharged. The notice was to take effect from 24 August 1907. In reply to this notice the General Secretary of the Boilermakers' Society stated that the Society's district delegate had tried unsuccessfully for four days to resolve the issue by negotiation and that this effort had been made before the strike began. The Society's letter was conciliatory and said that if the Federation would agree to inquire into the dispute the Society would instruct its members to resume work. In the meanwhile the Society instructed its members in all shipyards to cease overtime. Special branch meetings were called for 22 August. No firm assurances were received from the employers but discussions were not refused providing the men at Walker returned to work. An instruction to end the strike was then issued by the Executive Council.

The caulkers at Armstrong Whitworth's yard refused to carry out the instructions of the Executive Council and remained on strike. The Executive Council then sent a letter to all branches saying that if the lockout took place 'it would entail a weekly expenditure which it is utterly impossible for us to meet'. At least 25,000 men would be affected by the lockout. The Executive Council went on to say that 'it would mean a collapse of the struggle in its very early stages and spell ruin both morally and financially to the Society'. Members were asked to vote at special branch meetings in favour of reinforcing the Executive Council's instruction that the caulkers at Walker shipyard should return to work immediately.

Voting in the branches was in favour of the policy of the Executive Council. By 8,341 votes to 2,903 the branches voted for an immediate resumption of work. Immediately before the special branch meetings were held on 22 August the Executive Council had summoned a conference of representatives of district committees, together with district delegates and Executive Council members, to consider the threatened national lockout. The delegates to the conference were well aware that the mood among the membership was against a national dispute. The conference agreed that a delegation from the Society should meet the Shipbuilding Employers' Federation on the day before the lockout notice was due to take effect.

'RIGHT TO MANAGE'

At the conference the Shipbuilding Employers' Federation called not only for the ending of the strike at Walker but also for the acceptance of a procedure guaranteeing the 'right to manage'. The Boilermakers' Society decided that because of unemployment and their weak financial position they were in no position to take up the challenge. Provisional agreement was reached on the text of a new procedure for the industry. It represented a significant retreat by the Society. The agreement said that the Society withdrew from the position taken up by its members at the Walker yard of Armstrong Whitworth and, in addition, withdrew from positions taken by members in three other yards, two of them in Glasgow and one in Hartlepool.

The first clause of the provisional agreement said that there should be no stoppage of work before negotiations had taken place, first at yard level, then at local level and finally at national level between the Executive Board of the Federation and the Executive Council of the Society. According to the agreement it could be held that the Society's members were required to remain at work and to take their grievance through procedure even when conditions were changed by the employer.

The second clause in the provisional agreement said that there should be no interference with 'the working of such overtime as may be necessary'. The third clause said that journeymen should not be penalised by the Boilermakers' Society for carrying out their engagements with their employers during their apprenticeship. The meaning of this clause was that even if apprentices were put on 'black' work during their apprenticeship they were not to be penalised by the Society when their apprenticeship came to an end.

The final two clauses in the agreement said that there should be a further conference between the two sides to arrive at a permanent agreement and that all men who were then on strike should resume work immediately. Every representative of the Society attending the conference was required to indicate that he had accepted the provisional agreement and that he would recommend it and would do his utmost to secure confirmation of it by the Society's membership. In return for this undertaking the Federation agreed to withdraw the lockout notices. There could be no doubt that the terms of this provisional agreement represented a victory for the shipbuilding employers.

Even though the membership had voted strongly in favour of the instruction to the men at Walker to end their strike there was dismay at what was seen by many as the capitulation of the Society to the shipbuilding employers. There were indications of dissent from many areas. It was decided to put the terms of the Edinburgh provisional agreement to a ballot of the membership. The result of the ballot was a shock to the Executive Council: 2,215 members voted in favour of the agreement and 3,667 against.

The decision of the membership to reject the Edinburgh agreement was sent to the Shipbuilding Employers' Federation in a letter dated 13 September 1907. Four days later a reply was received from the Federation stating that the employers were not prepared to resume negotiations until the agreement was ratified by the membership. They gave notice that members of the Boilermakers' Society would be locked out from federated shipyards from 5 October.

After receiving this second notice of a national lockout the Executive Council of the Society decided that further meetings should be held in every branch. This time a special campaign of persuasion was mounted. Great emphasis was placed upon the financial weakness of the Society and the existing commitment to pay benefit to thousands of unemployed members. The Executive Council issued a circular strongly urging all members to accept the advice of the representatives at the Edinburgh conference by voting for the provisional agreement. Every effort was made to get a mass turn-out at the summoned branch meetings. On this occasion the voting in the branches was very much higher: 11,109 members voted for the agreement and 7,553 against. The total vote of 18,662 was a record for the Society. The majority in favour of the agreement was sufficient to stop a large scale revolt but it could not be regarded as providing overwhelming endorsement for the Executive Council.

In the annual report for 1907 the General Secretary said that the Society had been humiliated. It had been coerced by two threatened national lockouts. He complained of the industrial unrest of the time and suggested that it could be minimised by the adoption of new methods. He was 'firmly convinced that industrial peace is impossible without a law of compulsory conciliation and arbitration'. Contention, he said, upon piecework prices, demarcation and other minor matters was inevitable. These issues should be left to the employers and unions to settle within a fixed period. If there was no settlement then there should be compulsory arbitration.

The two threatened lockouts of 1907 represented a determined bid by the employers to regain managerial control over work practices. At one of the conferences held between the Shipbuilding Employers' Federation and the Boilermakers' Society the chairman of the Federation said:

> I don't think there is any manager who can propose the slightest alteration in work and in working conditions in the various yards without their action having to be approved by the Boilermakers' Society. Well now, employers have made up their minds that that condition of things must come to an end. There is no trouble, gentlemen, with any other Society but yours.

In relation to apprentices the General Secretary of the Society pointed out that apprentices were being put to work on jobs performed by men on strike. The chairman of the Shipbuilding Employers' Federation replied 'Yes, Mr Cummings, but even if what you say is true, were not these boys endeavouring to make themselves proficient in their trade . . . ?'

Shortly after the acceptance of the provisional Edinburgh agreement the Shipbuilding Employers' Federation submitted to the Society their proposals for a permanent agreement. The proposals set out a procedure for negotiations on lines similar to those contained in the provisional agreement. No stoppage of work was to take place until the procedure had been exhausted. The proposed permanent agreement also contained provisions relating to wages, piece-work prices, overtime, the employment of apprentices and disputes. On wages it was suggested that neither side should give notice of a general alteration in wages until six months after the date of the last alteration, and no general alteration was to exceed 5 per cent on piece-work prices or on time rates. Where there was a dispute about piece-work prices the employer was to give a temporary decision and work was to proceed on the basis of this decision. Members of the Society who wanted to challenge the employer's decision were required to remain at work and to invoke the negotiating procedure. On overtime it was suggested that the total amount should not exceed thirty-two hours per man in any four weeks but that allowance should be made for time lost through sickness, absence with leave or enforced idleness. An exception was, however, to be made for 'overtime necessary on account of breakdown, repairs, replacements, alterations for the employers or their customers, trial trips and repairs to ships, urgency and emergency'. The Society was required not to penalise anyone because an apprentice carried out the instruction of his employers (this was another way of saying that apprentices could be required to do the work of men on strike). The Federation maintained in the proposed agreement that they should have freedom of action in the event of any stoppage of work either in contravention of the agreement or after the procedure had been exhausted.

The events of 1907 evoked considerable criticism within the Society. The most serious outbreak was on the Clyde where an unofficial vigilance committee was established. The vigilance committee was very critical of the Executive Council. Towards the end of the year the Executive Council ordered the disbandment of the so-called vigilance committee and instructed branches not to discuss any circular sent out by the committee.

The Boilermakers' Society submitted a number of amendments to the employers' proposals for a permanent agreement for the industry. On the important issue of piece-work prices the Society suggested that if there was a dispute about a piece-work price there should not be a stoppage of work but that the workmen involved should be entitled to 'draw whatever amount it has been the custom of the firm to pay under the circumstances, or the disputed job can be done at rates agreed upon between the firm's officials and the district delegate'. Negotiations would then continue for the determination of a permanent price or rate. On the working of overtime the Society suggested that it should be optional for a workman to work two evenings per week, but that if a firm considered that more overtime was necessary the matter should be discussed between the employer and the district committee of the Boilermakers' Society.

The shipbuilding employers were in no mood to make concessions. Unemployment was rising and the employers were by now pressing for wage reductions. They were in no hurry to replace the

Edinburgh agreement which already gave them much of what they wanted.

WAGES

In the spring of 1907 a number of branches of the Society on the north-east coast had requested the Executive Council to submit a claim for a general increase in wages in shipbuilding. The Executive Council convened a meeting of branch representatives which favoured the submission of a claim. It was decided, perhaps rather rashly, to give one month's strike notice to the employers in support of a claim for an increase of 5 per cent on piece rates and 1s 6d per week on time wages. In June the Tyne Shipbuilders' Association rejected the claim and pointed to the depressed state of the shipbuilding industry. This reply was submitted to a conference of branch representatives who agreed to suspend the application for a wage increase. The branch representatives were aware of the fall in the number of orders received by firms on the north-east coast. By September the Society was still hesitant to proceed with the claim. Instead it was decided to ask other unions in the shipbuilding industry to join with the Society in pressing for a general increase in wages. This was really a way of delaying action and shifting responsibility to others.

Within a matter of weeks the situation had changed. It was now the turn of the employers to press for an alteration in wages. In a letter dated 2 December the Shipbuilding Employers' Federation gave notice of a 5 per cent reduction in piece rates and a 1s 6d per week reduction in time rates in shipyards on the Tyne, Tees, Hartle-pool, Barrow, Birkenhead and Hull. They also gave notice of a farthing per hour reduction in Scotland. These reduced wages were to take effect on 8 January 1908.

The Boilermakers' Society replied the following day protesting strongly against the action of the employers in giving notice of the pay reduction immediately before Christmas. The Federation rejected the Society's protest. Negotiations then took place on 11 December. The Federation refused to extend the notice of a wage reduction and the Society's representatives decided to submit the employers' notice to the branches.

At about the same time the Boilermakers' Society received notice of a reduction in piece rates and time wages from the north-east coast engineering employers. Shortly afterwards a similar notice was received from the Clyde engineering employers.

Representatives of the Boilermakers' Society met on the evening of Boxing Day 1907 to consider the ultimatum submitted by the employers, and in negotiations on the following day offered to recommend to the membership a settlement providing for 2½ per cent reduction in piece rates, a shilling per week reduction off time rates of 34s 6d and over, and 6d per week reduction off time rates under 34s 6d. The employers refused this offer and refused also to submit the dispute to arbitration. Further negotiations took place and the employers offered to make two concessions from their original demand. They agreed to defer the date of the wage reductions until 22 January and they agreed also that there should be no reduction in Scotland.

The Society decided to submit this revised demand from the employers to a ballot vote of the membership. They strongly recommended the membership to accept. The Executive Council said 'we wish to impress upon you the impossibility of fighting so gigantic a struggle successfully in the winter without plenty of ammunition in the shape of money, and we frankly admit it is impossible to pay dispute benefit . . .' They went on to say that to call a strike of some 20,000 men would be madness. It would, they said, mean defeat and disaster.

Following similar negotiations with the engineering employers the Society agreed to recommend acceptance of pay reductions amounting to 2½ per cent off piece rates, 1s per week off time rates of 26s and over and 6d per week off time rates of 22s and above and under 26s. The reduction was to take effect from the first full pay week in February 1908. In the ballot of the membership the Executive Council put the question not as for and against the proposed wage reductions but as for and against a strike of resistance. The result showed a comfortable majority against a strike: 6,083 members voted against and 2,168 voted for a strike. The wage reductions were accepted.

One of the lessons drawn from the humiliation suffered by the Boilermakers' Society was that much greater unity was needed between all engineering and shipbuilding workers irrespective of the union to which they belonged. The General Secretary of the Society, D. C. Cummings, said in his annual report for 1907 that in shipbuilding and engineering there were two powerful federations of employers, 'well organised, alert, and active in pursuit of what they conceived to be their special interest'. In contrast there were some thirty trade unions in the two industries, each having its own rules, usages and customs. The shipbuilding and engineering trade union federation was, he said, 'an imperfectly organised body'. For years it had been dealing with demarcation squabbles but from its very inception it had failed to promote trade union unity.

The General Secretary of the Boilermakers' Society also called for new ways of resolving disputes. He urged that there should be compulsory conciliation and arbitration when normal negotiations had been exhausted. He also urged that there should be 100 per cent trade unionism in all federated firms.

INADEQUATE RESERVES

With the growth of unemployment in the winter of 1906–7 it became ever clearer to the Executive Council that the finances of the Society were inadequate. A lengthy special financial report was published and circulated to the membership in May 1907. It said that unless the financial position of the Society was greatly improved the employers would 'take full advantage' of the Society's weakness. Those who refused to help to improve the finances were, said the Executive Council, playing into the hands of the employers.

The report prepared by the Executive Council tabulated the amount of money sent by each branch to the head office of the Society and the amount of money sent by the head office to each branch for the payment of various benefits. It revealed that over the previous ten years no fewer than seventy branches had received more money from the head office than they had remitted to it. In other words, these seventy branches had made no contribution to the administrative expenses of the Society. The subscriptions which they had collected had not even been sufficient to cover the benefits paid to branch members. The Executive Council went on to say that of these seventy 'insolvent' branches more than thirty had been 'insolvent' for more than twenty years. Moreover, the whole of the

Executive electoral district of Lancashire, including big branches in Birkenhead, Liverpool and Manchester, had paid out more in benefits over the previous ten years than they had received in subscriptions. The Executive Council said that the Lancashire electoral district was in a most deplorable condition.

Between 1902 and 1906 the funds of the Society had fallen from £415,000 to £317,000, representing a fall per member from £8 11s 7d to £6 1s 9d. The report drew attention to the biggest liabilities on the funds of the Society; they were for unemployment benefit, sickness benefit and superannuation benefit. The payment of superannuation benefit was imposing an increasing burden on the Society's funds. Ten years earlier it had cost £6,703 a year. At the close of 1906 it was nearly five times as great and the Executive Council found it impossible to calculate what the cost would be in a further ten years' time.

The Executive Council said that urgent action had to be taken. They did not propose, however, to call together the delegates of the General Council because they felt that this would itself add an unnecessary cost to the Society. Instead they proposed various changes in benefits which they submitted for ballot vote by the membership. They proposed that a levy of 6d per quarter should be paid by all first class members to supplement the funds available for superannuation purposes and that the scale of benefit should be reduced. The proposed new scale was from 7s per week after thirty years' membership to 10s per week after forty years' membership. As an alternative the Executive Council suggested that if superannuation benefits were to remain unchanged there should be a levy of 1s per quarter for first class members.

A further proposal was that unemployment benefit should not be paid for suspensions, breakdowns and bad weather. In addition, any member claiming unemployment benefit would have to produce a note signed by his foreman stating the cause of the unemployment, and benefit would commence one week after the date the member was discharged from his job. Benefit was to rise from 3s 6d per week for first class members with one year's membership to 9s per week for members with more than twelve years' membership.

Changes were suggested in the payment of sickness benefit and it was also proposed that branches should no longer pay fees to doctors who could be called upon to provide medical service to members. The Executive Council pointed out that no other trade union undertook this burden. Other changes suggested by the Executive Council related to the payment of compensation benefit for total disablement, the allocation of funds for benevolent purposes and the limitation of the age of entry of new members. It was proposed that first class members should not be accepted over 30 years of age and second class members not over 35 years of age.

A particularly important proposal was that ballots for all elections should be abolished, and instead that voting should be carried out by a show of hands at branch meetings. This, it was said, would save the cost of letters, ballot papers and postage, and also give a more open expression of opinion. The nomination of district delegates and Executive Council members was to be limited to branches in each district where an election was taking place but those nominated were to be voted upon by the whole of the Society. No literature was to be issued on behalf of candidates other than that published in the monthly journal. Violation of this provision was to disqualify a candidate. The General Secretary was to have power to refuse to publish any offensive or abusive references to any candidate.

A number of members of the General Council reacted unfavourably to the circulation of the report of the Executive Council and more particularly to the decision not to convene a meeting of the General Council. A copy of the report was sent by the Executive Council to the members of the General Council and only five out of twenty-one consented to its circulation. Seven were opposed and the others did not reply definitely in one direction or another. Subsequently ten of the twenty-one members of the General Council issued a manifesto severely criticising the Executive Council.

The response from the branches was very mixed. A number called for the convening of the General Council. Others suggested that a more widely representative delegate assembly should be elected and still others called for the setting up of a committee of experts to look at the Society's finances. A number of branches suggested that heavy levies should be imposed to restore the finances.

The Executive Council decided to submit to the vote of the membership the proposition that the General Council should be convened. The result was announced towards the end of 1907 and showed a very substantial majority against convening the General

Council. The number voting in favour was 1,431; the number against was 4,820. In the light of this decision the Executive Council decided to set up a special committee to be elected by the whole membership to deal with the financial problems of the Society. It was also decided by the Executive Council to submit to the membership a proposal that a 10s levy per member should be imposed immediately. By a majority of 5,286 to 2,114 the members voted in favour of the levy.

At the first meeting of the special committee to examine the financial position of the Society figures were presented revealing that in 1907 the average income per member was £3 14s 2½d but the average expenditure was £4 4s 1¼d. A detailed comparison with the income and benefits of the Amalgamated Society of Engineers showed that the Boilermakers' Society was paying out nearly twice as much per member in unemployment and sickness benefit and more than four times as much in benevolent benefits as the ASE. In addition, the cost of doctors' services amounted to 3s 3¾d per member whereas in the engineers' union there was no such benefit.

By the end of June 1908 it was reported that the funds of the Society had declined by more than £67,000 since the beginning of the year. The Executive Council decided to stop all payments from the benevolent fund and, in accordance with a rule which said that special steps should be taken when the funds of the Society were reduced to less than £4 per member, the Executive Committee asked the branches to consider the alternative of either increased subscriptions or reduced benefits. Despite this worsening of the financial position of the Society most of the proposals submitted by the Executive Council for changing the scale of benefits were defeated.

Towards the end of 1908, with the continuing worsening of the financial position, the special finance committee of the Society put forward further suggestions. It proposed that contributions should be increased by 3d per week for first class members, 2d per week for second class members and 1d per week for third class members.

It also suggested that superannuation benefits should be reduced. As an alternative to these proposals the special finance committee said that it would be possible to minimise the reduction in benefits if there were a more substantial increase in contributions. A suggestion for such an increase was put forward.

Early in 1909 it was reported that the membership had voted narrowly in favour of reduced benefits and increased contributions. Top rate superannuation benefit for example was reduced from 11s to 9s and top rate unemployment benefit from 11s 6d per week to 7s 6d per week. Contributions were also increased. First class members now had to pay 1s 9d per week instead of 1s 6d per week.

The full report of the special finance committee recommended the introduction of other important changes. All were accepted by votes of the members. One of the most radical was that the Executive Council should be reduced from seven to five members. The salary for each Executive Council member was to be £3 5s per week. Overtime payment for Executive Council members was to be abolished. The General Council was to be drastically reduced to only seven elected members. Membership of district committees was also to be reduced from seven to five. The Tyne, Wear and Tees district committees were to meet weekly if necessary, the Hartlepools, London, Mersey, Hull, Barrow, Belfast, South Wales and Manchester district committees fortnightly and the South Coast, Lincolnshire, Yorkshire and Staffordshire district committees monthly. In Scotland there was to be a central board to sit in Glasgow. It was to consist of seven members, including three from the upper reaches of the Clyde, three from the lower reaches and one from the east coast.

Changes were made in the rules relating to sickness benefit and unemployment benefit. The effect was to limit the number of members who were eligible for these benefits. A quarterly levy of 1s was introduced for superannuation and the benefit for accidents resulting in total disablement was reduced to £60. The Society's delegations to the TUC and the Labour Party conference were to consist of not more than two delegates together with the General Secretary. Ballots for elections were abolished and voting by show of hands introduced. Ballots were to be retained, however, on matters affecting industrial disputes. The effect of these changes was that by the final quarter of 1909 the income of the Society once again exceeded the expenditure.

ROBERT KNIGHT'S RETIREMENT ALLOWANCE

In the developments affecting the Society's finances there was an embarrassing controversy concerning the retirement allowance paid to the former General Secretary, Robert Knight. Following his retirement towards the close of the nineteenth century, Robert Knight was appointed consulting secretary at a salary of £3 10s per week. In 1900, however, the General Council abolished this office and there followed an exchange regarding the arrangements for Robert Knight's retirement. Robert Knight asked for a lump sum payment equal to 1s per member as an alternative to a weekly retirement allowance. This was defeated on a ballot vote by 23,493 to 12,295. A further ballot agreed, however, that he should be granted a lifelong retirement allowance of £3 10s per week. The number voting in favour of this allowance was 19,308 whereas 1,792 voted for £3 and 13,811 for £2 10s. At the time the Executive Council said that it should be understood that the retirement allowance would be for the length of Robert Knight's life and could not be changed by a future decision. Nevertheless, when the Society's finances deteriorated rapidly in 1907 and 1908 suggestions were received from no fewer than forty-five branches for a reduction in the retirement allowance.

These views were put to the finance committee and they decided to recommend a reduction of £1 per week in Robert Knight's retirement allowance. Robert Knight appealed against the recommendation and argued that the finance committee was legally and morally wrong. In June 1908 he wrote to the Society expressing willingness to accept a temporary reduction of £1 per week until the Society's income again exceeded expenditure. He said he made this offer without prejudice to his rights and on condition that no attempt was made to interfere permanently with his retirement allowance. He indicated that if this was not accepted by the Society he would contest the decision legally. The Society took legal opinion and it was advised that it would probably be unlawful for the finance committee to reduce the retirement allowance. After receiving this advice the Executive Council recommended to the membership that Robert Knight's offer should be accepted. They pointed out that Knight was now 75 years of age and that he should not be subject to further anxiety about his retirement allowance. By a large majority the membership voted in favour of the Executive Council's recommendation. The voting was 7,251 in favour of accepting Robert Knight's offer to reduce his allowance by £1 per week until income exceeded expenditure in the Society's funds. The number of votes cast against the proposal was 1,057.

UNEMPLOYMENT BENEFIT SUSPENDED

In 1909 trade remained depressed and the membership of the Society declined from 51,256 to 49,350. Towards the end of the year new proposals for changes in benefits were circulated. A number of options were put to the membership, of which the most radical was that unemployment benefit should not be paid in 1910. This proposal secured a narow majority on a ballot vote of the membership.

A table published in the December 1909 issue of the monthly journal listed the changes in rates of contribution since March 1871. It was as follows:

from March 1871 to April 1877	1s per week
from May 1877 to January 1879	1s 3d per week
from February 1879 to August 1880	1s 9d per week
from September 1880 to December 1881	1s 1d per week
from January 1882 to December 1883	1s per week
from January 1884 to December 1884	1s 1d per week
from January 1885 to May 1888	1s 6d per week
from June 1888 to December 1900	1s 3d per week

(In 1888 there was a special levy of 10s per member and special levies for various benefits.)

from January 1901 to December 1908	1s 6d per week

MORE DISPUTES

In 1908 trade remained depressed and in the middle of the year the Boilermakers' Society had more than 12,000 of its members unemployed. The wage reductions accepted by the Boilermakers' Society early in 1908 were rejected by the shipwrights. The majority of boilermakers were employed on piece-work whereas the majority of shipwrights were employed on time rates. Shipwrights, drillers, joiners, mill sawyers and finishing tradesmen in the north east struck work on 22 January 1908. The strike was made official by the Shipwrights' Society.

Despite the intervention of the President of the Board of Trade, Mr Lloyd George, the strike continued through the spring months. At the beginning of May the employers imposed a lockout in Scotland and the north of England in support of the north-east employers. The members of the Boilermakers' Society were affected by this stoppage and felt largely impotent to influence the outcome. Eventually, after the intervention of the TUC, a solution was found. Wage reductions were accepted and it was agreed that there should be a joint conference between the employers and the unions to establish new machinery to deal with disputes. Work was resumed on 1 June. The strike had lasted more than eighteen weeks and the eventual settlement was accepted on a ballot vote by only a narrow majority.

A parallel dispute took place in the engineering industry in the north east where proposed wage reductions were rejected by a number of unions. Mr Lloyd George again played a conciliatory role and managed to persuade the employers to withdraw some of their demands. The national leadership of the Amalgamated Society of Engineers was in favour of a settlement but the terms were rejected by the membership in the north east. In July the Engineering Employers' Federation threatened a general lockout, and in August, after a ballot vote of the national membership of the ASE, powers were given to the union's executive to settle the dispute. They accepted the proposed wage reductions, together with a guarantee that there should be no further wage alterations for six months. They agreed also to co-operate with the employers in revising the procedure agreement.

The Executive Council of the Boilermakers' Society complained that they had little influence on the course of the shipbuilding and engineering disputes in the north east and that the failure of the unions to unite in support of an agreed policy pointed to the need for stronger trade union co-operation. D. C. Cummings was also in favour of conciliation and arbitration and wanted to see a change in the law to give increased power to the Board of Trade to intervene in labour disputes.

At the 1908 Trades Union Congress the Boilermakers' Society moved a motion calling for the strengthening of the provisions of the 1896 Conciliation Act. It was suggested that compulsory powers should be given to the Board of Trade to inquire into any industrial dispute when requested by either party. Pending such an inquiry and the publication of its report no strike or lockout should take place. The motion was moved by D. C. Cummings on behalf of the Boilermakers' Society and seconded by Mr A. Wilkie, MP, of the shipwrights. The motion was opposed by the miners and on a card vote was lost by 978,000 votes to 616,000.

OFFICIALS

Early in 1908 John Rowat resigned his position as Assistant General Secretary. He had been seriously ill for some considerable time before his resignation. He survived for only a few months after his retirement and died in January 1909. He was succeeded as Assistant General Secretary by John Barker. At the time of his election John Barker was 38 years of age. He had been active in the Manchester area and joined the Society in 1891. He was also active in his local Labour Party and in the workers' educational movement.

In the spring of 1908 Mr J. H. Jose, district delegate in South Wales, was adopted as prospective Labour candidate for Cardiff. On a ballot vote the membership decided by 4,755 to 1,592 to give him financial support. In July, however, Mr Jose accepted a job with the Bristol Channel Employers' Federation. In accepting his resignation the Executive Council said that Mr Jose had always been a very able and efficient delegate.

In the autumn of 1908 the General Secretary of the Society, D. C. Cummings, submitted his resignation to accept a position in the Labour Department of the Board of Trade. It was part of the policy of the newly-elected Liberal Government to introduce trade unionists into the Labour Department of the Board of Trade. The disputes which had occurred in the closing months of D. C. Cummings's period of office may well have influenced his decision to accept

24

the offer of this job. He had been General Secretary since the resignation of Robert Knight in 1899. Though first elected as a critic of the authoritarian style of leadership of his predecessor, D. C. Cummings was not a militant. He consistently favoured a conciliatory policy. He is remembered to this day as the author of a commemorative volume to mark the diamond jubilee of the formation of the Boilermakers' Society. He departed from the Society with the good wishes of the Executive Council. In a note in the journal the Council said that D. C. Cummings would be able to help trade unionism in his new position.

Appendix to Chapter 1

Wage Rates in 1906

In 1906 the Boilermakers' Society conducted a survey of wage rates paid to members. The rates were summarised and published for various trade groups including angle ironsmiths, platers, riveters, holders-up and sheet-iron workers. The highest time rates in the United Kingdom were paid to ship-repair workers in London. The time rate for angle iron-smiths and platers was 51s a week of forty-eight hours. This was some five or six hours shorter than the normal working week in engineering, shipbuilding and many other industries. The time rate for riveters in London ship repair was 45s per week and for holders-up 39s per week. All were for a basic forty-eight-hour week.

Boilermakers employed in railway workshops were usually employed on wage rates towards the lower end of the national range for their trade. Angle ironsmiths and platers in railway workshops were usually on time rates varying between 32s and 40s per week, though rates for angle ironsmiths in the Gorton workshops of the Great Central Railway were 41s 6d per week, and in some of the workshops of railway companies around London were 42s per week.

In shipbuilding some of the lowest rates were paid in Aberdeen where angle ironsmiths and platers were employed on basic time rates ranging from 32s 9d to 35s 4d per week of fifty-four hours. Rates in Liverpool were high, and on repair work angle ironsmiths and platers employed by Cunard were on a basic time rate of 50s for a fifty-three-hour week. Rates in Hull for the same group of tradesmen were 41s or 42s for a fifty-three-hour week. On the north-east coast time rates varied between about 36s 6d and 42s for a fifty-three or fifty-four-hour week. On the Clyde the time rates for angle ironsmiths and platers varied between 36s and 40s 6d for a fifty-four-hour week. In Southampton the rates were higher and in most shipyards and boiler shops the time rate was 45s for a fifty-four-hour week.

In all areas the rates for riveters, caulkers and holders-up were less than for the more highly skilled trades. The time rates for holders-up, who were invariably at the bottom of the range, varied usually between

21s and 34s. The majority were in the range of 26s to 32s. As with the more skilled trades, the highest time rates were paid in London ship repair, Liverpool and Southampton.

Hourly rates for members of the Boilermakers' Society working in South Africa were substantially higher than in Britain. For angle iron-smiths, platers and riveters the time rates were between 78s and 84s for a forty-eight-hour week.

Average earnings of members of the Boilermakers' Society, *when working a full week*, were usually higher than the nominal time rate. The majority were piece-workers and earned piece-work bonus. Some also increased their earnings by overtime. Thus some members of the Society when in full employment had earnings exceeding £3 per week and a few had earnings in excess of £4 per week. Ship repair workers, who were among the highest paid, often had irregular employment.

In 1907 boilermakers, when in regular employment, were among the highest paid of all industrial workers. In 1906, for example, the median manual earnings for all men in industry, but excluding coal mining, were 26s 7d and the lowest quartile were 20s 9d. The average wage rate of all railway workers was about 24s but the lowest quartile of railway workers had wages averaging no more than £1 per week. The average earnings of piece-work platers, riveters and caulkers in ship and boat building and repair were £140 per year. No other group of manual workers had such high annual earnings.*

* For a much fuller discussion of these and many other figures of earnings see *Occupation and Pay in Great Britain 1906–60* by Guy Routh, Cambridge University Press, 1965.

Chapter 2

A New Militancy

Eleven candidates were nominated for the office of General Secretary following the resignation of D. C. Cummings. The two strongest were John Barker, the Assistant General Secretary, and John Hill, one of the district delegates in Scotland. It was thought that John Hill's chances of election might be damaged by the nomination of one of the other Scottish district delegates, James Conley. Of the election addresses circulated to the membership by far the most militant was that put forward by John Hill. In his address he said that the strike and lockout were brutal weapons but 'the combined power to demand a fair return or withdraw your services still remains in your hands to use when all other means fail to bring peace with honour'. He criticised recent national agreements, including the Edinburgh temporary agreement for the shipbuilding industry, and said that all had curtailed the rights of the membership. He recalled that he had fought for his workmates as a shop steward and as a branch officer and that he had been a district delegate on the Clyde for more than eight years. He was well aware that his strong association with the political Labour movement might lead some members not to support him. He asked that bias should not sway members in the ballot.

John Hill's election committee in a statement to members pointed out that he joined the Society in 1888 and had started work at 12 years of age. He had served his apprenticeship as a plater and had always been active in the Society. He had also fought two parliamentary elections as a Labour candidate. They said of John Hill that he was a trade unionist 'who has shaken off the shackles of prejudice and bigotry, which unfortunately have still a hold on the

28

minds of so many and keep them on their knees begging when they ought to be on their feet demanding'.

In contrast to the election address of John Hill the address of John Barker was platitudinous and uncontroversial. It made no criticisms in any direction nor put forward any suggestions for changes in policy.

The result of the first ballot was indecisive. No candidate had a majority over all others. John Hill came at the top of the poll with 4,046 votes and John Barker came second with 3,406. John Hill owed his majority largely to very strong support for him in the Clyde branches. He also received strong support from branches on the Mersey and the Humber. In the second ballot John Hill was elected with a decisive majority of more than two to one. He secured 9,434 votes against John Barker's 4,588.

JOHN HILL – TRADE UNION MILITANT

In his first annual report to the Society the new General Secretary reaffirmed his belief that it was essential to retain the right to strike. He recalled that on the railways a new system of conciliation and compulsory arbitration had been introduced and had been hailed as a great advance. The results, however, had not fulfilled the promise and there had been a decline in the membership of the railway trade unions. John Hill said 'leave us the ultimatum of the strike'.

In his annual report for the following year 1909 John Hill returned to the attack. Unemployment, he said, was the chronic corollary of capitalism. It was not due to the laziness and drunkenness of workers as had been fondly believed by 'those superior persons in ignorance who pride themselves that they do not live by labour but are of "independent" means or "gentlemen".' He went on:

The establishment of labour exchanges has demonstrated beyond question something of the enormity of this problem, and the next duty of the state is to supply as a civic right either work at trade union rates or maintenance in unwilling idleness . . .

The year 1909 rescued many thousands of our aged workers

from the stigma of pauperism and the horror of the workhouse. On the first day of January 1909 old age pensions were instituted by the state. Hitherto state pensions were the monopoly of professional party politicians and the descendants of frail royal darlings and certain other more or less deserving individuals. Over £7 million had annually been spent in this way. January saw an extension of pensions to many poor, deserving people. Our next step must be the abolition of the whole Poor Law system and its blighting influence. For too long have the latter years of the workers been rendered more bitter than death by the constant dread of the workhouse . . .

The year will also be remembered for the great Finance Bill, so full of possibilities for the workers, which was wrecked by our hereditary enemies, the Lords, with whom the trade unions had a big score to settle.

As General Secretary John Hill was responsible for editing the monthly report. He introduced a new radical note into it. On the inside front cover of the April 1909 issue for example he listed a number of 'labour proverbs'. They included:

Man realises himself only when he identifies his life with the common life. (Edwin Markham)

A man's labour power is his life and when he sells it he sells his life. (George D. Herron)

How can a man grow rich except on the spoils of others' labours? (J. A. Froude)

You are lost if you forget that the fruits of the earth are for all and that the earth belongs to no one. (Rousseau)

There are no millionaires – no professional, legalised, lifelong kleptomaniacs among the birds and quadrupeds. (J. Howard Moore)

No animal, except man, gloats over accumulations that are of no possible use to him. (J. Howard Moore)

I hold that the earth was meant for the human race and not for a few privileged ones. (Max O'Rell)

30

Your idea that it is proper for you to pocket as much of other men's earnings as the law allows is an idea which fills the world with poverty, starvation, diseases and death (Ernest Crosby)

In the issue of the monthly report for the following month John Hill came out strongly in favour of a Labour Party Bill to give financial support to the unemployed. He pointed out that it was opposed by 'the representatives of privilege and monopoly'. In the June 1909 issue of the monthly report an article was published attacking royalty payments to landowners on coal extracted from 'their' land. The article pointed out that when the *Lusitania* was under full steam the royalties on the coal consumed amounted to almost twice as much as the total wages paid to the 333 men employed as stoke hole crew. The article recalled that Mr Winston Churchill had said that there were only two ways in which people could acquire wealth. There was production and there was plunder. Coal royalties, said the article, represented colossal plunder, resulting from the private ownership of land and the unjust distribution of wealth.

The same issue of the monthly report commented sympathetically on a Bill introduced by the Government to establish labour exchanges. Every man in the building, engineering and shipbuilding industries was expected to register himself in a labour exchange immediately he fell out of employment. The article pointed out that the Government proposed to establish in 1910 a scheme of state insurance in building, engineering and shipbuilding so that unemployed workers would receive a weekly allowance. The Boiler-makers' Society urged that the control of these exchanges should be in the hands of equal numbers of trade unionists and employers, with a neutral chairman from the Board of Trade. Only in this way, it was said, would it be possible to 'prevent the labour exchange becoming a recruiting station for blackleg labour to take the place of men on strike'.

Month after month John Hill hammered away in the monthly report at the social evils of the time. On the inside front cover of the July 1909 issue he carried a report of an inquest on a child who had been burnt to death whilst its parents were out looking for work. Their income, week after week, had been no more than 2s 6d. Officials from the coroner's office had visited the room in which the husband, wife and three children lived. They found it extremely clean but it possessed no furniture except a table. There was not a scrap of food in the place.

In the following issue of the monthly report a poem was published in defence of workers who struck for decent wages. It criticised those in high places who used the law and troops against strikers. The same issue also carried a strong attack on the House of Lords. The Lords, it said, were continually taking away the rights of the common people. It was now time for trade unionists to march on Parliament and 'take that bauble away'.

Another short article in the same issue also attacked the Czar of Russia. The article said that trade unionists should refuse to touch the bloodstained hand of the Czar while the innocent victims of his tyranny were being slowly tortured to death. The fact that he was a relative of the British King was no reason why trade unionists should be silent. The rights of the common people everywhere had to be defended. British soldiers had shot down miners at Featherstone and in Belfast. Czarism was tainting the world. In closing, the article referred to the slogan of the labour movement, 'Workers of the world unite'.

Another article on the visit of the Czar to the British King described him as an unwelcome visitor. The history of the Czar of Russia, said the article, was written upon black and bloody pages. Between 1905 and 1909 the number of prisoners had increased from 85,000 to more than 181,000. In 1908 there had been 825 civilian executions and 59 suicides in prison. No fewer than 237 former members of the Duma (Russia's feeble equivalent of a parliament) had been condemned to various terms of imprisonment. Since the 1905 first abortive revolution 406 editors of newspapers and magazines had been condemned to imprisonment.

NEW SHIPBUILDING AGREEMENT

In 1909 there was a slow recovery in trade. The costly and punishing disputes of 1908 made both employers and the unions cautious of demanding changes in wages or conditions. There was, however, one other important development. In March 1909 a new procedure agreement was concluded in shipbuilding. One of its main features was that it applied to all federated shipbuilding employers and was signed by representatives of seventeen trade unions including the boilermakers, blacksmiths and shipwrights. The Boilermakers' Society commented sourly that they had insufficient influence in framing the new agreement but, nevertheless, they regarded it as an improvement on the temporary Edinburgh agreement of 1907. The new agreement wiped out three objectionable features of the Edinburgh agreement. The first was the requirement that trade union members should not interfere with alterations in customs introduced by the employers even though the effect of these alterations might reduce earnings.

The second was the requirement imposed on the Boilermakers' Society to admit to membership without penalty apprentices who had gone as 'blacklegs' from yard to yard during trade disputes. The third was the requirement on members to work overtime at the discretion of employers.

The new agreement gave full recognition to district delegates. It provided that no general fluctuation in wages should take place until after the lapse of six months from the date of the previous change in wages. The procedure for dealing with disputes provided for negotiations at yard, local and national level. The new agreement was submitted to the membership and approved by 14,514 votes to 9,563.

DRILLERS

Towards the end of 1909 the members of the Boilermakers' Society voted in favour of the formation of a drillers' section. The voting was 2,419 in favour and 539 against. This result was very pleasing to the Executive Council who described it as 'very satisfactory indeed'. They said that the membership had decided that future difficulties arising between drillers and other branches of the boiler-making trade would be settled within the Boilermakers' Society. The Society would thus be saved expensive demarcation and arbitration costs. This move to embrace the drillers within the Society proved, however, to be short-lived. The Executive Council drew up a proposed amendment to the rules to provide for the inclusion of drillers but the proposal was not immediately put to the membership because of strong and persistent protests from the Liverpool district.

The Executive Council pointed out in support of their proposal that changes in the organisation of work in shipbuilding and ship-repairing were taking place and that unless the Society embraced the drillers they would be recruited by other trade unions. Work which had been traditionally claimed by boilermakers would thus be lost to the trade. The proposed new rule said that anyone who had worked for five years as a hand or portable machine driller should be entitled to become a member of the Boilermakers' Society. In the November 1910 issue of the monthly report it was stated that most of the voting returns had been received by the Society and the result was 'an overwhelming majority against the acceptance of drillers'. The figures were not published. Clearly any suggestion that drillers might become full members of the Society and thus ultimately compete for employment in other branches of the boilermaking trades rather than constitute a separate and auxiliary section was unacceptable to the majority of members.

NATIONAL LOCKOUT

In the first half of 1910 trade recovered. The Society submitted a claim to the Shipbuilding Employers' Federation for wage increases amounting to 1s per week for men on time rates and 5 per cent for men on piece rates.

In the late summer of 1910 new local disputes shifted attention from the national claim. At two firms on the Tyne piece-work prices were reduced and the men stopped work. The employers argued that this was in breach of the new procedure agreement. There was also a dispute on the Clyde in the shiprepair industry where men would not start work on a vessel unless they were offered the same piece rates as paid on a previous vessel. The Boilermakers' Society argued strongly that in neither case were the men in breach of procedure because it was the employers who were introducing the changed conditions. The employers, on the other hand, argued that the men should remain at work and should take their grievance through the negotiating procedure.

The Employers' Federation served the Boilermakers' Society with a notice of a national lockout. The Society refused to capitulate and the lockout took place. About 15,000 members were immediately and directly affected. Within a short period more than half the total membership of the Society were out of work and dependent upon the Society for financial assistance.

The Boilermakers' Society were anxious to negotiate a settlement of the dispute because of their weak financial position. They proposed to the employers that a return to work could be agreed if machinery were to be established for the speedier settlement of piece-work price disputes. The Society urged that the period of settlement should not exceed six weeks and that during this period the average earnings of members affected by a dispute should not be reduced. In reply the employers proposed that every member of the Boilermakers' Society who stopped work in breach of the agreement (as they interpreted it) was to be fined £3 for the first offence and £5 for the second and any subsequent offences.

These fines were to be paid through the Boilermakers' Society to local associations of the employers who were, in turn, to hand them to local charities. Any member of the Boilermakers' Society who failed to pay a fine was not to be employed by any federated firm for a period of six months for the first offence and twelve months for additional offences. The Society rejected these proposals and imposed a 10s levy to help the funds during the lockout.

The dispute excited considerable national attention. In a speech at Clydebank Mr Keir Hardie, the foremost Labour politician of the time, said that it looked as if there was an understanding among the capitalist class to provoke trouble in order to prevent the working class movement from becoming unduly strong. He described the claim of the shipbuilding employers as too absurd for even serious consideration. The agreement as interpreted by the employers tied and bound the worker at every turn. He urged all trade unionists not to allow the boilermakers to be defeated.

One regrettable feature of the dispute was the intervention of the former General Secretary, Robert Knight, who made statements, published in the press, criticising the Boilermakers' Society. He was reported to have said at a shareholders' meeting on the Tyne that 'he hoped one day to see restored the methods which obtained when he was at the head of the Society, when each party dealt honourably and honestly with the other'. The Executive Council strongly criticised Robert Knight and said in the monthly report that in the greatest crisis in the history of the Society 'he is not with us'. They said he was not even neutral but actively and publicly opposed to the Society.

In October the Executive Council, faced with the rapid drain of the funds of the Society and widespread distress among thousands of members and their families, agreed to negotiate terms with the Shipbuilding Employers' Federation and to accept the principle that members of the Boilermakers' Society should be fined for contravention of the procedure agreement as interpreted by the employers. On 11 October a draft was accepted by representatives of the Society which said that any member who was party to a stoppage of work in contravention of the shipyard agreement should be fined for the first offence at the rate of 5s per day. An increased penalty was to be imposed for the second or subsequent offences. The fine was to be imposed by the Society and was to be used for the benefit of widows and orphans of the members of the Society.

The draft agreement also suggested that the negotiating procedure should be expedited so that a claim should be considered by a joint committee within seven days of a written request for a meeting, and by a local conference within fourteen days of notice of appeal. If agreement could not be reached at a local conference two local employers were to be called in to give a decision. The Federation also agreed to send a letter to the Society stating that when two local employers were called in under the provisions of the agreement they should take into account 'the average wages earned by the workman or workmen concerned in the same class of work on previous vessels in the yard or dry dock where the question has arisen'. Despite the desperate position of the Society this draft agreement was rejected on a ballot vote by 10,212 to 9,054.

Majorities against the agreement were recorded from branches on the upper reaches of the Clyde, from the Tyne and from Barrow and Hull; the Wear and Tees were about equally divided with a very slight majority against; and Lancashire was strongly in favour. The members also voted for new levies to help the funds.

The end of the lockout came unexpectedly after fourteen and a half weeks. Trade generally was recovering rapidly and the shipbuilding employers wanted to get back into activity and to make profits on the new orders for ships which they were receiving. Just before Christmas 1910 an agreement was concluded between the Federation and the Society. Both sides undertook to carry out the procedure agreement but the employers withdrew their insistence that men who broke the agreement should be fined.

Instead a new arrangement was established which provided that when an employer and the union were in disagreement as to whether or not a stoppage of work was in breach of the procedure the question should be referred to a committee of six representatives, consisting of three employers and three boilermakers. This committee was to decide who was responsible for the breach of the agreement. If the committee failed to agree the question was to be referred to an independent referee whose decision would be final and binding. The panel from which the referee was to be selected was to consist of persons acceptable to both the employers and the union. It was further provided that where it had been decided that a stoppage in breach of procedure had occurred the offending party, either workers or employer, was to be dealt with respectively by the union or the Federation. The settlement also provided for the speedier consideration of issues. Certain time limits were laid down. The terms of this agreement represented a significant victory for the Boilermakers' Society. The lockout had started on 3 September 1910 and had lasted until 14 December.

The victory of the Society was underlined by further events. Immediately after the resumption of work members secured wage increases in many yards and boiler shops. Firms in the north east, for example, offered an immediate advance at the end of the lockout of 1s per week on time rates and $2\frac{1}{2}$ per cent on piece rates, together with a further similar advance six months afterwards. The highest rate was to remain in force for no less than five years. John Hill pointed out that this offer gave the Boilermakers' Society higher rates than ever before during a period of good trade.

The struggle of the Boilermakers' Society in the shipbuilding lockout attracted wide support from other unions. The biggest donation of all, amounting to £2,000, came from the Amalgamated Society of Engineers whose members agreed by vote to impose upon themselves a levy of 1s per head as an act of solidarity with the boilermakers. Among other substantial donations were £500 each from the Ironmoulders and the Railwaymen, £300 from the Durham Miners, £250 from the Northumberland Miners, £100 each from the Weavers' Amalgamation, the Boot and Shoe Operatives and the Plasterers and £50 each from the Cotton Spinners, the Cardroom

Operatives in the cotton industry and from the Society of Tool-makers. Many other unions donated smaller amounts.

One important consequence of the shipbuilding lockout and the manner in which the Shipbuilding Employers' Federation had interpreted the procedure agreement was that many members of the Society were persuaded that there were disadvantages as well as advantages to trade unionists in procedure agreements. John Hill himself shared this view. Agreement with employers, he said, had been lauded as calculated to prevent stoppages of work and to provide machinery for obtaining fair wages without recourse to strikes. He went on:

> We prefer not to chop logic but judge from experience. While the national agreement did not prevent the most unwarranted lockout in our history, but was rather the justification from the employers' point of view for that lockout, there can be no doubt whatever that the national agreement prevented and is still preventing a legitimate advance of wages that trade warrants.

NEW CLAIMS

Throughout 1911 trade was good and wages were increasing. In March 1911 the Executive Council drew attention to the need to broaden the struggle for improved conditions and to press, in particular, for the introduction of an eight-hour working day. In the summer of 1911 the Executive Council said that the membership were prone to concentrate attention on wages and to overlook the ever more important question of hours of work. There was no trade, said the Council, in which an eight-hour day was more necessary than in boilermaking. They pointed out that the Society had put a motion on the subject on the agenda of the 1911 TUC.

In the late summer of 1911 the Society pressed a claim for wage increases in the shipbuilding industry and secured a 5 per cent advance on piece rates and 1s per week advance on time rates. The increase was payable from early in October. Additional wage increases were also secured in many individual yards and boiler shops. In his annual report for 1911 John Hill said that the year had been one of unrest. Wages had been increased for members of the Boilermakers' Society by between 5 and 10 per cent. On the other hand the rich and well-to-do were growing richer year by year.

He said that as a result of this contrast and with a big demand for labour the workers in all industries were in a state of revolt.

WHY A PROCEDURE AGREEMENT?

The shipyard national agreement was due to end on 9 March 1912 three years after it was introduced. Either side was required to give six months' notice to bring it to an end or to amend it. In January 1912 the Executive Council of the Boilermakers' Society decided to submit to a ballot vote of the membership four questions about the future of the agreement. They were:

1 Shall we continue the agreement as it is at present?
2 Shall we ask the employers to meet us in conference with the joint trades to have the present agreement amended?
3 Shall we as a Society have an agreement ourselves with the employers?
4 Shall we notify the employers that we desire no agreement?

In response to the first question there was an overwhelming majority against. Voting was 264 to continue the agreement, 3,861 against. There was also a majority against the second proposal. This was defeated by 2,748 votes to 2,000. In response to the third question the majority against was narrower but still decisive: 2,222 votes were cast against the proposition and 1,769 in favour. The response to the fourth question was the most significant of all. The membership voted heavily in favour of it. The voting was 2,927 in favour and 1,518 against. John Hill expressed himself strongly in support of the views of the membership. There may be those, he said, amongst the membership who look to the future with apprehension but 'no more wanton attack will ever be made upon our Society without an agreement than was made on us eighteen months ago under an agreement'.

CHANGES

Under the arrangements which had been agreed to reduce the expenditure of the Society it had already been accepted that the full-time Executive Council should be reduced from seven to five members. Elections took place in the early summer of 1910 for the newly constituted Council. Three of the members of the old Executive Council were elected outright on the first ballot. They did not have to compete against Executive colleagues. The other four were less fortunate. They had to compete for the remaining two seats.

This reduction in the size of the Executive Council and the consequent inevitable defeat of two of the existing members led to considerable dissatisfaction. A number of branches suggested that provision should be made to retain the services of the two former members of the Executive Council in some capacity or other. The Executive Council itself was sympathetic to this view and for a period retained the two defeated members at the head office on full pay. In the monthly report they said that they thought it would be the wish of the members 'to further consider the question'. The issue was put to the branches but a majority indicated that they wished to adhere to the decision to reduce the size of the Executive Council. Accordingly the two defeated members of the Executive Council, Mr D. Reid and Mr T. Waterton, were given notice. Mr Waterton had been a member of the Executive Council for thirteen and a half years.

This, however, was not the end of the matter. In the summer of 1911 the new Executive Council decided in response to requests from a number of members to submit to a ballot vote a proposal that a grant of £50 each should be made to Mr Reid and Mr Waterton. The former General Secretary of the Society, Mr D. C. Cummings, who was now employed at the Board of Trade, argued strongly in favour of such a grant being made. Despite this appeal the branches voted strongly against the proposed grants.

Early in 1910 there was a vacancy for a prospective Labour candidate for the Jarrow parliamentary constituency. The local Labour Party selected Mr John Barker, the Assistant General Secretary of the Boilermakers' Society. The Executive Council decided to ask the membership whether they were in favour of permitting John Barker to fight the seat. There was a low vote but it went in favour of the proposition. The number in favour of John Barker's candidature was 3,371 and the number against was 1,928. The voting in the seven branches in and around Jarrow was, however, less satisfactory; 137 votes were cast in favour of the candidature and 128 against. Indeed, of the Jarrow branches taken alone a majority was against. In view of these figures John Barker decided to resign as prospective candidate. In his letter of resignation John Barker referred to the marked division of opinion among the membership. He said that he would continue to strive to secure increased Labour representation in Parliament.

UNIONS AND POLITICAL ACTION

In December 1909 the House of Lords upheld a claim from a member of the Amalgamated Society of Railway Servants, W. V. Osborne, that the union should not spend its funds for political purposes. This was a serious blow to the trade union movement. The support given by trade unions to candidates pledged to favour legislation in the interests of working men and women was clearly in pursuit of trade union objectives. Moreover without the support of the trade union movement there was very little likelihood of Labour representation in Parliament. For all practical purposes there was no other way in which the labour movement could raise sufficient money to become an effective political force. Members of Parliament were at that time not paid for their duties. Labour Members had to depend upon trade union contributions. There were also no restrictions on wealthy individuals and private firms from giving money either to the Conservative Party or the Liberal Party. The Osborne decision was thus seen by the trade union movement as motivated entirely by the interests and prejudices of the ruling class.

The Boilermakers' Society took a very critical attitude towards the Osborne judgement of the House of Lords. In April and May 1910 the Society was required as a result of the Osborne judgement to put to the membership the question whether the parliamentary fund should continue to be used for the purpose for which it was collected. By 3,622 to 1,318 the members voted in the affirmative. This vote was accepted as providing a mandate for continued political action.

In Manchester the annual demonstration of boilermakers was revived after a lapse of five years and members marched in protest against the Osborne judgement in procession through the city. They were accompanied by a number of bands. About a thousand members of the Society attended the demonstration which was addressed by the General Secretary. At the demonstration a resolution was carried in the following terms:

> That in the opinion of this meeting the decision of the law courts prohibiting trade unions securing advantages through political action is a menace to progress and opposed to every democratic principle. We therefore urge the Government to grant facilities for the passage through Parliament of a measure to place trade unions on the same basis as other sections of the community. This is that the majority shall rule.

In the November 1910 issue the monthly report of the Society carried a statement from the General Federation of Trade Unions asserting that the Osborne judgement had proved that the law lords had not shed their prejudices or their class bias. This judgement, said the Federation, was 'based upon bad reasoning, bad law and bad policy'. Trade unions were claiming the same freedom for themselves as was already conceded to limited liability companies.

Though the Boilermakers' Society continued to support efforts for increased Labour representation it was also strongly sympathetic to many of the policies of the Liberal Government which it regarded as helpful to workers' interests. In this it was reflecting the point of view of many thousands of its members. John Hill welcomed the Government proposals for unemployment and health insurance. He said that the Government's schemes fell far short of the ideals of the Boilermakers' Society yet they marked 'a very distinct advance along the path of progress'. The Society also welcomed a decision by the Government to issue a statutory order, under the Factory and Workshop Act 1901, which provided that occupiers or contractors in shipyards should publish details of piece-work prices. Those covered by the order included platers, riveters and caulkers. It was strenuously opposed by the Shipbuilding Employers' Federation who, through their influence both inside and outside Parliament, were able to secure the exclusion from its protection of angle ironsmiths and others not actually employed in shipyards.

42

DEATH OF ROBERT KNIGHT

Robert Knight, former General Secretary of the Society and one of the dominating figures in the British trade union movement in the last quarter of the nineteenth century, died at the age of 78 years on 17 September 1911. He had been born in the village of Lifton in Devonshire. To this day the head office of the Boilermakers' Society is known as Lifton House. He started work at 12 years of age and became an angle ironsmith. He worked for fourteen years in the Royal Dockyard at Devonport and was then elected General Secretary of the Society. He remained General Secretary for twenty-nine years until his retirement in 1899.

Robert Knight made a great contribution to the development of the Society. He introduced administrative order into the head office and ensure that funds were protected, that they were properly accounted for and were wisely invested to meet the many financial calls of the membership facing unemployment, sickness, accidents and retirement. Towards the end of his period of office he became authoritarian in style and in the 1890s there were rumblings of revolt against him. In industrial policy he was a conciliator and his lack of militancy evoked considerable criticism. He was also an anti-socialist and took a leading part in resisting the influence of the new unionists and socialists in the late 1880s and 1890s. In this respect Robert Knight was overtaken by events.

The Boilermakers' Society dealt with him generously on his retirement but he was not forgiven for his open hostility to the Society at the time of the 1910 lockout. On the occasion of his death tributes to him were paid by the Society. Many employers, trade union and Liberal Party representatives were present at his funeral.

Chapter 3

The Great Unrest

The period from 1911 to the outbreak of the First World War was one of industrial turbulence. It was a stormy period of unrest affecting workers in many industries. In his book *A Short History of the British Working Class Movement** the late Professor G. D. H. Cole said that during this period 'trade unionism woke out of its long quiescence, and became class conscious, militant, aggressive.' Yet this judgement of Professor Cole could to some extent be misleading. The unrest was above all a movement of discontent from below. In many unions old leaders were still in charge and many of them were not in sympathy with the new radical mood. In the Boilermakers' Society, in contrast, the General Secretary, John Hill was himself a militant.

When the Trades Union Congress held its annual congress at Newcastle in 1911 the Society organised a welcoming demonstration. A march of 2000 members of the Society took place together with bands and the demonstration was addressed by the General Secretary, John Hill. It was a sign of a new mood among many trade unionists.

CONTRIBUTORY INFLUENCES

There were a number of contributory influences to the ferment in industrial relations. First and foremost was the fact that for a number of years living standards among most workers had not risen. For many of them there had been a decline. Industry had

* George Allen & Unwin, 1927.

44

been depressed and prices had been rising. With the recovery in trade in 1911 many workers turned towards a wages offensive. In 1912 trade boomed and in 1913 prosperity reached new heights.

The shipbuilding industry had more orders than ever before. In 1911 United Kingdom output was more than 2 million tons. In 1912 it was just under 2 million tons and in 1913 a new peak was reached with more than 2,200,000 tons. In each of these three years the output of ships in the United Kingdom was greater than the total output in the rest of the world. By 1913 the General Secretary of the Boilermakers' Society was saying that 'trade during the year has been more than good'. He referred to one large firm which, in a circular to its shareholders, stated 'the results of the year, without doubt, . . . have been beyond the dreams of avarice'. Prices for new ships were estimated to be at least 20 per cent higher than those quoted only two or three years earlier.

Another factor which influenced the mood of the trade union movement was the reaction against the over-optimism engendered by the election in 1906 of the first substantial group of Labour Members of Parliament. Though the Labour Members had supported the Liberal policy of social reform and the claims of the trade union movement for new legislation to help workers, the experience had demonstrated that the power of a group of political representatives within Parliament to bring about any significant change was limited. Many active trade unionists were beginning to understand that just as industrial action was not always an adequate substitute for political action so also parliamentary representation was no real substitute for trade union strength. Union militants urged workers to rely upon their own strength, particularly at workplace level.

This new radicalism was also stimulated by ideas brought from abroad. In the United States of America the Industrial Workers of the World propagated a crude Marxism which, nevertheless, served to rouse many class-conscious workers against the feebleness of craft unionism. The IWW advocated industrial unionism through which workers, irrespective of their skill or other differences, could express their solidarity. The IWW pointed also to the need to transform society from capitalism to socialism if any real change in the condition of workers were to be achieved. The IWW had no sympathy with the limited claims of the craft unions submitted on behalf of a labour aristocracy.

New ideas were also coming from France. These ideas emphasised the potential power of a general strike. By strike action involving millions of workers the power of the state and of its capitalist masters could be challenged. A general strike was seen by the advocates of these ideas to be a much more potent weapon than parliamentary representation.

The trade union movement in Britain was also affected by unrest in other walks of life. In political affairs there was a constitutional clash between the elected House of Commons and the hereditary House of Lords. The sovereignty of the elected chamber was challenged by the representatives of hereditary privilege. In Ireland, too, the struggle for home rule was reaching a new height and was in turn challenged by reactionary officers of the armed forces and landowners in the north. They refused to accept home rule even though both in Britain and in Ireland a majority of the elected representatives was in favour of it. It was the unconstitutional rebels in the north of Ireland who were later to be responsible for the establishment of the province of Northern Ireland which, despite geography, was torn away politically from the rest of Ireland. The problem remains unresolved to this day though thousands of Irish men and women in the province have since been killed and injured by civil strife.

A militant campaign was also being waged for the right of women to vote in elections. The suffragettes, as they were called, were themselves divided between a constitutional and a militant wing. It was the militant suffragettes who secured the most publicity and who in the end proved to be more effective. The campaign which they conducted hastened the day when women were to win the right to vote. The militancy of some of the suffragettes set an example to trade unionists of effective campaigning methods.

Finally, in the years before the First World War there were many indications of the preparation for war among the principal industrial powers. In the years 1911, 1912 and 1913 the building of warships accounted for about 20 per cent of the world's output of new ships. Early in 1911 the monthly report of the Boilermakers' Society carried a report of a special session of the Labour Party conference held to discuss the growing threat of militarism. The report stated that the delegates to the conference had unanimously pronounced 'against the ever-growing increase in naval armaments which do not add to our national security' and had denounced militarism.

In the following year the monthly report of the Boilermakers' Society recorded that the Labour Party conference had carried a resolution reaffirming its opposition to the growing burden of armaments and protesting against militarism in all its forms. The resolution went on:

> conference further expresses its approval of the proposals to investigate and report on whether and how far a stoppage of work, either partial or general, in countries about to engage in war, would be effective in preventing an outbreak of hostilities . . .

Trade unionists were thus beginning to discuss the use of the strike weapon for anti-war purposes.

NEW DEVELOPMENTS

In 1911 there were strikes in the mining industry, among printers, in shipping, on the docks and on the railways. Among many employers there was alarm at the spread of industrial unrest but the more far-sighted of them saw that if the unrest was to be contained without challenge to the existing social system, improved means of conciliation would have to be developed. Similarly some trade union leaders saw the situation as an opportunity to develop new conciliation machinery which would help the unions to secure settlements in disputes.

A number of trade union leaders joined with some prominent employers to establish a National Industrial Council. The initiative for the formation of the Council came from Sir Charles Macara, a prominent employer in the cotton textile industry. The Government responded to the initiative and called the Council into being. The purpose of the Council was to consider and inquire into matters referred to them affecting trade disputes and 'especially of taking suitable action in regard to any dispute referred to them affecting the principal trades of the country . . .' The National Industrial Council did not succeed in calming the industrial relations scene because the task was beyond its scope. It could not deal with the fundamental social problems which gave rise to the great unrest. Nevertheless, the Council was an interesting early example of an attempt to establish an institutional framework within which industrial relations problems could be discussed and resolved.

In the spring of 1911 a new daily paper, the *Daily Herald*, was established. It expressed a radical point of view and was supported by the militant wing of the trade union and labour movement. It was launched as a result of a printing strike in London. The Boilermakers' Society was one of the first organisations to give it support. John Hill agreed to contribute articles from time to time. The Executive Council commended the newspaper to members.

A few months later another labour paper was launched in competition with the *Daily Herald*. It was to become the *Daily Citizen*. The Executive Council of the Boilermakers' Society also supported this new initiative. Though the control of the *Daily Citizen* was to remain firmly in the hands of the right wing of the movement the Executive Council of the Boilermakers' Society welcomed the new newspaper and said that 'a press controlled entirely by capitalists has always been opposed to our interests as trade unionists . . .' They recommended that the Society should invest £1,000 in the new *Daily Citizen*. This was submitted to a ballot of the membership and a narrow majority was secured for it. The number of votes in favour was 3,107. The number against was 2,785.

The *Daily Citizen* started publication in October 1912 but it did not last long. By March 1913 a special conference had to be convened to attempt to rally support for the newspaper from the trade union movement. The boilermakers were represented by two delegates but significantly the delegation did not include the General Secretary. The conference was told that the newspaper was facing a financial crisis. As a result of this conference the Executive Council of the Society decided to recommend the membership to pay a levy of 1s per member per year for three years so as to ensure the continued publication of the *Daily Citizen*. The proposition for a levy of 1s per member per annum for three years was carried by a majority of 3,679 to 2,408.

The decision to introduce a levy to support the *Daily Citizen* was objected to by a number of members. An appeal against the levy was heard before a court in Dublin. The defence of the Boilermakers' Society was sustained and costs were awarded against the complainants. The complaint was then taken to the Appeal Court in Dublin and was again decided in favour of the Society. The Executive Council were able to point out that the levy on behalf of the *Daily Citizen* was introduced as a result of a vote of the members as provided in the constitution of the Society.

Despite the support given to it by the Boilermakers' Society the *Daily Citizen* was never successful. It had two years of life and finally went out of existence in 1914. Though it was under the official control of the labour movement it strongly opposed the much more militant views expressed by the *Daily Herald*.

JOHN HILL RE-ELECTED

Towards the end of 1911 John Hill was re-elected as General Secretary. He continued to express radical views. Early in 1912 one of his articles came under attack from the *North Eastern Daily Gazette*. In an article which he had written for the *Glasgow Herald* he had said that procedure agreements which provided for no stoppages of work until the machinery of negotiation had been exhausted took from workers their most effective weapon. The *North Eastern Daily Gazette* said that Mr Hill was condoning 'the refusal on the part of workmen to accept the indispensable concomitant of every bargain – submission to the terms agreed on. What he seems to favour is lightning changes and lightning results'. The *North Eastern Daily Gazette* noted that John Hill's article concluded with a strong advocacy of socialism.

In the February 1912 issue of the monthly report John Hill made it unmistakably clear that he was not to be regarded as a trade union leader who once elected to office began to preach moderation. When trade unionism became dangerous, he explained, the leaders were insidiously chloroformed and their hearts were destroyed with gifts. The exploitation of workers went on and trade unionism became 'respectable'. John Hill said that the rank and file were now awake and demanding justice. Their voice would not be stifled. The old game of choking the leaders with butter was useless providing the workers continued to march.

OVERSEAS REPRESENTATION

In 1911 the Prime Minister of New South Wales, Mr J. S. McGowen, a boilermaker by trade, visited Britain to attend the coronation of King George V. Whilst in Britain he spoke at the Derby branch of the Boilermakers' Society. In his speech he said that less than 1 per cent of boilermakers in Australia were non-unionists. The employers in Australia, he pointed out, were the same as in Britain and tried to pay as little wages as they could.

In South Africa the branches of the Boilermakers' Society pressed for a measure of autonomy. The remoteness of the branches had led to serious difficulty and there were a number of defalcations. Branches had to be closed, and in 1911 only three branches, Durban, Johannesburg and Germiston, remained. The total membership of the three branches was 375. The South African branches requested permission to set up a South African Council on lines similar to the Scottish Central Board of the Society. They also requested that a full-time delegate should be appointed.

The Executive Council responded sympathetically to the South African branches and suggested to the membership that they should accede to the request for a trial period of one year. By 3,047 votes to 1,197 the members voted in favour of the proposal.

In the winter of 1913–14 there was serious labour unrest in South Africa. The branches of the Boilermakers' Society were directly involved. As a result of a dispute in the railway workshops the members of the Boilermakers' Society, the Amalgamated Society of Engineers and the South African Railwaymen's Union decided to take strike action. The Government ordered the arrest of the entire Executive Committee of the Railwaymen's Union and of several other prominent trade union leaders. A number were sentenced and sent to prison. A ballot was taken among other workers and it was decided to support the railwaymen. The Government then declared martial law, prohibited all meetings and raided trade union property. The files of the branches of the Boilermakers' Society were taken by the police. A letter to the monthly report of the Boilermakers' Society said that all letters, telegrams and papers were censored and it was regarded as sedition to write a letter of encouragement to members on strike. The South African members appealed to the Boilermakers' Society to protest against the repression.

In the following issue of the monthly report, April 1914, it was announced that the South African employers and Government had retreated. In elections in the Transvaal Labour candidates had been successful and two prominent members of the Boilermakers' Society had been elected.

In March 1914 the South African Council reported on the result of the new scheme of organisation. Membership had risen to 491 and there were now eight branches. The South African Council acknowledged that the increase in the membership had not been as rapid as might have been expected. They had, however, faced very serious difficulties as a result of the South African Government's efforts to crush trade unionism.

The Executive Council responded sympathetically. They pointed out that in terms of membership the scheme of South African autonomy had not been successful. But this, they said, was due to the extraordinary circumstances obtaining in that country. They recommended that the scheme should be given a further year's trial. They expressed their solidarity with the South African boiler-makers who, they said, were 'fighting the organised tyranny of capitalism'.

In April 1914 a protest conference about the situation in South Africa was held in London. The conference carried a resolution stating that the actions of the South African Government were a menace to organised labour throughout the British Empire. It recommended that a special levy of ½d per member should be made towards a general defence fund. A resolution was also adopted by the House of Commons stating that the rights of British citizens contained in Magna Carta, the Petition of Rights and the Habeas Corpus Act, should be observed throughout the Empire. The members of the Boilermakers' Society voted heavily in favour of the levy to assist the struggle of the South African trade union movement. The number of votes cast for the levy was 5,203; only 770 voted against. The members also voted by a majority of approximately six to one in favour of continuing the autonomous organisational scheme for the South African branches.

MINERS' STRIKE - 1912

In 1912 the great unrest continued. In the spring there was the biggest strike ever to take place up to that time in British history. It was a miners' strike and involved over a million workers. The miners were seeking a minimum wage and were also pressing for the recognition of the Miners' Federation as the representative body of miners throughout Great Britain. The Government intervened in the dispute and introduced a Minimum Wage Bill. This Bill established machinery for the determination of district minimum wages. The miners did not win their central demand but a concession had been gained. Above all, the strike demonstrated the power of the miners when united nationally in support of a claim.

The Boilermakers' Society expressed their support for the miners. The Executive Council proposed that a 1s levy should be imposed on all members to support the miners' dispute fund. This proposal was supported by 4,248 votes to 864. The Society sent £2,000 to the Miners' Federation and, in addition, provided a loan of £10,000 to the Lanarkshire miners.

The miners also established an eight-hour working day in the pits including the time taken for one winding. The Parliamentary Committee of the TUC took up the campaign for an eight-hour working day and demonstrations were organised in cities throughout Britain. The Boilermakers' Society took a leading part in demonstrations held in the main shipbuilding areas.

HOURS OF WORK

The movement for the eight-hour working day gathered strength in 1913. The Boilermakers' Society initiated the proposal that if negotiations failed to secure an eight-hour day then the TUC should unilaterally impose a limit of eight hours in all industries. Efforts were also made in the House of Commons to secure legislation for an eight-hour day. Will Thorne, the leader of the gasworkers, introduced a Bill for a general eight-hour working day and Bills were also introduced dealing specifically with working hours on the railways, in baking and in cotton textile mills.

The TUC organised a ballot vote on the eight-hour day for members of affiliated organisations. The ballot was on four separate questions. The first asked whether members were in favour of an eight-hour day with a rigid restriction on overtime. The second whether they were in favour of obtaining an eight-hour day by negotiations. The third whether they were in favour of giving support through the TUC to any affiliated organisation which fixed a date after which members would not work more than eight hours in any one day. The fourth whether they were in favour of the TUC continuing to press for an Act of Parliament for a maximum eight-hour day.

Big majorities were recorded in the Boilermakers' Society for each of these four propositions. The results were:

Question 1	For 5,287	Against 578
Question 2	For 4,426	Against 607
Question 3	For 4,509	Against 675
Question 4	For 5,340	Against 581

The effort to win an eight-hour working day by negotiation yielded few results. John Hill, the General Secretary of the Society, made clear his view that rank-and-file action was needed. The constitutional way, he said, had led to imperceptible movement. He recalled that the nine-hour working day was obtained by rank-and-file action and 'leaders were left to follow their members'. History, he thought, was likely to repeat itself. The issue of an eight-hour day should not be delayed 'till our members dissatisfied with their leaders take irregular action to force the pace'.

John Hill returned to the subject in the April monthly report of the Society. He again emphasised that negotiations were getting nowhere. The question, he insisted, should be settled in the summer of 1914 otherwise events would be overtaken by another slump in trade. He warned that 'if we cannot settle by consent then we must pull our belts a hole tighter and use other means'. A few weeks later at a meeting with the Engineering Employers' Federation John Hill said that engineering workers were becoming tired of their leaders talking the question to death and never getting anything.

On the Mersey the members of the Boilermakers' Society took matters into their own hands. All overtime and night shift working was stopped and, after a short period, a forty-seven hour working week was conceded by the employers. John Hill underlined the importance of this example and urged all members to keep up the agitation for an eight-hour day.

In the summer of 1914 the Engineering Employers' Federation rejected the claim of the unions for an eight-hour day. The Boilermakers' Society were prepared to support a call for action to enforce the demand of the unions. Before this demand could be considered by the other unions war had been declared. The claim for an eight-hour working day was put aside.

INTERNAL DIFFERENCES

In the summer of 1912 the Executive Council of the Society and the General Secretary found themselves at odds on the question of a new procedure agreement with the Shipbuilding Employers' Federation. The Executive Council were in favour of an approach being made to the Federation for such an agreement whereas the General Secretary was hostile to it. He recalled that only a few months earlier the members had voted against such an agreement. The Executive Council decided to convene a conference of representatives of all the shipbuilding areas. This took place at the end of July. The majority favoured the course suggested by the Executive Council.

A further conference of shipbuilding representatives was held in September 1912. At this conference a resolution was adopted as follows:

> That we favour a national agreement between the Shipbuilding Employers' Federation and the United Society of Boilermakers for dealing with general fluctuations in wages and questions of an agreed general character or such as may be remitted from local conferences with the consent of both parties at local conference. All local questions to be dealt with locally and finally in localities. There shall be a neutral chairman at all conferences.

The conference also suggested that the members themselves should deal with issues arising in shipyards with or without the presence of the district delegate. They were also opposed to any scheme under which local questions could be remitted to a central conference with the Employers' Federation. Central conferences, the delegates felt, should deal only with questions of general application. These proposals were put to the membership and were supported by 3,691 votes to 1,328.

Despite the result of this vote the General Secretary remained strongly opposed to a new national agreement. In the February issue of the monthly report he pointed out that on a series of rule changes suggested by the General Council the members had voted overwhelmingly in favour of an amendment insisting that district delegates should not interview employers before interviewing the members. So far as agreements are concerned, said John Hill, the ordinary members have the gravest suspicion of all leaders.

Early in 1913 the Boilermakers' Society put their proposal for a new agreement to the Shipbuilding Employers' Federation. The negotiations were unsuccessful. In his annual report for 1913 the General Secretary recalled that the membership had wisely decided to be 'without many of the agreements which employers were slow to implement . . .'

At this stage interest in the negotiations for a new procedure agreement was overtaken by a demand for wage increases. A claim for a general advance in wages in federated shipyards was made in February 1913. In reply the employers predicted that trade would decline and that instead of a wage increase a counter claim would be submitted for wage reductions.

The prediction of a slump proved false. Trade continued to boom. Ultimately a wage offer was made by the Federation and, by a relatively narrow majority, was accepted by the Society. The voting was 4,184 in favour and 3,492 against. The General Secretary said of the increase that it was so small that it should not be regarded as an advance. Rather, 'in view of the great prosperity of the industry and the increased cost of living, it was an indignity and an insult to our intelligence'.

REVERSING THE OSBORNE JUDGEMENT

At the 1912 Labour Party conference the Boilermakers' Society moved a successful motion calling for the complete reversal of the

Osborne judgement. The motion stated that for forty years unions had had the right to levy themselves for the purpose of labour representation. This right, said the Boilermakers' Society, should be restored to trade unions. An amendment was also carried which advised all trade unions affiliated to the Labour Party to defy the law until such time as it was changed.

A few months later the Society suffered a setback when the members turned down a proposal that a levy of 4d per member for labour representation should be paid before the end of July 1912 and a further levy of 4d should be paid before the end of September 1912. The voting was 3,725 against the proposal and 2,505 in favour.

In the following year a new Act was passed by Parliament which recognised the right of trade unions to provide money for purposes of political representation providing that the members voted in favour of the creation of a political fund and providing also that members who did not want to contribute should be given the opportunity to contract out. The Bill had a stormy passage through the House of Commons but was eventually placed on the statute book. John Hill criticised the Act because he said that it enabled a minority to contract out of majority decisions.

Soon after the Trade Union Act 1913 was placed on the statute book the Boilermakers' Society drew up a resolution for the establishment of a political fund. This resolution was submitted to the membership and was accepted by 2,764 votes to 1,542. The members thus approved the furtherance of political objects within the meaning of the Trade Union Act 1913. Though there was a comfortable majority in favour of political action it was significant that many branches both in the north east and on the Clyde voted against. Of the thirteen branches in Sunderland, for example, only three recorded a majority in favour of political action. Not one of the Newcastle branches voted in favour. Shortly afterwards the rules for the setting up of a political fund were adopted by the narrow majority of 4,684 to 4,316.

DUBLIN

In 1913 trade was booming. The monthly report of the Boilermakers' Society described it as a year of unparalleled prosperity.

The membership rose to 66,288. Claims for wage increases were successfully pressed in many industries. The mood of militancy spread to many sections of the trade union movement. Trade union organisation was extended to many more workers.

In the late summer the focus of attention shifted to Ireland. In Dublin a dispute began which was to become one of the most memorable in the history of the British Isles. The cause of the dispute was the decision of one of Dublin's leading employers to dismiss from employment members of the Irish Transport Workers' Union. This union was led by James Larkin, a giant figure in the Irish labour movement.

Larkin was an advocate of industrial unionism. He was a militant and one of the most effective agitators ever produced by the labour movement. His supreme ability was to make workers conscious of the injustices of capitalist society. Larkin worked closely with James Connolly whose support for militant trade unionism was also associated with a deep understanding of social history. Connolly was a writer of talent and was strongly influenced by Marxist ideas.

The Irish Transport Workers' Union, though based in the transport industries, was prepared to organise workers of every occupation except those already covered by established trade unions. The union attached great importance to the strike weapon and relied on sympathy strikes, particularly from transport workers, in order to enforce their claims in newly organised establishments. The policy of the Irish Transport Workers' Union was successful and many significant improvements in wages and conditions were achieved. Wages in Dublin were considerably lower than in British cities.

In the summer of 1913 the owner of the Dublin Tramways, W. M. Murphy, embarked on a course to defeat the Transport Workers' Union. He controlled not only the tramways but a number of other enterprises in Dublin. He said that the Transport Workers' Union organised sympathetic strikes in breach of agreements with firms where the Union had already been recognised. Members of the Transport Workers' Union were dismissed from employment. Other employers then followed the example of W. M. Murphy. The Irish Transport Workers' Union accepted the employers' challenge and called a strike of members. A number of other unions supported the stand of the Transport Workers' Union. Many of the employers sought to obtain from workers an undertaking that they were not members of the Transport Workers' Union and would not join it.

The dispute in Dublin had special significance for British unions for two reasons. In the first place a number of British unions had members employed in Dublin and they became involved in the dispute. Secondly, even though some British union leaders had little sympathy with the views of James Larkin, the struggle in Dublin was seen as an attack on the fundamental right of workers to organise in trade unions. The Irish Transport Workers' Union also called for solidarity action from British workers, particularly those involved in handling goods exported from Ireland.

At the 1913 TUC held at Manchester the standing orders were suspended to enable the delegates to discuss the Irish transport workers' lockout before proceeding with the ordinary business of the Congress. A deputation of trade unionists from Dublin was received. A report in the journal of the Boilermakers' Society said that the Congress seethed with indignation. A resolution was carried condemning the Government and the Lord Lieutenant of Ireland for the brutal manner in which trade unionists in Dublin had been treated by the police resulting in the loss of two lives and injuries to several hundreds. The Congress agreed to send a delegation of three to Dublin to speak at meetings in favour of free speech and the right of trade union organisation and to inquire into the allegation of police brutality. One of the selected members of the delegation was John Hill.

Whilst in Dublin the delegation interviewed the Lord Mayor, the Lord Lieutenant, James Larkin, who was then in Mountjoy Prison, representatives of the Trades Council and the Irish Transport Workers' Union and representatives of the employers. The delegation reported on their visit and traced the cause of the dispute. They said that the Irish Transport Workers' Union had adopted a very aggressive policy, including sympathy strikes, and this policy had been met by the employers with an equally aggressive policy of a sympathetic lockout. Employers in Dublin had issued a form for employees to sign which required them to promise that they would not belong to the Irish Transport Workers' Union or any trade union affiliated with it. They were also required to promise to give one week's notice before joining any strike.

The delegation's report pointed out that Mr W. M. Murphy was also the proprietor of three Irish newspapers and was thus able to use the power of the press in a campaign against James Larkin and the trade union movement. The delegation said that on Saturday 30 August the police had broken up a meeting of trade unionists, two workers were battered to death and hundreds were seriously injured. The delegation were determined to assert the right of free speech, despite discouragement from the Lord Lieutenant and other government officials in Ireland. A mass meeting of trade unionists was successfully held in O'Connell Street. A vast crowd assembled and was addressed from three platforms. A motion was carried asserting the intention of trade unionists to defend the right of free speech and trade union organisation.

The delegation saw James Larkin in Mountjoy Prison and immediately afterwards were successful in arranging a conference between representatives of the Dublin Trades Council and employers to consider whether a way might be found to resolve the dispute. The meeting was adjourned but the employers then withdrew. The TUC delegation said that 'we are thoroughly convinced that the Dublin Employers' Federation are not prepared to make any kind of agreement with responsible trade union representatives and are determined to crush trade unionism in Dublin'.

The TUC delegation summarised the results of their mission by stating that they had asserted the right of free speech despite the warnings of government representatives. They also said that the right of trade union organisation was seriously menaced by the authorities who were using armed force to assist the employers to coerce trade unionists into abject subjection to the conditions laid down by the employers. They added that they had ample evidence to prove that the legal right to picket was being ignored by the authorities. Finally, they said that the persistent delay of the authorities in opening an inquiry into alleged police brutalities was justification for the gravest suspicion. The firm tone of the report owed much to the influence of John Hill, who, though the general secretary of a craft union, had strong sympathy with the militancy of James Larkin.

On the return of the delegation to Britain John Hill suggested to the TUC that British trade unionists should send a food ship to Dublin. This suggestion was adopted. John Hill reported this development to the Boilermakers' Society and said that two ship-loads of food would be sent to the starving wives and children 'of our comrades in dispute in Dublin'. It was, he said, a striking example of what could be achieved when workers were united. He pointed out that in Dublin men were working for 17s a week and women for 5s a week. He appealed to all trade unionists to support the Dublin workers. He spoke of the 'bloody outrages and murders of trade unionists in Dublin'. John Hill came in for some criticism from a number of members who were unsympathetic to James Larkin and the Dublin workers. John Hill stood his ground and said in the monthly report that he would never apologise. His heart, he said, had been full of indignation when he learned of the outrages committed against trade unionists in Dublin.

The Executive Council of the Boilermakers' Society proposed that an immediate grant of £200 should be made to the Dublin Transport Workers' Union. This was supported by the membership in one of the most overwhelming majorities ever secured in a vote in the history of the Society. The number of votes cast in favour of the proposal was 5,741, the number against was 9. Many branches urged the Executive Council to increase the grant and shortly after-wards it was decided to send an additional £300. Branches in the Manchester district urged the Society to send £200 per week and a number of branches decided to impose levies of 3d per week per member. The decision of the Executive Council in granting a further £300 to the Dublin workers was endorsed by 4,827 votes to 213. Shortly afterwards the members voted by 5,979 to 539 in favour of a levy of 3d per member to assist the Dublin workers. The TUC raised £83,000 to assist the Dublin workers.

By the end of 1913 many workers in Dublin and their families were facing near-starvation. Early in 1914 the dispute came to an end. Neither side won. There was not a negotiated settlement and to that extent the outcome might be interpreted as a victory for the employers. On the other hand, the resistance of the Dublin workers had been so great that some employers did not insist on the terms on which the dispute began. The great Dublin lockout of 1913 was one of the most stirring pages in the history of trade union solidarity. Larkin had been sentenced to seven months' imprisonment but there was such a wave of protest that he was released within days. In the history of the Dublin struggle the

Boilermakers' Society in Britain could be proud of the part they played. This was due in no small measure to the very firm leadership given by the General Secretary, John Hill.

MOVES TOWARDS AMALGAMATION

In the great industrial unrest of the years immediately preceding the First World War there was a strong movement for trade union amalgamation. Ideas about industrial unionism had considerable influence among active members of the trade union movement. In the summer of 1910, for example, a demonstration of 1,000 members of the Boilermakers' Society in Manchester, drawn from seventeen branches, passed a resolution calling upon the Executive Council to convene a conference 'of all engineering and ship-building trades to formulate a scheme of amalgamation'. In November 1910 the Federation of Engineering and Shipbuilding Trades discussed three resolutions from affiliated unions calling for amalgamation or a closer knit Federation. In 1911 the affiliated unions were asked to vote on the proposition that the Federation should become such a closer knit body. Boilermakers voted by 4,430 to 1,317 for the proposition. Letters discussing industrial unionism appeared regularly in the monthly journal of the Society. In 1912 the Boilermakers' Society took part in discussions for amalgamation with the Amalgamated Society of Engineers, the Ship Constructors and Shipwrights' Association and the Liverpool Shipwrights' Association. Only the discussions with the Liverpool Shipwrights' Association came to full fruition.

Early in 1912 the members of the Liverpool Shipwrights' Association voted in favour of a scheme of federation with the Boiler-makers' Society. The scheme was also accepted by the members of the Boilermakers' Society by 4,766 votes to 806. In August 1912 agreement was reached with the Liverpool Shipwrights' Society on the rules for the proposed Federation. It was agreed that members of the Liverpool Shipwrights' Society should pay a contribution of 1d per member per week to the central funds of the Boilermakers' Society. In return they would be entitled to dispute benefit of 8s per week for eight weeks. The Federation was to be managed by a joint committee consisting of the five members of the Executive Council of the Boilermakers' Society and two members of the

Executive Committee of the Liverpool shipwrights. The general secretaries of both organisations were also to be members of the joint committee. The members of the Boilermakers' Society voted in favour of the proposed new rules by 3,890 to 1,100. The Federation took effect from 1 October 1912.

The discussions with the Shipwrights' Association got off to a good start. It was agreed at the outset that the members of both organisations should be asked to vote on a proposal that the two unions should attempt to devise a scheme of amalgamation. In a circular to the membership the Executive Council of the Boilermakers' Society said that the ever increasing power of capital rendered individual action by trade unions less and less effective. It was only by a combination of industrial and political action that it would be possible for unions to win further reforms. Unity was essential. The members of the Boilermakers' Society voted by 4,379 to 1,247 in favour of the amalgamation discussions.

In the meanwhile the Boilermakers' Society had been exploring tentatively the possibility of amalgamation discussions with the Amalgamated Society of Engineers. The Shipwrights' Society objected to parallel discussions taking place. At the request of the shipwrights the boilermakers agreed to take no further steps towards amalgamation with the ASE whilst negotiations were proceeding with the shipwrights.

At the end of July 1912 the Boilermakers' Society called a special conference to consider amalgamation. The conference recommended the appointment of a joint committee with the shipwrights to draft a scheme of amalgamation and also carried a resolution favouring the principle of amalgamation with the Amalgamated Society of Engineers. The resolution said, however, that no overtures should be made to the ASE until an understanding had been reached with the Shipwrights' Society.

A meeting with the shipwrights was held in October 1912. The boilermakers submitted a scheme as a basis of amalgamation but the shipwrights put forward many counter proposals. One of the most serious difficulties was that the boilermakers favoured the principle of a full-time executive council whereas the shipwrights favoured the principle of a lay executive council. The differences between the two organisations were so wide that no further meeting was arranged for a number of months.

In view of the difficulties with the shipwrights the Boilermakers' Society turned once again to the possibility of developing closer relations with the Amalgamated Society of Enginers. A special conference between the two organisations was held in October 1913. It was agreed that joint action should be taken to extend trade union organisation among non-unionists. Particular attention was to be given to railway workshops. The two unions also agreed to undertake joint action on wages at local level.

During the following month a resumed conference on amalgamation was held with the shipwrights. At this meeting it was apparent that the differences between the two organisations were so wide that amalgamation was not an immediate possibility. There were differences not only on the composition of the executive council but on other rules, scale of contributions and benefits. Nevertheless, agreement was reached that a joint committee should be established to draft proposals for closer unity.

The proposals were put forward early in 1914. The general principle was that there should be joint action on all matters of mutual interest in the shipbuilding, shiprepairing and engineering industries. This was to include, in particular, joint action on working hours, wages, working conditions and the extension of trade union organisation. The two unions agreed to set up a joint fund and to pay into this fund a contribution equal to 3d per member every three months. Dispute or lockout benefit would be payable from this fund equal to 3s per week for eight weeks. This would be in addition to the dispute benefit paid by each society. A joint central board was also to be established consisting of five executive members from each organisation together with the respective general secretaries. Provision was also made for joint action at local level. Finally, provision was made for dealing with any differences arising between members of the two societies. The working agreement was submitted to the membership of both organisations and was accepted. The voting of the Boilermakers' Society was 5,141 in favour and 956 against.

DEMARCATION

The moves towards closer working between the Boilermakers' Society, the Shipwrights' Association and the Amalgamated Society

63

of Engineers were prompted not least by the experience gained from costly and damaging demarcation disputes. John Hill took his usual militant stand whenever and wherever the interests of boiler-makers were affected but never ceased to emphasise that demarcation disputes were damaging to trade unionism. He urged strongly that the unions themselves should resolve such disputes so that workers could combine together for the protection and advancement of their common interest. He objected in particular to any kind of demarcation arrangement under which an employer had the right to adjudicate between two trade unions.

In 1911 there was a particularly bitter demarcation dispute between the boilermakers and shipwrights at Short's shipyard, Sunderland. The dispute lasted for six months, from the beginning of May to the beginning of November. The roots of the dispute went back to the early years of Short's yard in the 1870s. When the yard was first opened the ironwork was done by members of the Boilermakers' Society. The management constantly complained of the cost of employing members of the Boilermakers' Society and when a dispute took place on piece-work prices the employer replaced the strikers with men whose training had been in wood. These men then formed themselves into a small local society. Many years later this small society was taken over by another local organisation and eventually by the national Shipwrights' Association.

At a later stage still the ironworkers in Short's yard asked to be allowed to join the Boilermakers' Society. Because they were members of the Shipwrights' Association and not of the Boiler-makers' Society they were not able to obtain work in other yards on the Wear or Tyne. The Shipwrights' Association refused the request for a transfer of union membership. The Boilermakers' Society then admitted them into membership. The men were dismissed by the employer and their jobs were filled by other members of the Shipwrights' Association. The shipwrights were not, however, able to fill all the vacancies because, according to the Boilermakers' Society, they did not have a single riveter in any federated shipyard in the United Kingdom. Some of the vacancies were then filled by non-union labour.

The Mayor of Sunderland intervened and attempted to arrange a settlement. Unfortunately it was unsuccessful. The case was then submitted to the Federation of Shipbuilding and Engineering Unions. After hearing both unions the Federation's officers submitted a recommendation that all men engaged in the dispute at Short's should resume work immediately and should be free to join whichever society they chose, it being understood that any man who left one society to join the other would carry out his financial obligations to the first society. This recommendation was accepted by the boilermakers but was rejected by the shipwrights. The shipwrights urged that a committee should be appointed to devise a scheme for an interchange of cards between the two unions for platers, riveters and caulkers. This counterproposal was rejected by the Boilermakers' Society who then urged strongly that the Shipwrights' Association should accept the recommendation of the Federation.

On 30 October the demarcation dispute was finally resolved. The terms of settlement were similar to the recommendation of the Federation. Short's, Sunderland, were free to employ members of either society on ironwork providing that consideration was given to existing employees of the firm. This, in fact, meant that the men who had joined the Boilermakers' Society would be given back their jobs. The Boilermakers' Society undertook to facilitate the re-employment of members of the Shipwrights' Society who had jobs there before the dispute began. An extremely important provision in the settlement was that any member of the Shipwrights' Society employed at Short's as a plater, riveter, caulker or holder-up would be required to take out a card of the Boilermakers' Society before obtaining employment at any other shipyard on the Wear. Finally, the two unions agreed that all members should clear any indebtedness to their respective unions.

Negotiations had also been proceeding with both the Engineering Employers' Federation and the Shipbuilding Employers' Federation for a demarcation agreement covering all trades. Talks had been going on for nearly three years. The employers requested that they should be given a voice in demarcation settlements. They urged that they should have the right to appoint three of their number to sit with three of each trade in dispute. The Amalgamated Society of Engineers were disposed to accept a settlement along these lines rather than to have no agreement on demarcation. The boilermakers on the other hand were opposed to the employers having a voice in demarcation disputes. John Hill pointed out that in a demarcation dispute the unions concerned were likely to take opposing views. If employers were to be represented on a demarcation disputes committee then the determining voice would probably be that of the employers. John Hill said that he disputed the claims of the employers to adjudicate in such matters. He said 'I have no right to decide whether a doctor or a dentist shall set my broken limb or pull my tooth and should I dare to call the wrong man these two professions would quickly settle the matter for me. All I would be allowed to do would be to pay and look pleasant, and what is good etiquette in the professions is good enough for us.'

The boilermakers suggested that three employers should be permitted to sit on a demarcation disputes committee providing also that there were three neutral trade unionists in addition to the trade unionists from the disputing unions and that the committee should be chaired by an independent person. The proposal of the boilermakers was opposed by the employers.

Despite the opposition of the Boilermakers' Society the other trades, largely under the leadership of the Amalgamated Society of Engineers, accepted a proposed demarcation agreement on the lines put forward by the employers. The provisional agreement said that in the event of a demarcation dispute there should be no stoppage of work and that failing settlement by direct negotiations the management should be entitled to give a temporary decision 'upon which the work shall proceed'. The dispute would then be considered by a disputes committee. The decision of the committee was to be accepted as final and binding.

As members of the Federation the Boilermakers' Society agreed to put the proposed agreement to a vote of the membership. The Executive Council made clear, however, their dislike of it. It had little resemblance, they said, to the kind of agreement suggested by the Boilermakers' Society. The members rejected the agreement by 2,309 to 1,720.

In the following year, 1913, the Boilermakers' Society accepted for contractors' work in H M Dockyards a demarcation agreement on lines similar to the agreement rejected by the membership for application in federated shipyards and engineering workshops. A demarcation disputes committee was to be established consisting of representatives of the unions in dispute and there was to be a chairman appointed by and from the Dockyard contractors. The chairman was to have the power of decision in the event of two unions being unable to agree. In accepting this agreement the Boilermakers' Society were reflecting their own weakness in H M Dockyards. Traditionally the platers in H M Dockyards were organised by the Shipwrights' Association.

In the following year, 1914, the Boilermakers' Society was able to conclude with Harland and Wolff Ltd, Belfast, the kind of demarcation agreement it favoured. The agreement was also signed by other unions represented among the employees of Harland and Wolff. Under the terms of the agreement each union involved in a demarcation dispute was to give evidence before a neutral chairman appointed by the Board of Trade. The employer was also asked to give evidence and thereafter the unions concerned, together with the neutral chairman, were expected to try to reach agreement. The employer was not to be represented in the discussions. If the unions concerned failed to agree then the task of making a decision fell to the neutral chairman. John Hill described this arrangement as 'perhaps the most remarkable agreement ever offered to trade unionism in our industry'. Demarcation disputes, he said, were the bitterest of all disputes and the unions should do all that was possible to bring them to an end.

APPRENTICES

The revival and then the boom in trade in the years preceding the outbreak of the First World War led the employers to demand an increased number of apprentices in shipyards. In April 1911 the Shipbuilding Employers' Federation gave notice to amend the existing apprenticeship agreement by eliminating the age limit. The Boilermakers' Society resisted this claim and pointed out that from the time when the previous agreement had been signed in 1901 there had been flagrant cases of breach of the arrangements by certain employers. Some employers had taken on a much higher proportion of apprentices to journeymen than was the general custom of the trade and they had also taken on apprentices outside the agreed age limit. Although, according to the Boilermakers' Society, evidence had been brought at various times to substantiate these charges the Federation had taken no action to uphold the agreement. The Boilermakers' Society insisted on their right to share in the control of apprentices. In a characteristic comment the General Secretary, John Hill, said that 'it was quite apparent that the question of making good tradesmen was a secondary question to the making of profits'.

The Boilermakers' Society was, however, aware of the shortage of holders-up in shipyards. Because of this shortage a number of riveters were also unable to obtain work. This in turn was delaying work for caulkers and platers. In discussion with the Shipbuilding Employers' Federation it became evident that the employers were very much concerned at the shortage of holders-up. The Society offered to amend their existing practices so that more holders-up could be recruited and could then be given the opportunity to graduate to other branches of the boilermaking trade. The Society also pressed the Shipbuilding Employers' Federation to adopt a proper system of indentured apprenticeship. This was not acceptable to most of the employers because, as they pointed out, a proper indenture system would require them to maintain apprentices in employment in bad years as well as good.

The outcome of these discussions on apprenticeship was that the Boilermakers' Society decided to introduce a new scheme from the beginning of 1912 for the registration of apprentices. The employers were resolutely opposed to this policy but the Society, nevertheless, went ahead. The employers wanted unlimited entry to apprenticeship according to the state of trade, whereas the Boilermakers' Society wanted a controlled entry sufficient to supply an adequate number of well-trained tradesmen. 'Adequacy' was to be defined by the long-term trend and not by reference to any one year, whether prosperous or depressed. A vote of the branches resulted in almost unanimous approval for the apprentice registration scheme. Rules were also prepared for an apprentice section of the Society. Apprentices were able to join between the ages of 16 and 22 years. Apprentice members were entitled to sickness, unemployment and funeral benefit.

Because of the failure to reach agreement on apprenticeship with the Boilermakers' Society the Shipbuilding Employers' Federation submitted a claim for the control of apprenticeship to all unions in the shipbuilding industry. A conference was called for this purpose.

The other unions were reluctant to attend the conference because they were well aware that the real issue of contention concerned the boilermaking trades. The conference did not lead to an agreement.

RIVETERS AND HOLDERS-UP

The shortage of holders-up in shipyards had another consequence. The holders-up were dissatisfied with their piece-work earnings and pressed for a higher proportion of group piece-work earnings. This meant, in effect, that more would have to be given from group earnings by riveters to holders-up.

So serious did this issue become that a special national conference of riveters and holders-up was called by the Boilermakers' Society. Representatives attended from all the main areas. The General Secretary submitted to the conference information about the time rates of wages of riveters and holders-up in different areas. The highest time rate for riveters was in London and Southampton, 38s per week. The lowest was in the north east and on the Mersey, 35s a week. The highest rate for holders-up was at Northwich, 35s a week, and the lowest in Scotland, 28s 2d. The rules of the Society stipulated that any member working in a squad and employed on piece-work should share squad piece-work earnings in proportion to the time rates of wages. It was clear from the figures produced by the General Secretary that there were, nevertheless, fairly wide variations in piece-work earnings of holders-up in relation to the earnings of riveters. On average, however, holders-up received 16s 8d for every pound paid to riveters.

Representatives from Sunderland stated that the officially recognised proportion of piece earnings payable to holders-up was 75 per cent of the earnings of riveters. A standing notice issued by the Sunderland District Committee stated that anyone paying more than 15s to the pound would be fined, yet it was acknowledged that the customary proportion was 18s per pound. There was not a single squad of riveters who were paying 15s to the pound.

At the conference the representatives of riveters agreed that the wages of the holders-up were too low but they also argued that riveters wages were not sufficiently high to enable them to pay out of their group earnings a higher proportion to the holders-up. Eventually agreement was reached on a resolution recommending that piece-work earnings of holders-up should be in the proportion of 10½d to each 1s earned by riveters, that is, 17s 6d to the pound. In order to provide the money for this increase it was agreed to make a claim on the employers for a 4 per cent advance in riveting piece rates. In support of this claim the riveters complained that they were required to work harder because of the increased weight of plates, harder rivets, deeper counter-sinks and thicker plates.

By the end of the year the shortage of riveters was so acute that a notice was published in the monthly report of the Society stating that any cases of 'notorious bad time-keeping' by riveters would be severely dealt with by district committees. When an individual riveter was absent from work the remaining members of the riveting squad were not able to follow their normal employment. This then affected the employment of platers and caulkers. The Executive Council also instructed branches to give members every facility in changing their cards from other branches of the trade to those of riveters and holders-up.

This shortage of labour encouraged the Boilermakers' Society to press for the abolition of what were known as discharge notes. Without one of these notes no man could transfer his employment from one federated yard to another. They were first introduced on the Clyde and were extended to the north east coast in 1909. The case for them put forward by the Shipbuilding Employers' Federation was that it enabled an employer to indicate whether a particular employee had a bad time-keeping record. They were, however, very much resented by members of the Boilermakers' Society. The discharge notes frequently referred not only to time-keeping but other matters which might result in the victimisation of a particular worker. The Boilermakers' Society sought to abolish the discharge note system but were unable to secure the agreement of the Federation. Finally, the Society decided that from 1 January 1912 no member should either accept or tender these notes for employment. The employers refused to accept this unilateral act of the Society but after a few weeks they found it impossible to impose their will. The Society was successful and in February 1912 the discharge note system was finally withdrawn.

The claim for a 4 per cent increase in piece-work prices for

70

riveters met with a blunt rejection from the employers. Two national conferences were held with the Shipbuilding Employers' Federation but on both occasions the employers refused to make any special concession to riveters. The Society was reluctant to call a strike on the issue because a stoppage of work would have affected not only riveters but also platers, anglesmiths, caulkers and other tradesmen. Opinion in the main shipbuilding areas appeared to favour a ban on piece-work rather than a strike. This reluctance to engage in strike action on a special claim for riveters was reinforced by the knowledge of the membership that a general wage claim was being simultaneously pursued on behalf of members. The alternative of a strike or a ban on piece-work was put to the membership and there was a majority in favour of a ban on piece-work. The voting was 4,316 for the ban and 1,914 against. By 2,351 to 1,529 the members rejected the alternative of a strike.

The claim for a general advance in wages was successful. Agreement was reached for 5 per cent on piece rates and 1s per week on time rates payable from Saturday 31 August 1912. This took some of the steam out of the riveters' claim, but early in 1913 a new agitation began. Another special conference of riveting representatives was held on 25 February. At this conference the General Secretary submitted a number of detailed calculations to show that if there were a $2\frac{1}{2}$ per cent increase on piece-work prices for riveting it would be possible to pay holders-up $10\frac{1}{2}$d for every 1s of the piece-work earnings of riveters without the riveters having to suffer a reduction in pay. The special conference decided to modify the earlier claim for a 4 per cent increase in piece-work prices and instead to claim a $2\frac{1}{2}$ per cent increase.

A GENERAL CLAIM

By this time a further claim was being advanced by the Boilermakers' Society for a general increase in wages for all members of the Society. The claim was for 5 per cent on piece rates and 1s per week on time rates. This claim was said to be without prejudice to the special claim of the riveters. Three national conferences were held on this general wage claim and on each occasion the employers rejected the claim. They said that members of the Boilermakers'

Society lost approximately 19 per cent of all working time through bad time-keeping, absenteeism and disputes. If this lost time were eliminated the members of the Society could secure for themselves a substantial increase in pay.

The Boilermakers' Society rejected the arguments of the employers and pointed out that the alleged loss of working time was in many cases attributable either to bad management by employers or factors outside the control of the workers. When men stopped work in disputes it was often because of changes introduced unilaterally by the employers without negotiation. The Society also pointed to the large amount of overtime which the employers were requesting. Because of the refusal of the employers to make any concessions at the three national conferences on wages the Society introduced a ban on overtime from 1 May 1913.

The Executive Council also asked the membership for authority to submit strike notices in support of a claim for a wage increase. This was approved on a vote of the membership by a ten to one majority. The authority for strike action was also extended to the claim for the special increase of $2\frac{1}{2}$ per cent on riveting piece rates.

The very heavy majority in favour of giving the Executive Council authority to call a strike in support of the two wage claims had the desired effect Negotiations were re-opened and in July 1913 agreement was reached for a general increase of 1s per week, together with a special increase of $2\frac{1}{2}$ per cent on riveters piecework prices. The increase of 1s per week was not to the satisfaction of many members and when the agreement was put to a vote it secured a relatively narrow majority in favour.

HM DOCKYARDS

The Boilermakers' Society continued to make representations to the Government for the reclassification of riveters, caulkers and men engaged on the bending, punching, shearing and drilling of plates in H M Dockyards. Traditionally these men had been classified as skilled labourers and not as tradesmen. The only boilermakers classified as tradesmen in H M Dockyards were men actually employed in the manufacture of boilers. The platers were organised by the Shipwrights' Association. Almost every year the Boilermakers' Society were responsible for a successful resolution at the TUC urging the Government to bring their practice in H M Dockyards into line with that of private shipyards.

The Government's case for the practice in H M Dockyards was that the riveters and caulkers were recruited not from apprentices but from boys who came into the Dockyards in the hope of learning a semi-skilled occupation. The Admiralty claimed that by classifying them as skilled labourers it could transfer them from one semi-skilled occupation to another. The Admiralty were thus able to give them continuity of employment, whereas if they had followed the practice of the private shipyards men would have been thrown out of work periodically according to the phasing of various jobs.

The Boilermakers' Society rejected this defence put up by the Government and said that the real reason for the Admiralty practice was that it provided cheap labour. The basic rate for a skilled labourer in H M Dockyards was 22s or 23s a week whereas the rate for a riveter employed by a private contractor in any of the Dockyards was 40s 6d per week. The Government said that the Boilermakers' Society's figures were misleading. The skilled labourers were on a scale of pay, and this scale could rise to a maximum basic rate of 28s per week. They claimed that the average earnings of skilled labourers employed on piece-work were more than 34s a week.

Despite frequent representations to the Government no progress was made on the claim of the Boilermakers' Society. The Society's representatives were, however, embarrassed in their discussions with the Government by the rules of the Society which did not provide for Dockyard riveters and caulkers to be full members. They were organised in what were known as auxiliary branches. From time to time these auxiliary branches were called together by the Boilermakers' Society to discuss matters of mutual interest to skilled labourers employed on riveting, caulking, drilling, bending, punching and the shearing of plates. One such conference of auxiliary branches held in 1912 was joined by delegates from the regular branches of the Boilermakers' Society organising boilermakers in H M Dockyards. At this joint conference a resolution was adopted calling for closer association between the regular branches and the auxiliary branches. The representatives of the regular branches also carried a resolution expressing support for amalgamation with the Shipwrights' Association.

In the summer of 1912, after the Executive Council had again been embarrassed by the Government pointing out that the Society did not admit Dockyard riveters and caulkers into full membership, it was decided to ballot the members on a proposal that the rules should be changed. Unfortunately the membership rejected the proposal by a substantial majority. The voting was 4,107 against the proposal and 1,619 in favour.

In 1914 the issue was again raised by the Boilermakers' Society. The Government were pressed to give skilled status to riveters and caulkers in the Dockyards but once again the Admiralty were able to point out that the Boilermakers' Society did not recognise the skilled labourers as eligible for full membership of the Society. A number of branches on the south coast urged the Executive Council to take the initiative and to urge the membership to vote in favour of a change in the rules. They also urged that an additional district delegate be appointed for the purpose of extending the organisation of the Boilermakers' Society among all who might be eligible to join in the Dockyards.

The Executive Council responded to the request and issued a statement pointing out that men working as riveters and caulkers in the Dockyards had been organised only in auxiliary branches. The Society had appealed year after year to the Admiralty to recognise these men as tradesmen but the Society had itself refused to give them recognition. The Executive Council said that the Society should act consistently and give recognition to men who were legitimately entitled to recognition as tradesmen and as full members. The Executive Council also gave publicity to statements adopted by the London and South Wales District Committees expressing support for the proposals of the Executive Council. The EC concluded their statement with the following words:

It lies with you, worthy brothers, first, to recognise men who are truly and legally entitled to that recognition, and thereafter we may rest assured these men will be enabled, without help, to wipe out the stigma of inferiority which the Admiralty has continued to place upon our craft as iron shipbuilders in all parts of the country as well as in Royal Dockyards. We appeal, therefore, to your sense of brotherhood and fair play and also to your respect for your own craft, to vote in favour of this organisation scheme.

This time the response of the membership was overwhelmingly favourable to the point of view of the Executive Council. By 4,471 votes to 870 the membership voted in favour of the proposal of the Executive Council. Even so, the Dockyard authorities continued to refuse skilled status to the men concerned.

AN APPROVED SOCIETY

The passing of the National Insurance Act 1911 was of very great significance for the trade union movement It established a contributory scheme to insure workers against sickness, and a similar scheme, though less comprehensive in scope, for insurance against unemployment. Friendly societies and other organisations including trade unions could become approved societies for the purpose of the administration of the benefits. The contributions were 4d per week for men and 3d per week for women, 3d per week from the employer and the equivalent of 2d per week from the state. It was from this arrangement that the phrase '9d for 4d' came into common use. The separate insurance scheme for unemployment did not cover all employed persons but it embraced workers engaged in shipbuilding, engineering and the vehicle building trades among others. Again the principle was that contributions should be made by employees, employers and the state.

Under the health insurance scheme benefits were intended to cover all necessary medical attendance, special treatment in a sanatorium for sufferers from tuberculosis, and a payment of 10s a week for twenty-six weeks and 5s a week after twenty-six weeks up to the ages of 70. There was also to be a payment of 30s in the case of a confinement where either the mother herself or her husband was insured.

The trade union movement welcomed this new measure though not uncritically. John Hill described it as the greatest Act which had ever been placed on the statute book but it was, nevertheless, he said, 'seething with imperfections'. The greatest of all its failings was, he contended, that those who needed insurance most, the unhealthy and the casual workers, were not satisfactorily insured at all. Contributions would be placed to their credit when they were working but when the credits were exhausted no one would take responsibility for them beyond continuance of medical benefit for the current year.

When the Bill was going through Parliament the trade union movement made representations on a range of detailed matters including, for example, the arrangements under which a worker might decline to work at less than recognised rates, the effect on contributions and benefits of men engaged in strikes or lockouts, the effect on men and women who were suspended from work and the arrangements made for securing new work. The craft unions, particularly in engineering and shipbuilding, were opposed to the provisions for the training of workers who were lacking in skill and knowledge. The unions feared that adult training schemes might lead to a surplus of skilled men and the subsequent reduction of wages.

In its annual report for 1911 the Boilermakers' Society recalled that for seventy-seven years it had undertaken responsibility to provide financial benefit for sick or unemployed members. The new Act, said the annual report, stipulated that in future employers and the state would have to share these burdens with society. This was a principle with which trade unionists would agree, but the Society warned that the control and administration of the scheme should not be taken completely out of the influence of trade unionists. It was here, said the report, that the danger lay. Trade unionists would have to be alert to ensure their full representation on local committees concerned with the administration of the new scheme. The annual report predicted that in time there would be a demand for the state to provide wholly against sickness and unemployment. Trade unions would then be able to concentrate on protecting and improving wages and conditions.

In 1912 the members voted in favour of the Boilermakers' Society becoming an approved society for the purpose of the National Insurance Act. The voting was 5,489 to 338. A statement was published to the membership showing that the financial effect of the new scheme would be to the benefit of the Society. Indeed, the Society stood to gain financially more than any other trade union, largely because of the high rate of benefit paid by the Boilermakers' Society. The Boilermakers' Society was also one of the very few organisations that paid the fees of doctors called upon to administer to the needs of members. The Executive Council calculated that the introduction of the new scheme under the National Insurance Act would benefit the Society to the extent of more than £54,000 per year.

In the annual report for 1912 it was pointed out that the new scheme had resulted in a very great increase in the amount of work falling on branch secretaries. It might have been possible to centralise the work at the head office of the Society but the Executive Council deliberately rejected such a policy. It would, they said, kill the fellowship and comradeship of branch life. It would have relieved branch officials but would have demoralised the Society.

The annual report for 1912 welcomed the National Insurance Act but warned that the primary function of a trade union was to defend the trade interests of members. The time and strength of active trade unionists should not be expended on subsidiary questions such as health insurance. Might it not be better, asked the annual report, if these functions were administered separately through local committees? The employing class, said John Hill, had reason to bless and not to curse the new National Insurance Act 'as it has filled men's minds with hope and filled trade union leaders' heads with work'.

John Hill soon became an authority on the administration of the new scheme. He continued to support its general principles but warned against the illusion that it satisfied trade union objectives. At one large meeting which he addressed on Tyneside he predicted that approved societies would ultimately drop out of existence and the cumbrous machinery of the Act would be cast aside in favour of a non-contributory scheme financed by the state. An intelligent government, he said, would organise the nation's industries in the interests of the producers and consumers, and sharks who gambled on the Stock Exchange would be eliminated 'even as Christ whipped the traffickers from the Temple of Jerusalem'.* John Hill answered Labour Members of Parliament

* One of John Hill's favourite quotations was from Abraham Lincoln's first annual message to the United States Congress: 'Labour is prior to and independent of capital. Capital is only the fruit of labour, and could never have existed if labour had not first existed. Labour is the superior of capital, and deserves much the higher consideration.'

who expressed criticism of trade unionists because they did not subscribe to the view that all problems could be solved by political
action, legislation and arbitration. In reply, for example, to Mr
Philip Snowden, one of the foremost leaders of the Labour Party,
John Hill said:

> We are all willing to admit that Mr Snowden is one of our intel-
> lectuals but the fault of our Labour Members is the assumption
> that they and they only know what is good for the workers and
> in this they are agreed with the employing class, who supply
> compulsory education, compulsory drill, compulsory vaccination,
> compulsory compensation and insurance, all for one purpose,
> namely, that we may be more profitable tools in their hands.

John Hill said that the workers would continue to struggle against
their fetters and would use all means at their disposal including
industrial as well as political action.

The implementation of the National Insurance Act and the
establishment of the Boilermakers' approved society led to the
introduction of new scales of contributions and benefits. From 15
January 1913 first class members paid a contribution of 3s per
fortnight. In return they received sickness benefit of 10s per week
from the Society and 10s per week from the state. This total of £1
per week lasted for the first twenty-six weeks of sickness. Afterwards the benefits were reduced by one half. Members unemployed
received 7s per week from the Society and 7s per week from the
state, making a total benefit of 14s per week payable for eleven
weeks. Thereafter for four weeks the member received 7s per week
benefit from the state. Members also received superannuation
benefit. Reduced scales of benefit were payable to second class and
third class members. There was also provision for apprentice
members. Special scales of state sickness benefit applied to all
classes of members over 50 years of age. One other change introduced as a result of the National Insurance Act was the election
by the Society of a national insurance secretary.

SOLIDARITY

The Boilermakers' Society continued its tradition of solidarity with other workers engaged in industrial disputes. The high points of this solidarity were the support given by the Boilermakers' Society to the miners in their national dispute in 1912 and to the Dublin workers in 1913.

These, however, were not the only examples of support given by the boilermakers to workers engaged in industrial disputes. In 1911 money was sent to assist miners in South Wales not only by the Executive Council of the Society but also by branches. The monthly report stated for example that the Selby branch sent £23 from its very small membership. In 1912 two grants of £20 each were made by the Executive Council to workers involved in a dispute in the transport services in London. Further money was sent from branches amounting altogether to about £75. Branches also sent money to London building trade workers engaged in a dispute against non-unionism in 1914.

Chapter 4

The Boilermakers' Society
in the First World War

In the years immediately preceding 1914 the labour movement in
Europe had pledged itself to oppose militarism and the preparation
for war. It was argued in the labour movement that any new war
between the great powers in Europe would be caused by imperialist
rivalry. Britain had acquired a huge empire by conquest and this
gave advantage and profitable outlets to business interests. This
domination was being challenged by Germany whose industrial
strength had developed at a later stage and was already overtaking
that of Britain. The German industrialists and financial interests
looked with envious eyes on the imperial possessions of Britain and
saw also new possibilities of domination in the Middle East, Africa
and in Eastern Europe. Thus Germany needed to challenge the
power of Britain, France and Belgium in the west and of Russia
in the east.

When war came in August 1914 the resistance of the labour
movement to the military preparations largely collapsed. In Britain
most of the workers were persuaded to support the war on the
grounds that it was a struggle for the defence of democracy. It
mattered little that Britain was by far the world's largest colonial
power and that it was allied with Tsarist Russia, which was one of
the most repressive regimes in the world. In Germany, likewise, the
majority of workers were persuaded to support German war aims
on the grounds that the fatherland was struggling against Tsarist
autocracy and seeking an equal place in the sun with the dominant
colonial power, Great Britain.

80

There were some exceptions to this capitulation of the European labour movement to the war plans of the rulers of the main imperial powers. In Russia an important section of the labour movement, led by Lenin, came out strongly against the war and expressed its full support for the pre-war anti-militarist declarations of the international labour movement. In Germany some of the left-wing leaders of the labour movement, led by Karl Liebknecht, made a historic stand by voting in the German Parliament against the granting of war credits to the Kaiser's government. In Britain the Independent Labour Party, including its leader Ramsay MacDonald, did not support the war, though their opposition was much more on pacifist than on socialist grounds. A small number of left-wing members of the British Socialist Party (one of the fore-runners of the Communist Party) also opposed the war.

BOILERMAKERS' RESPONSE

The response to the war of the majority of the members of the Boilermakers' Society was no different from that of the rest of the British working class. There was an immense barrage of publicity to convince British citizens that the real purpose of the war was to defend Belgium which had been trampled underfoot by the might of the German war machine. The General Secretary, John Hill, wavered. He was a socialist and a militant. He was not widely read in socialist theory but he had a strong belief in international class solidarity. In August 1914 he described war as 'the greatest curse of nations' and said that notwithstanding the lengthy explanations of statesmen it was exceedingly difficult for working men 'to understand what we are fighting for'. He expressed his opposition to the expansionist aims of Germany but he said that it was hateful to every lover of liberty that Britain should be associated with Serbian assassins and Russian tyrants. As workers, he said, 'we have no quarrel with the workmen of Europe and when the workers of all countries are wise they will cease to become the pliant tools in the hands of ambitious warlords . . .'

By the following month John Hill's position on the war had become more equivocal. He reaffirmed that he did not trust the aims of the statesmen and military leaders, but the workers, he argued, were offering themselves in the cause of liberty and democratic institutions. He went on '. . . when we have fought and won, as we must win, we must fight against those even of our own nation who would rob us of the result of a war in which so many of our class have staked their all'.

As the pro-war propaganda mounted during the opening months of the war John Hill became more committed in his support for the war. By October 1914 he was talking of maintaining and increasing Britain's fighting forces until victory was won. But his faith in the common interests of working men of all countries still remained. At the end of the year he wrote that hundreds of the members of the Boilermakers' Society were already in the front line facing boilermakers and shipbuilders from Germany who had no more responsibility for the outbreak of war than the members of the British Boilermakers' Society.

In the early weeks of the war the membership voted in favour of a levy of 1s per member per quarter for the relief of members' dependants adversely affected by the war. They also voted in favour of a grant of £300 to a war fund launched by the Prince of Wales.

In December 1914 the Executive Council decided to relax the regulations regarding the admission of holders-up. A special national conference was held to deal with the problem of the shortage of riveting squads and a number of suggestions were put to employers for the better use of riveters and the making up of riveting squads where labour was not available.

At the beginning of 1915 the Boilermakers' Society protested against profits being made out of the war. John Hill said that there was no loyalty amongst employers or financiers. Contractors were putting defective material into soldiers' huts, and footwear manufacturers were supplying boots which went to pieces after a week's wear. Shipowners carrying coal and grain had raised their freight rates threefold and were netting profits of many thousands of pounds after each voyage.

The January 1915 issue of the monthly report of the Boilermakers' Society carried a reprint of a letter from a Gateshead soldier serving with the British army in France. In this letter he described the fraternisation between the British and German soldiers on Christmas Day 1914. The fraternisation, he said, had been started by the Germans who lit up their trenches and shouted their

Christmas greetings to the British troops. The British soldiers responded and then some of the soldiers walked out into no man's land and met their 'enemies' halfway. They wished each other Merry Christmas, shook hands and declared a truce for Christmas Day. Later some of the British soldiers started to kick a football outside the trenches and a number of German soldiers joined them. The Gateshead soldier said that 'to cut a long story short it finished up with meeting one another half way, shaking hands, exchanging cigarettes, souvenirs, and parting the best of friends. One has given me his address to write to him after the war. They were quite a decent lot of fellows, I can tell you.'

John Hill greeted this report of fraternisation and said that if it were left to the working men of Britain and Germany there would be no war. Common men of all nations must take the affairs of state into their own hands. Fortunes were being made by rich shareholders from the manufacture of guns which were then used to blow the workers of each country to eternity.

WAR-TIME CHANGES

By the early weeks of 1915 the steep rise in the cost of living had led to serious unrest among engineering and shipbuilding workers, particularly on the Clyde. A strong rank and file movement developed and for the first time the term 'shop steward' became familiar to newspaper readers. The demand for higher wages was led by rank and file workers' representatives. Many of the shop stewards on the Clyde came together to form the Clyde Workers' Committee. Strikes took place and eventually wage increases were conceded. In the shipbuilding industry an increase of 4s per week was conceded to time workers and a 10 per cent increase in piece-work prices was conceded to piece-workers.

In 1915 the Government appointed a Committee on Production to consider ways of increasing the output of ships and munitions of war. The committee proposed that no stoppage of work by strike or lockout should take place on work for government purposes and that, subject to certain conditions, all demarcation arrangements between skilled trades on government work should be suspended. Employers were asked to give an undertaking that any departure from trade practices would be only for the period of the war. In return for the suspension of the right to strike the committee proposed that any dispute not resolved through the normal machinery of negotiations should be referred for arbitration.

In one of its reports the Committee on Production proposed that where suitable skilled men were not available, greater use should be made of upgraded semi-skilled or unskilled workers. This became commonly known as dilution. The proposals of the Committee of Production were put to a conference of engineering and ship-building unions and were then considered at a meeting with the Chancellor of the Exchequer and the President of the Board of Trade held in March 1915. The recommendations for the suspension of the right to strike, the introduction of arbitration, the relaxation of trade practices and the dilution of labour were accepted by the unions and recommended to their members.

In the summer of 1915 Parliament passed the Munitions of War Act 'to make provisions for furthering the efficient manufacture, transport and supply of munitions for the present war'. The Minister of Munitions was given the power to declare any factory or yard engaged on war work a 'controlled establishment'. Lockouts and strikes in such establishments were prohibited. All the normal machinery for dealing with grievances was continued but if the grievances were not resolved they had to be referred to the Board of Trade for arbitration. Any rule, practice or custom tending to restrict production was to be suspended and any person inducing another worker to comply or continue to comply with such a rule, practice or custom was guilty of an offence under the Act. Departures from normal trade custom were to be recorded and were to continue only for the period of the war.

A national conference of representatives of the Boilermakers' Society was convened to consider the new legislation. It received a report on the representations made by trade unionists to secure amendments to protect workers' interests. The conference adopted a resolution stating that the trade union representatives had done all in their power to make the legislation as fair and equitable as possible under the circumstances.

In July 1915 an appeal was issued over the signatures of a number of trade union leaders, including John Hill, condemning any restrictions of output on war work. The appeal said that the national need was paramount and urgently called for maximum output from every worker engaged on war work.

In November 1915 the Boilermakers' Society convened another national conference of representatives to consider possible amendments to the Munitions of War Act. Attention was concentrated on four points. First, that employment of unskilled and semi-skilled labour upon work previously performed by skilled men should last only so long as skilled labour was unobtainable. Secondly, men should not be taken from higher paid work to lower paid work. Thirdly, apprentices should be allowed to change jobs when their apprenticeship was completed. Fourthly, men should not be prevented from leaving civilian work in a controlled establishment if they could find employment on shipbuilding or munitions production.

Though John Hill had signed the appeal to lift restrictive practices during the war he was still reluctant to associate himself with war propaganda. He refused to attend any of the conferences or meetings called on the first anniversary of the outbreak of the war. He said that he did not care to take the responsibility of deciding whether another million or so of the best men in Europe would have to give up their lives. Nevertheless, he said that looking back over the year he thought that Britain's decision 'to stand by Belgium . . . was our only honourable course . . .'

John Hill did, however, accept an invitation to visit the front line in northern France. He wrote a moving account of his experiences which was published in the monthly report of the Society. In the October 1915 issue he wrote of the contrast between the troops and the workers in industry on the one hand and the owners of Britain's shipbuilding industry on the other. He published a table showing the steep increase in profits of a number of leading engineering, shipbuilding and coal-mining companies.

At the 1915 TUC John Hill spoke in support of a resolution recording appreciation of 'the magnificent response made to the call for volunteers to fight against the tyranny of militarism'. The resolution went on to oppose conscription. Another resolution carried by the TUC expressed support for Great Britain and her allies in the war against German militarism. The Boilermakers' Society also moved a successful resolution at the 1915 TUC calling for the introduction of a Bill for a general eight-hour working day. Such a Bill, it was argued, was needed to educate public opinion.

OFFICIALS

Shortly after the outbreak of war John Hill had been returned unopposed as General Secretary. In his letter of thanks to the membership he said that he had sought to encourage and assist his colleagues to secure higher wages, shorter hours and better conditions of employment for the membership. He had also tried to widen the outlook of the Society.

In March 1915 the members voted in favour of a 5s per week increase in salary for the Executive Council members and the Assistant General Secretary. They also agreed to an increase for the General Secretary. When, however, the district delegates applied for an increase of 15s per week there was a substantial majority against the proposal. The claim of the district delegates was then reduced to 10s per week and this was accepted by 2,320 votes to 846.

Early in 1915 an appeal was made for a retirement allowance to James Conley, who had been the Clyde district delegate since 1887. He had served as a full-time official for about twenty-eight years. Before that he had been an active lay member of the Society almost immediately after joining in 1872. He was the Society's first nominee as a parliamentary candidate and in 1906 contested the Kirkdale constituency of Liverpool.

Three alternatives were put to the membership. The first was that there should be a levy of 2d per member and that the sum raised should be given to James Conley. The second was that an allowance of 25s per week should be paid to him and the third was that an allowance of £1 per week should be paid. The appeal was widely supported by a number of active members from Clydeside branches.

As soon as the appeal was published it met with a number of protests. One of the protesting London branches said that they had no ill-feeling towards James Conley but they were opposed to the establishment of a precedent. The Society's funds they said should be 'immune from life pensioners'. They referred in particular to the unfortunate experience when it had been decided many years earlier to give a life pension to the former General Secretary, Robert Knight. The former General Secretary had shown strong reluctance to accept any reduction in his pension when the Society was in financial difficulties. He had also opposed the policy of the Boilermakers' Society in one of its major disputes with the employers.

The effect of the protests was seen in the voting on the proposal for a retirement allowance to James Conley. It was defeated by 2,679 to 1,861. Even worse was to come. James Conley decided to stand again for election as one of the Clyde's district delegates. He suffered the humiliation of coming at the bottom of the poll among three candidates. His vote was barely one third of the successful candidate, W. Mackie.

The election of William Mackie was a reflection of the discontent felt by many members on Clydeside. The committee sponsoring him in the election said that he had sought to lift the class to which he belonged. He had taken a prominent part in the shipbuilding lockout in 1910 and had been a leader and organiser in the demonstrations and strikes which had taken place on Clydeside in 1915. James Conley was nominated by only one branch. In contrast William Mackie received nominations from thirteen branches.

The defeat of James Conley shocked many active members of the Society. At a national conference of Society representatives held in October 1915 a resolution was carried placing on record the appreciation of the Society for the valuable services rendered by James Conley for a period of more than forty years. It viewed with profound regret the decision of the membership not to give him a retirement allowance. The conference asked the Executive Council to submit a new proposal to the membership. This the Council did, and suggested that every member of the Society should pay a levy of 2d to be given to James Conley 'as a small recompense for his long and faithful service to the Society'. This time the proposal was carried, but only by a relatively narrow majority. The voting was 1,854 in favour and 1,550 against.

The presentation to James Conley was made in Glasgow in April 1916. Among those present was Arthur Henderson who by this time was a Labour representative in the Coalition Government. It was pointed out that James Conley had been a member for forty-four years and had held office for almost the whole of that period.

87

ORGANISATION

In September 1915 the Society decided very narrowly, by 2,146 votes to 2,082, to admit drillers into membership. The terms of admission were to be arranged at a special national conference. This conference took place towards the end of October. The terms of admission stipulated that drillers could be admitted in accordance with the rules of the Society but that no driller 'can progress to any other section of the trade'. It was also stipulated that all persons admitted as drillers were to confine themselves to their own section of work and would have to observe all existing demarcation practices. These conditions were put to the membership early in 1916 and were adopted by 1,583 to 934.

Another structural change in the organisation took place at the end of 1915 with the winding up of the South African Council. Since the setting up of the Council in 1911 the membership in South Africa had risen from 375 to 455. Even this figure, however, was doubtful and the finances of the South African branches were in poor shape.

The Executive Council of the Boilermakers' Society decided to bring the South African Council to an end and to terminate the services of the full-time organiser in South Africa. An appeal against this decision was made by the South African members. This appeal was put to the branches and was overwhelmingly defeated.

UNREST

In the 1915 annual report written early in 1916 the General Secretary said that the most distinctive feature throughout the year, apart from the war itself, had been the extraordinary rise in the cost of living. This had reduced the purchasing power of wages by something like 30 per cent. John Hill contrasted the sacrifices of trade unionists and the men in the front line with the increased profits made by the employers. He pointed out that during 1915 there had been very few disputes involving members of the Boilermakers' Society and the amount paid out in dispute benefit was the lowest for a period of thirteen years.

In March 1915 skilled men in shipbuilding received an increase in wages of 4s per week on time rates and 10 per cent on piece rates. This increase was awarded by the Committee on Production after the employers had rejected a claim by the unions and following stoppages of work among engineering and shipbuilding workers on the Clyde. One year later in March 1916 the Boilermakers' Society, together with other trade unions representing skilled trades in shipbuilding, applied for a further general increase in wages. No settlement was reached in negotiations with the employers and once again the dispute was referred to the Committee of Production. In August the Committee awarded an increase of 3s per week to time workers only. The Executive Council of the Boilermakers' Society expressed strong regret that the wages of piece-workers had not been increased.

In the spring of 1916 there was serious unrest among engineering workers on the Clyde. Thousands of workers were involved in stoppages of work. There was no single cause of the dispute though the immediate irritant was an argument at Beardmore's Parkhead, about the facilities to be afforded shop stewards in carrying out their duties. Behind this immediate cause, however, were other grievances including wages, dilution, and the system of leaving certificates which impeded the mobility of labour. Leaving certificates were particularly unpopular. Workers who obtained a certificate might find it endorsed with comments from an employer about unsuitability, unpunctuality or with other unfavourable observations. Leaving certificates were not abolished until October 1917. There were also many workshop grievances which were being taken up by shop stewards. The stewards were giving leadership to workers on issues where the official trade union leadership felt inhibited from taking action because of wartime legislation and their support for the war. Many of the leading shop stewards on Clydeside were opponents of the war.

In the April 1916 issue of the monthly report John Hill said, in referring to the recent wave of unrest, that a very large number of members had been in doubt as to whether 'they should be swayed by local influences to leave work in sympathy or should be loyal to their brothers in the trenches and to the advice of their

Executive . . .' John Hill added that he wished to make it clear that in his opinion there were no grievances that could justify the cessation of work for a single day.

The unrest on the Clyde in the early months of 1916 was regarded very seriously by the Government. At the beginning of February a school teacher, John McLean, who wielded considerable influence among leading shop stewards and active trade unionists on the Clyde, was arrested. McLean was an opponent of the war, a revolutionary socialist and an effective educationalist and propagandist. He lectured regularly at public meetings and classes for workers on the Clyde and his sessions were extremely well attended. He was later sentenced to three years' imprisonment for sedition. After the Russian Bolshevik revolution in the autumn of 1917 he was appointed a diplomatic representative of the revolutionary government.

A few days after the arrest of John McLean a journal issued by the Clyde Workers' Committee was suppressed and a number of prominent members of the Committee were arrested. Two of them were later sentenced to twelve months' imprisonment. In March, immediately following the Clydeside strike arising out of the dispute at Parkhead, another group of leaders of the Clyde Workers' Committee were arrested and deported from Glasgow. There were further strikes on the Clyde and the Government gave an assurance that there would be no further deportations.

One of the deported engineering workers was David Kirkwood, the convenor of shop stewards at Beardmore's Parkhead. Subsequently he was elected as a delegate of the engineers to the January 1917 conference of the Labour Party. In their report of the conference the boilermakers' delegates said that David Kirkwood contributed at the conference 'a manly and dignified statement concerning the deportation of his colleagues and himself'. The delegates, according to the boilermakers' report, were roused to anger. There was a demand for the immediate return of David Kirkwood and a committee were elected to investigate the cause of the deportation. John Hill, General Secretary of the Boilermakers' Society, was elected as a member of the committee. Immediately after the Labour Party conference Kirkwood returned to Glasgow but was deported again. It was not until the end of May 1917 that the deportation order was rescinded.

90

In the October 1916 issue of the boilermakers' monthly report it was pointed out that since the outbreak of the war the basic wages of members had risen by about 15 per cent. In the same period, it was said, the cost of living had increased by about 45 per cent. Food prices alone had risen by 62 per cent between July 1914 and June 1916. Many of the workers in shipbuilding and engineering were working long hours of overtime and this alone enabled them to keep their earnings in line with the rise in the cost of living.

Through the winter of 1916–17 the Society continued to urge upon the Committee on Production the need to award an increase for piece-workers in line with the 3s per week awarded earlier to time workers. The Committee on Production agreed to receive representations from the Boilermakers' Society and from other trade unions in May 1917. After listening to the unions they deferred giving an award and said that the claim should be considered in conjunction 'with proposals for general changes in wages in the shipbuilding and engineering trades' which were about to be submitted. Shortly afterwards the unions representing skilled workers submitted a claim to the employers for an increase of 25 per cent on time rates and 25 per cent on piece-work rates. This claim went to the Committee on Production, who awarded 5s per week to both time workers and piece-workers payable from April 1917.

Towards the end of March 1917 the Engineering Employers' Federation and the various engineering unions, including the Boilermakers' Society, agreed to suspend for the period of the war the normal operation of the procedure for dealing with general changes in wages. During the period of this suspension it was agreed that, with the consent of the Committee on Production, consideration should be given at four-monthly intervals to the level of wages in the engineering industry. The awards made by the Committee on Production were to be applied in all federated firms.

Early in 1917 the Federation of Engineering and Shipbuilding Trades accepted, at the request of the Government, proposals to extend the system of payment-by-results in the shipbuilding industry. The purpose of these new proposals was to increase output in the shipbuilding industry. British merchant shipping was under strong attack from German submarines.

In the early summer of 1917 the Society signed with Messrs Green and Silley Weir Ltd an agreement on apprenticeship. The agreement was also signed by the juvenile employment committee of the Ministry of Labour. The Society and the employer regarded this as a model agreement and it was commended to all other firms in the industry. It covered riveters, including occupations subsidiary to riveting, caulkers, cutters, angle ironsmiths, platers and draughtsmen. The agreement included clauses relating to age limits, the period of service, the regulation of the number of apprentices, the division of labour, wages, provision for continued education and for the joint control of the apprenticeship scheme.

The unrest in Scotland in 1916 and 1917 brought to the fore in the Boilermakers' Society a number of leading militants. One of them was J. M. Airlie. When there was a vacancy for a district delegate for the south side of the Clyde in the summer of 1917 he ran for election. In his election address he said nothing about the war effort but instead stressed that the interests of the employers and the workers were directly opposed to each other. The need of the capitalists, said Airlie, was to get plenty of cheap labour, to avoid strikes and to get big dividends. The need of the worker was to get a living wage, decent working conditions, the right to sell his labour to the best advantage and a shorter working week.

Airlie was at a disadvantage in contesting the election for a Clyde district delegate because he came from Edinburgh. When the result of the election was announced J. M. Airlie was one of the unsuccessful candidates. There were, however, allegations of irregularities in voting and, following an investigation by the Executive Council, the election was declared void and a new election was held. Two of the leading candidates were declared ineligible. This gave Airlie a new opportunity. He again fought the election as a militant and this time he was successful. Again there were allegations of irregularities, particularly in one of the branches where strong support had been given to Airlie. These allegations were again investigated and once again the Executive Council ordered a new election. A third election was then held and J. M. Airlie was again successful. His majority was narrow. He secured 863 votes against 740 for his competitor, R. D. Reid. Two branches which would have voted heavily in favour of J. M. Airlie were disqualified because they did not take the vote on an ordinary meeting night.

SCHEME FOR UNITY

The problems faced by the engineering and shipbuilding unions during the early period of the war underlined the need for unity. Towards the end of 1915 the Federation of Engineering and Shipbuilding Trades put forward a number of proposals designed to bring about closer working between affiliated unions. The proposals were submitted to a ballot vote of the membership of the Boilermakers' Society and were supported by 2,026 votes against 292.

The unity scheme of the Federation of Engineering and Shipbuilding Trades covered seven proposals. The emergency committee of the Federation was to be the authority to carry out the policy of the Federation between annual meetings. The membership of each signatory union was to remain inviolate, and lapsed or expelled members were not to be admitted into another union until the union to which the lapsed or expelled member had originally belonged had been consulted and all subscriptions fully paid. Propaganda work was to be undertaken to recruit non-union labour, and district rates of wages were to be maintained by joint action between the unions. Any union which was proposing to put in a claim for improved wages or conditions was to give notice to other unions and the opportunity was to be given for other unions to co-operate. Finally it was emphasised that the Federation was to have no responsibility on demarcation problems or in respect of 'partial sectional disputes'.

At the beginning of 1917 the Boilermakers' Society and the Ship Constructors' and Shipwrights' Association entered into a joint working trade agreement. The purpose of the agreement was to promote joint action on claims affecting wages, hours of work and shipyard conditions, and the extension of trade union membership. Joint district boards were established consisting of not more than five representatives from each union together with the full-time officials of each union.

At the beginning of 1918 the joint working agreement with the shipwrights was extended to include the blacksmiths. Preliminary discussions also took place on the possibility of an amalgamation between the three unions. Each of the unions undertook to ballot its members on amalgamation before the end of 1918.

During 1918 discussions took place between the three unions about amalgamation. They made little progress. There were basic differences between the unions in their structure, methods of organisation and scales of benefit.

As part of the campaign for amalgamation the Devonport district joint working board of the three unions called a mass meeting in Plymouth Guildhall. Representatives of each of the three unions spoke at the meeting, including John Hill on behalf of the Boilermakers' Society. A member of the Boilermakers' Society moved a successful motion welcoming the 'spirit of closer unity indicated in the joint trades working agreement' and urging the three unions to accelerate complete amalgamation.

John Hill was a strong supporter of the amalgamation proposals. In his annual report for 1918 he said that throughout the year continued efforts had been made towards the unification of all workers in the shipbuilding and engineering industries. He hoped in particular to see progress towards an amalgamation between the shipwrights, the separate union for Liverpool shipwrights and the Sheet Iron Workers' Society.

SACRIFICES

As the sacrifices of war increased John Hill continued to be tormented between, on the one hand, his opposition to German militarism and, on the other, his consciousness of the misery caused by the slaughter. In the annual report for 1916 he argued that the longer war went on the less hope there was for a better world in the future. He quoted with approval a manifesto issued by the Russian Council of Workers and Soldiers' Deputies saying:

> Workers of all countries, in extending to you a fraternal hand over mountains of brothers' corpses, across innocent blood and tears, and through the smoking ruins of towns and villages, and the destroyed treasures of civilisation, we summon you to a renewal of international unity. Therein lies a gauge of our victory and of our complete freedom.

John Hill said that a word from the Czar at the beginning of the war would have avoided the conflict. He also referred with approval

94

to the efforts made by President Wilson of the United States to bring the war to an end. He recalled that President Wilson had been supported by the American Federation of Labor but had been snubbed both by Britain and by Germany. Sections of the British press, he said, had 'howled with indignation at President Wilson'.

Early in 1916 the Boilermakers' Society took a prominent part in the public discussion of Government proposals for compulsory military service. A special national conference of the Society was held on 5 January 1916 at which a resolution in favour of compulsory military service was carried by a large majority. The majority of the delegates felt that this was the fairest way to ensure equality of sacrifice.

On the following day the representatives of the Boilermakers' Society attended a national conference of trade union and labour organisations to discuss the Government's proposals for compulsory military service. A motion was put forward by the Parliamentary Committee of the TUC reaffirming opposition to compulsory military service. The motion drew attention to 'the magnificent success of the voluntary principle which, in so short a period, has supplied this country with an army of 4 millions of free men'. The boilermakers moved an amendment to this motion calling for compulsory military service for fit single men but it was defeated by 2,121,000 votes to 544,000. The NUR then put forward a further amendment which re-affirmed opposition to compulsory military service, expressed pleasure at the success of the voluntary principle, and recommended the Labour Party in Parliament to oppose compulsory military service. This amendment was carried, and was then adopted as a substantive motion with a majority of more than two to one.

In February 1916 the Boilermakers' Society wrote to the Prime Minister urging that the Government should assume ownership of new merchant shipping. The Society pointed out that Britain was in urgent need of ships and their effective utilisation could not be obtained without direct and full national control. Ships had risen steeply in price because of the increased profits that they were now capable of earning. It was unreasonable, said the Society, that these extra costs should come out of the national purse.

The contrast between the high profits made by the employers and the limitations on the wages and mobility of workers was underlined by John Hill in the July 1916 issue of the monthly report. The law of supply and demand, he said, was too sacred to be interfered with when it applied to the employers, but in the case of the workers the law simply did not exist in war-time conditions. The worker was chained to his employment and his pay was controlled.

John Hill returned to the same theme when at the 1916 TUC he moved a motion viewing with alarm the increase in the cost of living and expressing indignation that the Government had not taken direct control of a number of essential industries.

At the same Congress the Boilermakers' Society repeated their success at the 1915 TUC by moving a further motion calling for legislation for an eight-hour working day to be introduced immediately at the end of the war. The resolution urged the TUC to organise demonstrations in various parts of the country in support of this principle. Another resolution moved by John Hill on behalf of the Parliamentary Committee of the TUC called for the extension of public ownership to railways, waterways and mines.

Early in 1917 John Hill reported on a visit which he had made to France as a TUC delegate to the French TUC. During his stay there he went to the battlefield on the Somme. He recalled words used by the British Prime Minister who described the Somme as 'the furnace of hell into which the many thousands of our best and bravest marched to suffer cruel wounds and oblivion'. Shortly afterwards the membership of the Boilermakers' Society decided by an overwhelming majority in a ballot vote to buy and donate an ambulance for use on the Western Front.

In March 1917 the Boilermakers' Society wrote to the Secretary of State for the Colonies protesting against an Act of Parliament prohibiting the formation of trade unions in the British West Indies. The attention of the British trade union movement to this legislation was drawn by Mr Samuel Gompers, President of the American Federation of Labour. The Boilermakers' Society asked for the Act to be repealed. They also sent a circular about the legislation to every branch.

WAR AIMS

At the end of 1916 John Hill warned that the final destruction of all forms of militarism would not be accomplished by the sword but by a union of the workers of the world. He was not to wait long for the first rumblings of revolution. In February 1917 the Czar was overthrown in Russia and a new government was brought to power under Kerensky. It was not a revolutionary socialist government and, indeed, it pledged itself to continue fighting the war. Nevertheless the February revolution was an indication that the old order was crumbling. John Hill welcomed the February revolution and said in the monthly report that he was grieved to think that the trade union movement in Britain 'is still dead to the appeal of new Russia'. He welcomed what he described as the emancipation of Russia. In a short struggle the Russian people, he said, had freed themselves from a yoke of centuries.

After the February 1917 change of government in Russia it was proposed that a number of trade unionists should visit that country. John Hill was suggested for this delegation. The proposal was put to the membership who voted in favour of it by 2,831 to 1,030. Shortly after his vote was taken it was announced that the visit of the delegation to Russia had been deferred. In the meanwhile four members of the Council of Workers' and Soldiers' Delegates of Russia visited Britain and met representatives of the TUC. Following this visit of Russian representatives the Parliamentary Committee of the TUC sent a cable to the President of the Council of Workers' and Soldiers' Delegates stating:

> that we congratulate the workers of Russia on the overthrow of the old regime and assure them of our willingness to co-operate with them in the direction of strengthening the powers of democracy and trade unionism for the purpose of securing the economic and political emancipation of the people.

John Hill was the President of the Trades Union Congress in September 1917. In his presidential address he spoke critically of the origin of the First World War. He recalled that a member of the Royal House of Hapsburg had been murdered at Sarajevo. 'Had the murdered man belonged to the class represented here today,' said John Hill, 'we should never have heard his name, but the blood of a royal prince must be avenged and the nations of the murdered man and the murderers took sides upon the question.' John Hill went on to say that he believed in the need to rescue a small gallant nation from the outrages of a tyrant. It was for this reason that he supported the war, but he did not support the ambitions of kings and capitalists. Our quarrel, he said, is not with the working men and women of Germany but with a system and a government which has created fear and suspicion in Europe.

In his report on the Congress to the members of the Boilermakers' Society John Hill drew special attention to a resolution which had been adopted by the delegates stating that an international conference would be of the greatest service and was a necessary preliminary to the conclusion of a lasting and democratic peace. In all the countries of Europe, said John Hill, labour had been divided against itself into majority and minority camps. He was pleased that at the TUC both the right and the left had supported a resolution calling for an international conference as a necessary preliminary for a lasting and democratic peace.

The resolution on the need for a peace conference arose out of a controversy over a proposal for an international labour peace conference to be held at Stockholm in the summer of 1917. There was both support and opposition to this proposal within the trade union movement. John Hill was among those who supported the proposal to attend the conference. He was supported in this by the members of the boilermakers' parliamentary panel. A proposal was then put to the membership of the Boilermakers' Society that delegates should be sent to the Stockholm conference. This, however, was defeated by 2,971 votes to 1,932.

At the end of 1917 John Hill was re-elected unopposed as General Secretary of the Society. He continued to be very critical of the war aims of the Allied Powers even though he supported the war against German militarism. At the end of December 1917 delegates of the Boilermakers' Society joined with more than 800 other delegates at a special conference of the labour movement to discuss war aims. A declaration of war aims was moved by Arthur Henderson, MP, on behalf of the Labour Party and seconded by John Hill on behalf of the TUC. The declaration said that the fundamental purpose of the British labour movement in supporting the continuation of the war was that the world should henceforth be safe for democracy. The labour movement, it underlined, had no sympathy with attempts to convert the war into an expedition of conquest. Germany should pay reparations for damage to Belgium, and Alsace and Lorraine should be allowed to determine their own political future. The declaration also made observations on the situation in the Balkans, Italy, Poland, the Turkish Empire, the colonies of tropical Africa and on the Jews and Palestine. An important part of the declaration dealt with the problems of peace and emphasised that it was the duty of every government to take immediate action not merely to relieve unemployment but to prevent it.

The memorandum of British war aims put forward by the labour movement conference in December 1917 was submitted to the branches of the Boilermakers' Society and was approved by 1,813 votes to 287. The Labour Party and TUC shortly afterwards launched a campaign to bring the declaration on war aims to the attention of the public. The Society, and John Hill in particular, played a part in this campaign.

In October–November 1917 there was a further revolution in Russia. This time it was a socialist revolution which sought to transfer political power to the councils (soviets) of workers, peasants and soldiers' representatives which had come into existence in many parts of Russia. The leaders of the revolution called for peace and for the withdrawal of Russia from the war. Despite opposition internally from the vested interests of the old order, despite civil war and economic chaos, and despite the hostility and intervention of the ruling class of many other countries, the revolution succeeded.

In the February 1918 issue of the monthly journal of the Society John Hill argued strongly that there must be 'a people's peace'. He recalled that immediately after the revolution in Russia the workers' delegates had said that the common enemy was not the people of the belligerent countries but their governments. The Russian revolutionaries had overthrown their own government and the workers of Austria and Germany were rising in spite of the despotism which held them in subjection. War, said John Hill, was a European quarrel for imperial expansion and capitalist exploitation. No sane workman believed any longer that this was a war for democracy.

This article, written under the immediate influence of the Russian Bolshevik revolution of October–November 1917, reflected a change in John Hill's outlook. He concluded his article by saying 'we the workmen of all lands have been in a maze of lies and misrepresentation. Russia calls upon us to come out, and the Labour Party of this country points the way to international negotiations and peace'.

John Hill's strongly expressed views on the aims of the war and the need to win the peace came under some criticism from a number of members. He replied to these criticisms in the June 1918 issue of the monthly report. He reaffirmed his belief that a conference of the workers of the belligerent powers would have been helpful. An honourable and lasting peace, he said, had been possible early in 1917. That, however, was not to be, even though, alleged John Hill, the British Government had been in touch with the Kaiser and his colleagues.

John Hill said that he was against the Kaiser and his class but he had still some faith in the common people, including the common people of Russia and Turkey, Bulgaria, Austria and Germany. The workers, he said, could not possibly have made a worse mess than the governing classes. The workers' representatives of the belligerent nations had declared that the war was the outcome of years of capitalist greed and imperialist ambition. All governments shared in the responsibility. He felt it would be preferable to build a new international of workers' representatives. He concluded by asking the membership to help in this effort to bring together the workers of all lands.

At the 1917 Labour Party conference John Hill spoke on the restoration of trade union conditions at the end of the war. A resolution was adopted reminding the Government that it was pledged unreservedly to restore after the war all rules, conditions and customs that prevailed in the workshops before the war. At the 1918 TUC John Hill spoke against a motion from the Sailors' and Firemen's Union condemning atrocities committed by Germany on the high seas. The General Secretary of the Sailors' Union, Mr Havelock Wilson, said that his union not only condemned the Kaiser and his government but the whole of the German nation. John Hill dissociated himself from such sentiments.

In the summer of 1917 John Hill was approached to accept the Order of the Companions of Honour. He received a letter from Buckingham Palace dated 30 June 1917 stating that his name had been recommended for the Order and he was asked to complete a form and return it at his convenience. John Hill's reply was as follows:

Sir,

I acknowledge receipt of your favour of 30 ultimo and thank you for the honour it is intended to confer upon me.

I have always felt that I am a citizen of no mean country, and my endeavour has been to serve my country by the efficient discharge of my duties of citizenship.

My work lies among my own class and I recognise that whatever I can do for their betterment is of national service. I hope to continue that work, and the acceptance of any title might cause me to be misunderstood, and render my work less useful. I therefore respectfully ask to be excused.

Faithfully yours,
John Hill

John Hill's forthright statement of views continued to arouse opposition from a section of members. In the December 1918 issue a letter was published from a member in Plymouth stating that the General Secretary had been asked to resign by a small section of members. The member from Devonport defended the General Secretary and he said that John Hill had reached his zenith in the eyes of his admirers when in his letter declining an honour he had used the words 'my work is with my class'. The letter went on to express solidarity with the new Soviet Government in Russia and urged members of the Boilermakers' Society not to vote for Liberals and Conservatives in the forthcoming general election.

INDUSTRIAL RELATIONS

Early in 1918 the Society concluded an agreement with the Shipbuilding Employers' Federation stating that any rule or custom which had been relaxed during the war would be restored at the end of the war. The employers also undertook not to employ anyone who was not a member of the Society; not to retain any non-member in employment whilst members of the Boilermakers' Society were available; and not to induce any member to leave the Society. A new procedure was concluded for the settlement of differences between federated firms in shipbuilding and members of the Boilermakers' Society. Any grievances which could not be settled domestically at yard level were to be referred to a joint committee. If the joint committee was not able to reach agreement the dispute was to be referred to a conference of representatives of the Federation and of the Society, together with a chairman appointed by the Chief Industrial Commissioner.

Wage claims continued to be submitted from time to time to the employers in accordance with the established war-time procedure. Rarely, however, was it possible to reach a voluntary negotiated settlement. The claims had then to be put before the Committee on Production. By the summer of 1918 the wage increases given since the outbreak of war amounted to about 25s per week for time workers. Time rates before the war averaged, according to the Boilermakers' Society, about £2 per week.

In December 1918 the Committee on Production awarded a further increase of 5s per week to adult male workers in the engineering industry. Wage increases had been granted at four-monthly intervals since the institution of the scheme under the Committee on Production. Wage increases had been granted in March, July and November 1917 and July 1918.

The members of the Boilermakers' Society voted in favour of a 25 per cent increase in the wages of all full-time officials. This applied to district delegates, members of the Executive Council, the Assistant General Secretary and the General Secretary. The increase was back-dated to the end of September 1918.

In 1918 the Boilermakers' Society began to campaign vigorously for a reduction in the length of the basic working week to take effect immediately at the end of the war. The Society urged that the basic working week should not exceed forty-four hours, that systematic overtime should be illegal, that the maximum overtime to be worked in any one month should not exceed thirty-two hours per worker, and that no person under 18 years of age should work overtime. In the summer of 1918 the Society approached the Shipbuilding Employers' Federation to negotiate a shorter working week to be introduced at the end of the war. The Federation were at first reluctant to meet the Society for such negotiations, but some weeks before the war ended they agreed to discuss hours of work with the shipbuilding trade unions. In these discussions the employers accepted the principle of a shorter working week after the war and proposed that the negotiations should be conducted jointly with the Engineering Employers' Federation.

At the September 1918 TUC a lively debate took place on hours of labour in which the Boilermakers' Society pressed for a forty-four-hour working week. They moved an amendment to a proposal from one of the general workers' unions that there should be a forty-eight-hour working week. On a card vote the proposal for the forty-eight-hour working week was carried by 2,108,000 to 2,091,000.

The war finally came to an end in November 1918. The engineering and shipbuilding unions pressed immediately for a reduction in working hours. At a conference held on 24 December 1918 agreement was reached between the engineering employers, the shipbuilding employers and unions affiliated to the Engineering and Shipbuilding Trades Federation for the introduction of a forty-seven-hour week from 1 January 1919. The new agreement came in for much criticism, not least from members of the Boilermakers' Society. The unions decided to submit the new agreement to a vote. On a ballot of the membership of the Boilermakers' Society the proposed agreement was rejected by a heavy majority. The vote against the agreement was 9,848 and the vote in favour, 3,974. On a total vote of the unions, however, the majority went the other way. The new agreement was accepted by 329,793 votes to 157,375. The Boilermakers' Society accepted the majority decision of the engineering and shipbuilding unions.

At the end of the war the membership of the Boilermakers' Society had reached more than 90,000 and at the end of 1918 the Society had a financial balance of £740,000. The annual report for 1918 recorded that the Society was continuing its efforts towards the unification of all workers in the shipbuilding and engineering industries. The hope was expressed that in the coming year the Society would be able to bring about amalgamation with the shipwrights and the sheet iron workers. The annual report concluded by commenting that the workers had as yet only dimly realised the power in their hands. Trade unionists were now more alive to the value of the power that was theirs providing they were properly united and honestly led. The objectives of the workers were not the objectives of the employers.

Chapter 5

A Short-lived Boom

The post-war period opened with a boom in trade. Among the members of the Boilermakers' Society there was virtual full employment and for the first time in history the membership rose to more than 100,000. In 1919, despite heavy expenditure on industrial disputes, the funds of the Society increased by more than £30,000. By the end of the year they amounted to £772,000.

With the ending of the war the industrial workers in Britain looked forward to full employment, improved working conditions and better social services. They were prepared to take up the struggle to achieve these objectives. In 1919 the Boilermakers' Society spent over £100,000 on industrial disputes. The number of disputes affecting members of the Society, said John Hill, disproved the claim of the employers that 'we are all brothers now'. The share of the wealth produced by labour would depend, he said, as in the past, on the effectiveness of the demands made by workers on the class who owned and controlled the nation's industries.

At the beginning of 1919 John Hill urged the members of the Society to recognise that they had it within their own hands in the shipyards and engineering factories to exert much greater control over industry. He complained that for many years the trend of negotiations had been to take power out of the hands of the men directly concerned and put it in the hands of officials who met far away from the workshops where disputes had their origin. He pointed out that there was now a revolt in the shop stewards' movement. The stewards were saying to the trade union officials that they were too slow and compromising. John Hill felt that this was a question of importance for the Boilermakers' Society and that the constitution of the Society should be such that the members should have conscious control of their own affairs in their branches and in the workshops.

HOURS OF WORK

The introduction of the forty-seven-hour working week was regarded by many active trade unionists, particularly on the Clyde, as an unnecessary compromise in the demand for a forty-hour week. The shop stewards on the Clyde led a revolt against the new agreement and by the end of January 1919 almost every engineering factory and shipyard in and around Glasgow was involved in a strike for the immediate introduction of a forty-hour week. A demonstration of some 50,000 workers in St George's Square, Glasgow, was attacked by the police, the Riot Act was read, and a number of the main leaders of the demonstration, including David Kirkwood, later Labour Member of Parliament, Emanuel Shinwell, later a Labour Cabinet Minister and William Gallagher, later a Communist Member of Parliament, were arrested. Troops were sent to Glasgow and the city was placed under martial law. The severity of the measures taken against the leaders of the strike, together with the opposition to the forty-hour movement of many of the official trade union leaders in London, finally brought the strike to an end in the middle of February. Nevertheless, the campaign had the effect of compelling the union leaders to re-open negotiations for a shorter working week.

In the early summer of 1919 the members of the Boilermakers' Society voted overwhelmingly in favour of a claim for a forty-four-hour week. The voting was 17,357 to 303. Negotiations were to continue for many months afterwards but no further progress was made. In the negotiations for the forty-four-hour week the employers relied mainly on the argument that Britain could not afford shorter hours because of German competition. German industry, the employers said, was undercutting British industry by some 35 to 40 per cent. John Hill was outspoken in his condemnation of the attitude of the employers. He asked them if this was evidence of their declaration of the new brotherhood between employers and workers. The war promises of the employers, he said, were of no more value than scraps of German paper.

In the midst of the negotiations on the claim for a shorter working week the Boilermakers' Society criticised strongly the views expressed by some of the representatives of the General Federation of Trade Unions who had condemned as 'unrealistic' the forty-hour-week claim. This body, it will be recalled, was originally established with the goodwill of the TUC to act as a means of pooling support for unions in disputes. The attitude of the Executive Committee of the GFTU, said the Boilermakers' Society, was 'painful to everyone who is honestly striving for the unification of labour forces'.

The shipbuilding employers were as opposed to the claim for a shorter working week as the engineering employers. The claim was put to the employers on behalf of the shipbuilding unions by John Hill but the employers replied by urging the unions to withdraw the claim for two years.

Negotiations dragged on without any real progress being made. Towards the end of 1919 there was a division between the unions about a call for an inquiry into the claim for a shorter working week. The Boilermakers' Society favoured a public inquiry but the majority voted in favour of a private inquiry. The Boilermakers' Society were sceptical about the possibility of such an inquiry leading to any change in conditions. John Hill argued that the issue would not be resolved without a ballot vote of the membership on a proposal for strike action.

Early in 1920 the Society wrote to the President of the American Federation of Labor, Samuel Gompers, to inquire about the experience of the forty-four-hour week in the shipbuilding industry in the United States. Samuel Gompers replied in a letter dated 3 February 1920. He said that 90 per cent of shipyard employees in the USA worked a forty-four-hour week. A shorter working day had proved more productive. In his reply Gompers quoted a statement from Henry Ford:

Employers who are hostile to the 8 hour day do not know their business. Eight hours is long enough for anybody to work. A man can't work more than eight hours and do good work. We've proved it often. We have had the eight hour day in force in the Ford factory for three years and we have made more money each succeeding year under it . . .

106

WAGES

Not only did the British employers oppose any reduction in the working week below forty-seven hours at the end of the war but they also sought to reduce the wages of both shipbuilding and engineering workers. The unions put in a counter-claim for an increase of 15s a week both for time workers and piece-workers. Under the arrangements then in existence the employers and unions agreed to the claim being submitted to arbitration. The claim was heard on 24 June 1919. The arbitration court decided to reject both the claim of the employers for wage reductions and the claim of the unions for wage increases. In their award the court said that in comparison with pre-war rates there had been an increase in shipbuilding of 28s 6d a week for time workers and 21s 6d for piece-workers. In addition, piece-workers had received upwards of 10 per cent on piece rates. There had also been special awards providing additional increases to both piece-workers and time workers. Despite the complex nature of the earnings structure the court also rejected the claim of the unions for wage consolidation.

Following the rejection of this national wages claim the Boiler-makers' Society decided to pursue a series of local claims. By the autumn wage increases had been secured in many districts. Towards the end of 1919 the unions again put in a national claim. This time they were more successful and an increase of 5s per week was awarded by the arbitration court.

Four months later the unions secured another increase in wages as a result of arbitration. This time the increase was 6s per week for time workers and 15 per cent on net piece-work prices. This award was in response to a claim from the unions for 15s a week with an equivalent increase in piece-work prices. In the early summer of 1920 the unions submitted another claim for wage increases. The arbitration court rejected the claim. This was the last of the arbitration awards made under the agreement of February 1917 which provided for a review of wages every four months.

In bringing the arbitration agreement to an end the unions were expressing the widespread dissatisfaction of their members. Workers felt that their wages were not keeping up with the rising cost of living and that the arrangements for resolving wages disputes

107

through arbitration ensured that the unions could not exert their full strength.

By the late summer of 1920 the Boilermakers' Society was engaged in a number of major disputes. On the Mersey, shipwrights and drillers were on strike to enforce a claim for a minimum wage of £6 per week. The strike was not given official backing by the union but John Hill argued strongly that the claim was reasonable. On the Clyde, platers' helpers were engaged in a dispute about wages and two shipyards were stopped. The dispute threatened to involve all west of Scotland shipyards. The strike was brought to an end with wage increases being granted to the helpers. Trade union organisation among platers' helpers had been extended from the north-east coast, where they had been organised since the 1890s, to the Clyde. The principal union involved was the National Amalgamated Union of Labour.

The prominent part played by shop stewards in the wages movement of the immediate post-war period enabled the unions to secure full recognition for them. An agreement to this effect was concluded with the Engineering Employers' Federation in the summer of 1919. It said that members of the various engineering unions employed in federated establishments could appoint representatives to act on their behalf and these representatives were to be known as shop stewards. The method of appointment of shop stewards was to be determined by the trade unions concerned. The names of the stewards and the constituency which they represented were to be notified officially by each union to the management.

The agreement also provided for the setting up of works committees, consisting of not more than seven representatives of the management and seven shop stewards. The stewards selected for this purpose were to be nominated by the shop stewards in the establishment. The agreement made it clear that shop stewards were to be subject to the control of their union and were to act in accordance with the rules and regulations of their union and the agreements with employers. Facilities were to be provided to shop stewards to deal with questions raised in the shop in which they were employed. This new agreement superseded an earlier agreement of 20 December 1917 made between the Engineering Employers' Federation and the engineering unions.

DISPUTES IN OTHER INDUSTRIES

In 1919 Britain was faced with a major dispute in the mining industry. The miners claimed a six-hour working day, a 30 per cent increase in wages and the public ownership of the industry. The coal owners and the Government strongly opposed these demands but the miners in a ballot voted overwhelmingly in favour of strike action to enforce them. In the spring of 1919 the Government compromised by agreeing to appoint a commission of inquiry under Sir John Sankey. The strength of the miners was sufficient to persuade the Government to agree that the miners' union should nominate some of the members of the commission.

John Hill complimented the miners on their insistence on the right to nominate one half of the members of the commission. When the names were announced he said that he had great expectations about the report. On the other hand he warned that the idea of appointing commissioners to head off unrest was 'as old as government itself'. It was not only old, he said, but it was 'hoary with deception'. Commissions were often appointed for bogus purposes to waste money and time 'in their endeavour to hide the truth'.

The commission divided half and half on the question of nationalisation but the chairman came down on the side of the miners and recommended that the principle of state ownership of the mines should be accepted. The commissioners were unable to agree on recommendations about pay, but the chairman suggested a number of concessions which were subsequently accepted by the Government. The Government did not, however, accept the recommendation in favour of nationalisation. Once the immediate threat of a stoppage on wages had been averted the Government consigned the Sankey report to the files. The trade union and labour movement conducted a public campaign in favour of public ownership but the Royal Commission had served the Government's purpose by averting an industrial crisis primarily on the issue of wages.

In the autumn of 1919 the storm centre shifted to the railway industry. In confused negotiations it appeared that the Government were seeking to enforce wage reductions on the railwaymen. The railwaymen resisted and eventually a stoppage of work took place.

The Government made careful preparations to try to break the strike by the use of volunteers and soldiers for the distribution of various goods. All this was, as usual, very strongly condemned by John Hill. He referred to secret circulars which had been sent to commanding officers in the army asking them to find out how many of the soldiers under their command were trade unionists and how many of them could be relied upon to act as strike breakers. He said the Government had also enlisted in their secret service other men who were prepared to act as spies and traitors to their own workmates. He described these men as unprincipled renegades.

John Hill declared his support for the railwaymen but echoed the complaint voiced by other trade union leaders, whose members were affected by the railway dispute, that they ought to have been consulted. The Boilermakers' Society had 15,000 members working for railway companies and these members were daily seeking advice from the Society. Unfortunately the Society had no official information and had not been able to take part in any negotiations. When the stoppage of work took place in the railway industry the Executive Council of the Boilermakers' Society instructed its members to continue normal working but not to do the work of any men directly engaged in the dispute. The dispute, finally came to an end because of the intervention of other unions, principally the transport workers. A settlement was reached under which wages were not reduced. Thus the resistance of the railwaymen, together with the support which they eventually secured from other workers, was sufficient to resist the pressure for a wage reduction.

AMALGAMATION?

In the period immediately following the First World War the mood of most workers was favourable to social reform and industrial change. This mood affected their attitude towards the structure of the trade union movement. Moves were made to bring about trade union amalgamations in the engineering and shipbuilding industries. In the engineering industry the Amalgamated Society of Engineers invited other unions in the industry to discuss amlagamation proposals which they had drawn up and which had been approved by their membership. This development led eventually to the forma-

1 The Newcastle headquarters of the Boilermakers' Society as they were originally built and as they remained throughout the period covered by this volume.

2 John Hill, General
Secretary, 1908–36.

3 Mark Hodgson, General
Secretary, 1936–

4 The centenary
demonstration of the
Boilermakers' Society held
in Manchester in 1934.

5 In the centenary
demonstration in 1934 pride
of place to lead the march
was given to the Bolton
branch. The Society was
formed in Bolton in 1834.

6 Another view of the centenary demonstration. A group of superannuated members were conveyed in the Salford state

tion of the Amalgamated Engineering Union. It came into existence on 1 July 1920. The Boilermakers' Society was one of the few unions not to participate in the engineering amalgamation.

The Boilermakers' Society decided to concentrate its efforts on bringing about an amlagamation in the shipbuilding industry. At the time many active trade unionists favoured industrial unionism but there were still strong feelings of craft identity among members of the Boilermakers' Society. This encouraged insularity and opposition to amalgamation with other organisations catering for less skilled workers.

In the first half of 1919 the Boilermakers' Society agreed to an amalgamation with the Sheet Iron Workers' and Light Platers' Society. The Sheet Iron Workers' Society had a membership of just under 1,300 and central funds amounting to more than £7,000. The General Secretary of the Sheet Iron Workers' Society, Mr Alexander Richmond, was appointed as the organiser of light platers and sheet iron workers within the Boilermakers' Society. The members of the Boilermakers' Society voted by 5,677 votes to 962 in favour of the amalgamation. In the Sheet Iron Workers' Society the majority was much narrower. Support for the amalgamation was approved by 501 votes to 323.

By far the most important development, however, affecting the Boilermakers' Society was a proposed amalgamation with the shipwrights and blacksmiths. The talks between the three organisations made good progress and it was agreed to form an Amalgamated Union of Shipbuilding, Engineering and Constructional Workers. At the outset this was to take a federal form. Proposals for the new amalgamated union were drawn up in the early part of 1919 and agreed by representatives of the boilermakers, shipwrights and blacksmiths at a joint meeting on 25 April 1919. The proposals envisaged an amalgamated union with one executive council consisting of twelve members. It was intended that the amalgamated union should appoint a general president, a general treasurer and a general secretary. It was intended that the three existing general secretaries would fill these offices.

Each of the three amalgamated unions was to remain in existence and each was to have its own executive council. Strikes, however, were to be authorised only by the executive council of the amalgamated union. The amalgamated union was also to be responsible for

111

the payment of dispute benefit, for the control of all full-time officials, and for the district committees. From 1 January 1920 there was to be a common membership and contribution card.

The Boilermakers' Society was by far the strongest of the three organisations. In 1918 the Boilermakers' Society had more than 95,000 members and funds amounting to nearly £746,000 whereas the shipwrights had just over 41,000 members and funds of £261,000 and the blacksmiths just over 19,000 members and funds of £34,000. In a letter to the membership the provisional joint executive council of the three unions said that:

> Capital is organised as it has never been before in the history of industrial undertakings and if labour is to meet on anything like equal terms and solve the problems which have arisen as a result of war conditions it can only be by a closer unity industrially and thus be able to meet organised employers on more equal terms.

The members of the three unions voted in favour of the amalgamation proposals. The majority in the Boilermakers' Society was overwhelming. The number of votes for the proposal was 46,738 and the number against 4,488.

At the end of 1920 the Amalgamated Union of Engineering, Shipbuilding and Constructional Workers appeared to be set on an expansion course. A special recruitment campaign was launched, for example, among apprentices. An identical membership card was issued for apprentice boilermakers, shipwrights, drillers and blacksmiths.

By the end of 1920 the Executive Council of the Boilermakers' Society was sufficiently optimistic about the progress of the Amalgamated Union of Engineering, Shipbuilding and Constructional Workers to predict that in future years the Amalgamated Union and not the Society would be responsible for the publication of the customary annual report. John Hill reported that the effort to amalgamate the principal unions had entailed endless sacrifice and patience, but that the unions were now through their labours. 'We shall be part and parcel of a society,' he said, 'enrolling in its membership all the principal trades in shipbuilding and ship-repairing.' By this time John Hill was acting as the General Secretary of the new amalgamation, Alex Wilkie of the shipwrights was acting as Chairman and Bill Lorimer of the blacksmiths was acting as General Treasurer.

So strongly was opinion moving in favour of closer working among trade unions that towards the end of 1920 the Boilermakers' Society, the shipwrights and the blacksmiths joined with a number of other unions to propose the formation of a wider federal body to be known as the General Combination of Ship Constructional and Engineering Workers. To some extent this new organisation was seen as a rival to the new Amalgamated Engineering Union. The other unions party to this new proposal included the Amalgamated Carpenters, the General Union of Carpenters and Joiners' Society, the National Amalgamated Sheet Metal Workers' and Braziers' Society and the General Union of Braziers' and Sheet Metal Workers' Society. The draft proposals referred to the need to overcome the problems of craft demarcation. The intention was that each constituent union should make a limited financial contribution to the new General Combination. Money would then be available to any of the constituent unions in the event of a strike or lockout. Provision was also made for the formation of district committees of the General Combination and for dealing with demarcation disputes.

It was characteristic of the mood of trade unionists during the immediate post-war period that among supervisors there was also strong feeling about the need for union co-operation. A Federation of Foremen's Associations had been formed between organisations called the National Foremen's Association, the Amalgamated Managers and Foremen's Association and the Scottish Foremen's Protective Association. In the late summer of 1920 the Federation of Foremen's Associations concluded an agreement with the Amalgamated Union of Shipbuilding, Engineering and Constructional Workers designed to promote co-operation between the constituent organisations. The agreement said that in the event of a dispute between the employers and any of the parties to the agreement the members of the other unions would observe strict neutrality and would not take the place of those who were engaged in the dispute. The agreement also contained a clause calling for co-operation in the event of the victimisation of any member.

The Federation of Foremen's Associations also encouraged their members who belonged to the crafts covered by the Amalgamated

113

Union of Engineering, Shipbuilding and Constructional Workers to join or retain their membership in the Amalgamated Union. Conversely the Amalgamated Union undertook to encourage their members who accepted positions as foremen or supervisors to join or retain their membership of one of the constituent unions in the Federation of Foremen's Associations.

In 1921 all these developments towards amalgamation and unity suffered a severe setback. The cause was unemployment. Trade became rapidly worse and depression bit deeply into industry. The trade unions became defensive. The richer unions became more concerned about the preservation of their funds to meet commitments to their existing membership rather than with the wider unity of workers.

The Boilermakers' Society was no exception. The attitude of many of the members towards amalgamation changed rapidly. Some members became increasingly concerned about the ability of the Society to meet demands on its funds for the payment of unemployment benefit. They were much less inclined to extend these benefits to members of other unions. By the summer of 1921 when the members were asked to vote for further proposals on amalgamation they recorded only a very small majority in favour. The number voting for amalgamation was 12,615 but the number voting against was 11,208. Only six months earlier they had recorded a majority of more than three to one, 5,104 to 1,504, in favour of a federation with the joiners and with the braziers in the proposed new General Combination.

Towards the end of 1921, following difficulties with the Shipwrights' Association, proposals were put forward for an amalgamation with the blacksmiths only. The terms were regarded as favourable to the Boilermakers' Society. The members of the Boilermakers' Society voted in favour of this proposal by 35,939 to 6,090. Unfortunately this represented less than 50 per cent of those entitled to vote and thus the amalgamation could not be carried out because it did not comply with the legal requirements. Moreover, in the Blacksmiths' Society a majority of those who voted were against the proposal. The proposal for amalgamation was defeated by 4,210 votes to 3,807.

The moves towards further amalgamation in engineering and shipbuilding finally came to an end with the national engineering

114

lockout of 1922. The Boilermakers' Society were dissatisfied at being outvoted by other unions in the Engineering and Shipbuilding Federation. The Society were opposed to what they felt were unnecessary concessions made by some of the other engineering unions in negotiations with the Engineering Employers' Federation. These developments are described in Chapter 7.

Chapter 6

Post-war Political Action

The first General Election after the ending of the First World War was held on Saturday 14 December 1918. A coalition of Conservatives and Liberals was returned with a huge majority of seats even though coalition candidates secured under 48 per cent of the total votes cast in the election. The largest opposition party was Sinn Fein with seventy-three seats. Next was Labour with fifty-seven seats. The opposition Liberals secured twenty-eight seats.

Five members of the Boilermakers' Society stood as Labour candidates in the election but only one, Mr A. Short, who was the candidate at Wednesbury, was elected. He was the first boilermaker to become a Member of Parliament. Commenting on the outcome of the election John Hill said that the blame, if any, lay with the workers in the constituencies who failed to support their own class at the polls. In his annual report for 1919 the General Secretary said that the political efforts of the Society had never been more than half-hearted. This, he suggested, was due, perhaps, to the industrial strength of the Society and its success in direct industrial action. Nevertheless, John Hill called upon members to support the political work of the Society.

Alfred Short, the new Member of Parliament, had been an active member of the Boilermakers' Society for many years. He had represented the Society as a delegate at the TUC, the Labour Party conference and the General Federation of Trade Unions. For eight years he had served as the secretary of the Sheffield branch of the Society. He had been a member of the Boilermakers' Society for sixteen years before he was elected to Parliament. He first came to prominence during the shipbuilding lockout.

116

With the return of peace and with the victory of the coalition in the General Election of December 1918 the prevailing mood in Britain was to abolish the controls of the war period. The short-lived boom encouraged those who had little sympathy with the proposals which had been made for a more planned reconstruction. Controls were lifted and there was a 'free-for-all' atmosphere in the economy. In 1921 the railways were returned to private ownership. The existing companies were consolidated into four new giant companies, the London, Midland and Scottish, the London North-Eastern, the Great Western and the Southern.

HANDS OFF RUSSIA

Despite its 'half-hearted' political efforts the Society was soon to play a significant part in a major international issue of concern to the labour movement in every continent, though the battleground was to be found much more in industry than in Parliament. The issue was that of military intervention by the major capitalist powers against the Russian revolution. After the revolution of November 1917 these major powers, including the United States, France and Britain, supported and engaged in armed intervention in Russia with a view to overthrowing the new government.

A worker who played an outstanding role in eventually stopping British military intervention against the Soviet Republic was a prominent lay member of the Boilermakers' Society, Harry Pollitt. Pollitt was born in November 1890 in Manchester. He started work as a boilermaker apprentice in 1905 at the Gorton Works where the locomotives of the Great Central Railway were made and repaired. It was popularly known as the Gorton Tank. Pollitt, strongly influenced by his parents, became an active trade unionist and socialist. In 1912 he became a foundation member of the British Socialist Party. This was the main forerunner of what eventually became the Communist Party.

During the First World War Pollitt was for a period a shop steward of the Boilermakers' Society at Armstrong Whitworth's works in Openshaw. Some 8,000 men were employed there. In 1917 at the time of the Russian revolution Pollitt was working in a small boilershop in Manchester and in January 1918 he moved to London to work on ship repair. He shared a room in Poplar with Alf Whitney, who, many years later, was to become a member of the Executive Council of the Boilermakers' Society. Pollitt was elected as delegate from the London No. 11 branch of the Society to the London District Committee and on 1 January 1919 he was elected secretary of the London District Committee. It was a lay post.

The name of Harry Pollitt was to become very closely associated with the national campaign to stop the war against Russia. He worked tirelessly to this end. Not only was he extremely energetic but he had an attractive personal style, very strong socialist and trade union convictions and he was also an excellent speaker. The campaign to stop the war against Russia had the support of many active members of the Boilermakers' Society including the General Secretary, John Hill. In April 1919 Hill said in his monthly notes that the miners had struck one of the best blows ever landed by a trade union when they passed a resolution against war with Russia. In the June issue of the monthly report it was recorded that many resolutions had been received from branches urging the withdrawal of British troops from Russia. In the July issue John Hill said that the object of the military campaign against the Russian revolution was sinister.

In the same issue a letter was published from Harry Pollitt under the title 'Hands off Russia'. In his letter he said that the working men of Russia had overthrown their age-long tyrants, but that the Government of England was sending soldiers, shells and aeroplanes to defeat them. The workers of Russia, he continued, had succeeded in establishing the first socialist republic in the world. In his letter Pollitt urged the members of the Boilermakers' Society 'to get busy in your branches and get our members to refuse to touch any ship that is to carry munitions to Russia'.

In June 1919 the Boilermakers' Society had been represented at the annual conference of the Labour Party at which a resolution was carried by a two to one majority urging the National Executive Committee to consult the Parliamentary Committee of the TUC with a view to effective action being taken to enforce the demand for the ending of intervention in Russia. The resolution called for the unreserved use of political and industrial power.

In September 1919 the national Hands off Russia Committee, of which Harry Pollitt was a leading member, circulated a letter to trade unions urging branches to pass resolutions demanding the immediate withdrawal of British troops from Russia, the stopping of supplies to the counter-revolutionary armies, the raising of the blockade against the new Soviet Republic and the establishment of diplomatic relations between the new Soviet Republic and Britain.

John Hill, the General Secretary, gave support to the campaign to stop the war against Russia. In the November monthly report he said that Britain was using armed troops to re-establish Czarism and to kill a working-class government. In the same issue there was another letter from Harry Pollitt urging members to compel the British Government to stop supplying Czarist reactionaries with munitions.

In December 1919 a special TUC was held to consider the nationalisation of the mines, the cost of living, unemployment and the war of intervention against Russia. On the last item a resolution moved by the Boilermakers' Society was carried. It called upon the British Government to consider the peace overtures of the Soviet Government, to raise the blockade against Russia and to give passports to a delegation from the TUC to enable it to make an independent inquiry into conditions in Russia. Towards the end of January 1920 a letter was sent from the Boilermakers' Society to the TUC urging that every effort should be made to persuade the British Government to make peace with the Soviet Union and to open up new trade relations.

In March 1920 John Hill spoke of 'the miracle of Russia'. He said that the mass of common humanity were awakening. The people of Russia – in ignorance, poverty and despair – had thrown off their despots, had defied the united forces of militarism and capitalism and were reconstructing their whole social system. This was an example of what was possible for the workers of all lands. On the eve of May Day 1920 Pollitt wrote to the monthly report of the Boilermakers' Society urging the members in all branches to work for the transformation of society from capitalism to socialism. He linked this struggle with the immediate demand for the introduction of a forty-four-hour working week.

In the summer of 1920 the campaign to stop the war against Russia developed rapidly. London dockers refused to load an arms ship destined to Poland, and a special congress of the TUC called upon workers not to carry out any operation for the manufacture, repair or transport of war material. In August representatives of the TUC, the National Executive Committee of the Labour Party and the Parliamentary Labour Party said that the whole industrial power of organised workers would be used to defeat the continuation of the war against Russia. A Council of Action was formed which demanded an absolute guarantee that the armed forces of Britain would not be used in support of the Polish Government or in support of any other military or naval expedition against the Soviet Government. It authorised strike action to support this policy. Hundreds of local councils of action to stop the war against Russia were established in different cities and towns.

The Government finally gave way to this pressure from the labour movement. The war against Russia was brought to an end. In this struggle the role played by Harry Pollitt was outstanding and his name became known in many countries.

POLLITT'S OTHER ACTIVITIES

Pollitt's activity was not restricted to the campaign to stop the war against Russia. He was also a vigorous activist within the Boilermakers' Society. Following his service as a shop steward, district committee delegate and his election as secretary of the London District Committee he was nominated in March 1919 for the parliamentary panel of the Society. The nominating branches were London No. 11 and East Ham.

In his letter of acceptance Pollitt said that for years he had taken a very active part in the labour movement. He felt that it was more than ever necessary for the trade unions to be represented politically as well as industrially and this could only be done by trade unions returning to the House of Commons men whose whole time could be given to safeguarding the interests of their members. He described himself as a determined opponent of capitalism.

In the voting for the parliamentary panel Harry Pollitt was unsuccessful. He stood as a candidate in the no. 5 district, covering roughly the South of England and South Wales. He secured a majority vote in the London area but this was not sufficient.

In the September 1919 issue of the report Harry Pollitt had an article on trade unions and politics. He argued that it was necessary to press 'for something higher than wages and hours'. He referred to the long and bitter fights that had taken place between trade unions and the courts and he said that those fights had proved that the unions had to resort to political pressure to get their grievances remedied. The February 1920 issue of the monthly report carried a letter from Pollitt urging that a special national conference should be called to organise a claim for wage increases, a forty-four-hour working week and resistance to paying income tax on incomes below £250 per year.

Pollitt was, of course, by no means the only active member of the Society who saw a clear and close relationship between trade unionism and politics. The big growth in unemployment in the winter of 1920–1 served to emphasise that collective bargaining alone was not sufficient to protect workers' interests.

ACTION AGAINST UNEMPLOYMENT

The Trades Union Congress and the Labour Party called a special conference to consider what should be done. It was held towards the end of January 1921. Two resolutions were carried. The first condemned the Government for not having taken action to prevent unemployment, and said that the growing number of jobless was due largely to the failure of the Government to secure the resumption of trade with Russia and central Europe.

The resolution called for remedial measures to stimulate employment, and urged that unemployed workers should be given adequate maintenance. It put forward a number of suggestions to create employment. It called for the expansion of education and other public services, schemes of afforestation, the development of agriculture and the launching of projects for harbour improvement. The resolution said that in a period of unemployment the policy of the Government should be one of expansion and not of contraction. It also suggested that overtime should be kept to an absolute minimum. It called for the ending of unnecessary expenditure by bringing to an end British military adventures abroad and by terminating military oppression in Ireland.

The resolution concluded by stating that unemployment arose

from the very nature of the capitalist system and could be solved only 'on the principles so repeatedly enunciated by Labour'. The second resolution said that the decisions of the conference should be sent to the Prime Minister, to every Member of the House of Commons, and to trade unions and local Labour parties.

POLLITT AND THE BOILERMAKERS' SOCIETY

At the beginning of 1920 Pollitt was nominated for General Secretary. He declined and supported the re-election of John Hill. In the summer of 1920 Pollitt was again nominated for the parliamentary panel of the Society, this time by seven branches. He declined nomination but said that he deeply appreciated the honour that had been extended to him. He believed he could do more good in the workshop and in the Boilermakers' Society than he could by 'the use of the present parliamentary machine'.

In the September issue of the monthly report Pollitt urged the need for a boilermakers' national conference. He pointed out that national conferences were held by the miners, dockers and railwaymen. At these conferences programmes were formulated and when the delegates returned to their branches the decisions were popularised. Pollitt urged that the objectives of a boilermakers' national conference should be to press for wage increases, to suspend overtime, to consider a standard rate for all districts, to consider removing the general office of the Society to London, and to consider what action should be taken to obtain the forty-four-hour working week. He also said that the Society should define its attitude towards the pressing questions of peace with Russia, nationalisation, conscription and Ireland.

In the November 1920 issue of the monthly report Pollitt had another letter published in which he paid tribute to the work done by John Hill, the General Secretary. Pollitt urged the Executive Committee to provide more facilities to the General Secretary to enable him to give time and attention to the business of the TUC. It was essential, he argued, that the trade union movement should develop its unity. No union by itself was powerful enough to defeat the employers.

Pollitt's decision to decline nomination for the parliamentary panel because of the need to concentrate on trade union business was not the only indication in the Society that trade union militants judged their industrial activity to be rather more important than election to parliament. In Scotland Mr W. Mackie resigned from the parliamentary panel. In his letter of resignation he said that he had not lost faith in political action but he felt that he could do better work 'on behalf of the progressive movement where I am'. Mr Mackie's resignation was followed by the election of another militant, John M. Airlie, to the parliamentary panel. His was the only nomination.

In the March 1921 issue of the monthly report Harry Pollitt urged members of the Society to press for affiliation to a new international organisation of trade unions whose headquarters were in Moscow. He said that British unions should sever all connection with the International Federation of Trade Unions which he described as the 'reformist Amsterdam International'. This International, said Pollitt, had never functioned, beyond issuing a few pamphlets and occasionally collecting money to help a trade union during a strike. During the war the Amsterdam International deserted its ideals and the leaders in each country 'flocked to the support of their respective capitalist governments'. Pollitt said that on 1 May 1921 a world congress of trade unions would be held in Moscow and he urged the Society to be represented at it.

By this time Pollitt had established a national reputation in the Boilermakers' Society both as a trade union militant and as a political radical. In the ballots for delegates to the Labour Party conference, the TUC and the General Federation of Trade Unions Pollitt was successful. In each of the elections he came second in the voting. His largest vote was for the Labour Party conference delegation.

In September 1921, following a visit to Russia, Pollitt published an appeal to the membership of the Boilermakers' Society to assist the people of the Soviet Republic. He said that there could be no doubt about the very desperate needs of the Russian people but that the workers, peasants, soldiers and sailors were supporting the revolutionary government. The present crisis in Russia was due, he said, to the breakdown of economic life following the revolution, the blockade imposed on Russia by the British Government, and the sabotage of economic life by the counter-revolutionaries

123

who were receiving aid in materials and money from the leading capitalist governments. He appealed for money to help the Russian people in the midst of famine and called upon the workers to prevent reactionary intervention by the British Government.

With the very steep rise in unemployment in 1921 many members of the Boilermakers' Society suffered wage cuts. At the beginning of 1921 over 10,000 members of the Society were unemployed. By July this figure had risen to more than 40,000. In a letter in the monthly report Pollitt said that the policy of wage reduction was in full swing. He pointed out, nevertheless, that many firms were making large profits and quoted facts to substantiate his contention.

Pollitt's activity and propaganda was thus many-sided. He sought to arouse the membership on workshop, national and international issues affecting working-class interests. He recognised the importance of the trade union movement and of influencing the policy of his own union. In this respect his efforts were distinctive. Many earlier left-wing socialists had taken a sectarian view of trade union activity and had tended to discount it.

In 1922 Harry Pollitt was elected at the top of the poll for each of the Society's delegations to the TUC, the Labour Party and the General Federation of Trade Unions. It was an impressive achievement and there was by this time no doubt of his standing and popularity within the Society.

In the spring of 1922 nominations were sought for the five electoral districts for the Executive Council of the Society. Pollitt accepted nomination for the district covering his home base in Manchester even though he was still living in London. He declined nominations for the Scottish district and for the district covering London. In his letter accepting nomination Pollitt said that his opinions, politically and industrially, were known to the membership and he had no desire to solicit support under false pretences. He stood, he said, for industrial unionism and he pointed to his experience in railway workshops, construction shops and in shipbuilding and ship repair.

Pollitt would have been a strong candidate in the Executive Council election but the Council decided that he was ineligible to stand. They said that they had given the matter long and careful consideration but had felt compelled to declare Pollitt ineligible

124

because one of the rules of the Society had been violated. They said:

> The facts are briefly that Bro. Pollitt was employed outside our trade for a period of over twelve months before nomination, and for a long period had not signed the book; and only began to sign some weeks after nominations had been asked for.

During that period Pollitt had been working full-time in the 'Hands Off Russia' movement.

Early in 1923 the term of office of the London district delegate, J. T. Husband, expired. Mr Husband accepted nomination for re-election but Harry Pollitt was also nominated. His nomination was supported by Alf Whitney, who by this time was London district secretary. The committee supporting Pollitt referred, in a letter which they sent to the monthly report, to his integrity, his practical experience and to his reputation as an organiser, negotiator and public speaker.

The election eventually went to a second ballot. J. T. Husband was narrowly re-elected by 512 votes to 462. He owed his re-election largely to the support he received from branches in the outer London area. Pollitt secured a majority in most of the inner London branches.

After the election Pollitt wrote to the monthly report to wish J. T. Husband every success in his further term of office. He said that it was now the duty of all members 'to support to the full Brother Husband'. The members, Pollitt urged, 'must all pull together'.

Chapter 7

The Post-war Slump and the Employers' Offensive

The year 1920 was a peaceful period for the Boilermakers' Society. The membership rose by the end of the year to 104,448 and only £6,205 was paid in dispute benefit. Towards the end of the year, however, unemployment began to rise and the amount distributed as unemployment benefit in 1920 was 50 per cent higher than in the previous year. By the end of 1920 about one million workers were out of a job.

It was a sign of the change in the economic situation that when in November 1920 the Engineering and Shipbuilding Federation submitted a claim to the Engineering Employers' Federation for an increase in wages of 6d per hour and the consolidation of war bonuses they met with an emphatic refusal. The unions decided not to call a strike in support of their claim but to re-submit it in six months' time. They felt that in view of the growth in unemployment it would be unwise to try to enforce the claim.

The situation did not get better; indeed, it grew worse. Early in 1921 the Executive Council of the Society drew the attention of branches to the rule which prohibited overtime in any town where more than 10 per cent of the membership were signing the vacant book. Systematic overtime, said the Executive Council, must be stopped though they recognised the need for overtime to meet emergency repairs. On a ballot vote the Society decided by 7,747 to 1,021 to introduce an unemployment benefit levy.

The growth in unemployment aroused John Hill to make one of

his most trenchant attacks on the capitalist system. In a message to the membership on the eve of May Day 1921 he pointed out that German workers were being compelled to work long hours to pay war reparations whilst British and French workers were without jobs. It was not the aristocrats of Germany who were being made to suffer but the workers of the various countries. The workers, said John Hill, had one cause in common. They must control the workshops and establish political power. It was not the guns of the capitalists that were to be feared most, continued John Hill, but their 'insidious, lying press' and their agents who spread religious and political bigotry to divide the workers.

WAGE REDUCTIONS

By the end of March 1921 11·3 per cent of the twelve million workers insured under the Unemployment Insurance Act were registered as unemployed, and an additional three-quarters of a million insured workers were on short time. There were wage reductions in many industries. The Shipbuilding Employers' Federation called for wage reductions in all federated firms and, after negotiations, the Federation of Engineering and Shipbuilding Trades decided to submit to a ballot of members of affiliated unions a proposal from the employers that a 6s per week increase secured in 1920 should be withdrawn in two instalments. The first reduction was to take place early in May and the second reduction a month later. The leaders of the unions recommended the proposed reductions. The members of the Boilermakers' Society voted by 13,819 to 4,771 to oppose the reduction. They were, however, outvoted by the members of other unions. The aggregated vote showed 45,169 for acceptance of the reductions with 35,913 against.

Despite heavy unemployment among members the Boilermakers' Society responded generously to an appeal from the miners who in the summer of 1921 were involved in a national strike. The maximum grant which could be given under the rules by the Executive Council was £20. They decided, therefore, to send £20 to each of the sixty-one county and other local unions which constituted the Miners' Federation of Great Britain. This was equivalent to a national donation of £1,220.

By mid-summer 1921 more than 40,000 members of the Boilermakers' Society were out of work. More than £20,000 per week was being distributed in unemployment benefit. Many members had exhausted their benefit. The Executive Council introduced an immediate weekly levy of 6d to help to meet the drain on the funds.

In March the Engineering Employers' Federation demanded a reduction in wages. The unions said that the proposed reduction, made up of different elements, would amount to 16s 6d per week from time workers and 40 per cent from the earnings of pieceworkers. The unions rejected the demand and proposed instead that the Minister of Labour should set up a court of inquiry. The Boilermakers' Society confirmed this rejection by 19,186 votes to 4,420. Further discussions, however, resulted in a draft agreement for wage reductions similar to those introduced in shipbuilding. This proposal was accepted by the Boilermakers' Society by 11,515 votes to 8,417.

In the late summer of 1921 the shipbuilding and engineering employers proposed further wage reductions. The unions sought to negotiate to minimise the reductions whilst accepting in principle that a reduction would have to be conceded. Unemployment was widespread and wages had been reduced in many other industries. The employers insisted on their demand. The members of the Boilermakers' Society voted by 9,864 to 7,894 to reject the proposed reductions, but they were outvoted by the aggregated vote of the other unions. The aggregated vote showed a majority of 170,471 votes to 147,636 in favour of accepting the reductions. The largest single union, the AEU, voted, like the Boilermakers' Society, to reject the employers' demand. Among other smaller craft unions opinion was divided but among the general workers' unions, which at that time were joined together in the National Federation of General Workers, voting was heavily in favour of accepting the reductions. Successive wage reductions took place on 1 November and 1 December 1921 and again on 1 January 1922.

In 1921 the Society lost less than 4,000 members. This was an achievement in a year of heavy unemployment and wage reductions. About £283,000 was distributed in unemployment benefit and benevolent grants. The funds of the Society fell by more than £230,000.

At the end of the year the Society reported that there had been no previous year in the history of the shipbuilding industry when such drastic reductions had been enforced. The loss to time workers amounted to 17s per week. Piece-workers lost an even higher proportion from piece-work prices. These general reductions, said the Society, did not include the hundred-and-one smaller reductions and withdrawals of allowances, some of which had been in existence for as long as older members could remember. There could be no justification, said the Society, for further general reductions.

SHIPBUILDING DISPUTE

In 1922 the employers' offensive continued. At the beginning of the year further demands were made for wage cuts. The shipbuilding employers suggested a reduction of 26s 6d per week. By 26,405 votes to 3,698 the members of the Boilermakers' Society voted against any further wage cuts. On an aggregated vote of the shipbuilding unions the employers' demand was rejected by 113,547 votes to 11,062. The shipbuilding employers responded with a threat of lockout to commence from 15 March 1922. The employers said that they would enforce the reduction in two stages. The first reduction was to take effect in March and a further reduction was to take effect on an unspecified later date.

The unions protested against the employers' attitude. The employers agreed to resume discussions and modified their claim for wage reductions. They suggested that there should be a reduction of 10s 6d per week on 29 March and a further reduction of 6s four weeks later. The unions were not prepared to accept this suggestion but they agreed to submit it to their members without a recommendation. The employers insisted, however, that during the time the vote was being taken the unions should bind themselves to take no action to influence their members to cast an adverse vote. The unions refused to accept this stipulation and the negotiations were again broken off.

The employers sought then to enforce the proposed wage reductions but the shipbuilding workers refused to accept them. The industry came to a standstill. The employers said that it was a strike and the unions said that it was a lockout.

129

On 25 April the shipbuilding employers and the shipbuilding unions reopened discussions. A recommendation was made that the reduction of 10s per week which had come into operation on 29 March should remain. The further reduction of 6s per week, which the employers insisted should be made, was to take effect in two instalments. There was to be a reduction of 3s per week on 17 May and a reduction of a further 3s per week from 7 June 1922.

This recommendation was rejected by the members of the Boilermakers' Society by 17,483 votes to 9,456. The aggregated votes of the members of the shipbuilding unions showed, however, a much narrower majority against acceptance of the recommendation. The voting was 46,302 against the recommendation and 41,264 in favour. The rules of the Engineering and Shipbuilding Trades Federation required a two-thirds majority to continue a dispute and, in accordance with these rules, it was held that the dispute should be terminated. Telegrams to this effect were sent out to the membership. The Boilermakers' Society felt they had been let down by the other unions. The Executive Council said that the question of affiliation to the Federation would be put before the membership.

ENGINEERING LOCKOUT

In the engineering industry events took a different course. In 1921, with the growth of unemployment, a number of district committees of the Amalgamated Engineering Union sought to restrict the amount of overtime being worked. Disputes also took place about the employment of semi-skilled men on certain machine tools without consultation with the union, and about the employment of apprentices on payment-by-results also without consultation with the union. The overtime issue was, however, by far the most important of the differences between the union and the employers.

The employers said that the AEU was seeking to interfere with managerial functions and the unions argued that their members had a right to be consulted on matters affecting their interests. Some district committees banned overtime. In the spring of 1921 a national lockout was threatened by the employers. The AEU decided to resist but, because of the large number of members who were out of work, they made every effort to negotiate a settlement. The union made a concession and the lockout threat was withdrawn.

The truce did not last long. Towards the end of the year the employers asked the union to accept the right of management to introduce certain changes in working arrangements without prior agreement or consultation. They also claimed that management and only management could determine whether overtime should be worked. After prolonged negotiations the Executive Council of the AEU decided to recommend the membership to accept a memorandum embodying these proposals. This advice was rejected on a ballot vote by 50,240 to 35,525. The engineering employers decided, in reply, on a national lockout of AEU members from 11 March 1922.

The engineering employers then requested that all the other engineering unions should sign the memorandum which had been put to the AEU. John Hill said that the action of the engineering employers was the most drastic and unreasonable he had ever known. He defined it in the following terms:

The employers claim the right to exercise managerial functions: that is to tell any man to come here or go there. An employer may change any custom or rule or method of working and the men concerned must go on. He may make the job more difficult and expect you to do it in the same time and for the same money, and you must go on. He may ask you to work overtime, and you must work. You may send a protest or a claim for more money to a conference, and in a month, or in several months, your protest may be heard, but in nine cases out of ten there will be no settlement, and in the tenth one that is settled, it may not be settled to your satisfaction. This is militarism in the workshops and Prussian militarism at that.

The membership was overwhelmingly opposed to the engineering employers' demand. By 35,255 votes to 3,107 they rejected the employers' memorandum on managerial functions. At this point the unions in the Engineering and Shipbuilding Trades Federation (but not including the AEU) urged the Government to appoint a court of inquiry into the dispute. The Federation appeared to be rather more conciliatory than the AEU and for a short period the lockout notice to the federated unions was lifted. The Government finally decided to appoint a court of inquiry and it began its work towards the end of April 1922.

At the court of inquiry the federated unions, together with the unions in the Federation of Foundry Workers, gave their evidence jointly, but the AEU decided to stand apart. The AEU felt that in the earlier negotiations the other unions had shown weakness towards the employers. The Boilermakers' Society regretted this division between the unions and said that it 'left an opening for the employers which they took full advantage of throughout the course of the enquiry'. The court of inquiry reported sympathetically on the employers' demands.

Meanwhile, the employers and the federated unions had made no further progress in their discussions. Members of federated unions were locked out from 2 May 1922.

When the lockout began against the members of the federated unions the employers continued to offer employment to anyone who would accept their conditions. There were, however, few blacklegs. The action of the employers was described by the Boilermakers' Society as 'the most insidious and dangerous blow at trade unionism . . . in the history of the industry'. The members of the Society responded almost without exception to the call of the Executive Council to stand firmly with the other unions against the demands of the employers.

Following the publication of the report of the Court of Inquiry negotiations wcre reopened between the employers and the unions. Unfortunately, there were still differences between the AEU and the other unions. In the negotiations it became clear that certain of the unions, but not the Boilermakers' Society, were prepared to accept a settlement very much on the lines wanted by the employers. It was decided by the unions to put proposals for a settlement to a ballot.

The Boilermakers' Society decided to call a representative conference of the Society to consider these developments. The conference was held on Friday 26 May, and it adopted a resolution regretting that the proposed terms of settlement of the lockout were being put to a ballot vote of the members of all unions. The resolution said that 'We are of the opinion that the acceptance

132

of these proposals would be disastrous'. The conference said that it could not recommend the proposals to the membership, and, more important, it could not accept that the Boilermakers' Society should be party to a pooled vote upon the proposals.

A letter was then sent to all branches stating that the ballot vote of the Boilermakers' Society would not be pooled with the votes of members of other unions in the Engineering and Shipbuilding Trades' Federation. The members of the Society voted by more than a five to one majority to endorse the attitude of their Executive Council and their representative conference in rejecting the employers' proposals. The voting was 22,433 against to 4,196 in favour.

In contrast to the result of the vote among the members of the Boilermakers' Society the vote among members of the other unions in the Engineering and Shipbuilding Trades Federation went heavily in favour of accepting the employers' terms. The vote in favour of acceptance was 99,313 to 46,881. This vote did not include the figures of the Boilermakers' Society. The Federation decided to meet the engineering employers to arrange a resumption of work. The lockout against the members of federated unions came to an end on Tuesday 6 June.

The members of the AEU and the Boilermakers' Society were still locked out. Both unions, however, were in a weak position. In the AEU tens of thousands of members were unemployed and the funds were at a very low level. Moreover, some of the local associations of engineering employers had put pressure on Boards of Guardians to cut relief payments made to locked-out engineering workers. At the end of May the AEU suspended the payment of all benefits except to sick and superannuated members. It was in these circumstances that early in June the members of the AEU decided by 75,478 votes to 35,453 to accept the employers' terms of settlement. The members of the AEU returned to work on 13 June. The lockout had lasted more than thirteen weeks.

This left the Boilermakers' Society in isolation. It was now the only union standing out against the employers' terms. A special conference of the Society was called for Saturday 17 June 1922. The conference took note of the isolated position of the Society and observed that in many factories the employers were insisting that work previously done by boilermakers should in future be carried out by workers from other unions who had returned to work on the employers' terms. The delegates to the boilermakers' conference decided, regretfully, in the circumstances that to continue the struggle in isolation would only bring further hardship to the membership but with no possibility of success. They adopted a resolution advising the membership to resume work.

One immediate consequence of the defeat sustained by the unions in the engineering lockout was a demand inside the Boilermakers' Society for disaffiliation from the Federation of Engineering and Shipbuilding Trades. Many members of the Society, who had voted for continued resistance to the employers, felt let down. The Executive Council responded to this demand by agreeing to a ballot vote on the issue. They issued a statement, however, opposing disaffiliation. They said that though there was every reason for dissatisfaction it should be remembered that the Boilermakers' Society had been one of the principal founders of the Federation and had taken the lead in joint action in resisting wage reductions or any encroachment on hours of work or conditions of employment. It was not always possible, said the EC, for each separate union successfully to resist the employers.

Support for the point of view of the Executive Council came from some of the more militant members who had been foremost in calling for resistance to the attacks of the employers. Harry Pollitt, for example, in a letter in the monthly report, said that to achieve power workers 'must use every institution they possibly can, and they will find that one of their best weapons will be the trade unions when the trade unionists have learned to amalgamate their forces instead of being divided into so many different sections as we are at present'.

The result of the ballot was a majority for continued affiliation to the Federation. The voting was 2,922 to 2,248.

MORE WAGE CUTS

Almost immediately following the return to work at the end of the lockout the Engineering Employers' Federation demanded a new round of wage cuts. The employers proposed that wages should be reduced by 5s 6d per week at the end of July, by a further

5s 6d per week four weeks later, and by a still further 5s 6d per week after another four weeks. The unions put this demand to a ballot vote of their members. The Boilermakers' Society voted by 6,793 to 4,752 to reject the demand. The members of the AEU also voted for rejection. The aggregated votes of all the engineering unions showed a majority against the employers' demand of 70,900 to 43,937.

This was a remarkable result in the immediate aftermath of the defeat of the unions in the lockout. The engineering employers were, however, determined to press home their advantage. They indicated that they were not prepared to make any concession and insisted that the wage cuts, should be implemented. The AEU decided not to take another ballot and advised their members to remain at work. The employers succeeded in cutting wages. The resistance of not only the AEU but of the other unions had been broken.

It was much the same story in shipbuilding. The employers demanded that the war bonus should be withdrawn. The unions balloted their members but, although on an aggregated vote there was a majority against accepting the demand, there was not the required two-thirds majority for resistance. The Boilermakers' Society voted by 10,085 votes to 7,200 to reject the employers' demand. Wages were reduced in four successive stages over a period of about nine weeks.

The Engineering Employers' Federation also pressed for new national arrangements on overtime and nightshift working. They also submitted proposals to the unions on payment-by-results. These proposals gave employers the right to introduce payment-by-results providing that workers were guaranteed a minimum of day rate wages irrespective of their piece-work earnings. Other important clauses in the proposals were:

Piecework prices and bonus or basis times shall be fixed by mutual arrangement between the employer and the worker who is to perform the work. In the event of a worker taking exception to any piecework price or bonus or basis time allowed, and no arrangement being come to in settlement, the matter shall be dealt with between the management and a deputation of work-people consisting of the worker affected and two others engaged

135

in the branch of trade in the shop concerned. The decision shall be retrospective to the commencement of the job upon which exception is taken. The management shall, if they desire, be entitled by demonstration to justify the proposals they have made.

In the case of jobs not previously done in the shop and jobs for which no piecework price, bonus or basis time has previously been fixed, the employer shall, either before, or as soon as possible after the job has been given out, see the worker concerned with a view to arranging the piecework price, bonus or basis time. A sufficient period shall be allowed for proving the piecework price, bonus or basis time.

No piecework price, bonus or basis time hereafter established may be altered except for the following reasons:

(a) A mistake has been made in the calculation on either side;
(b) The material, means or method of production or the quantities are changed, provided that the modification shall in no case be such as to effect a reduction in the earnings of the workers concerned; or
(c) A mutual arrangement has been come to between the employer and the worker engaged on the job in the same manner as a new price is arranged.

Pending an arrangement being come to regarding the piecework price, bonus or basis time, the worker shall proceed with the job in accordance with the piecework price or bonus or basis time allowed by the management.

Piecework prices and bonus or basis times shall be such as will enable a workman of average ability to earn at least $33\frac{1}{3}$ per cent over time rates (excluding war bonuses).

In the event of a depression of trade in any establishment, systematic short time shall be worked if practicable in preference to discharging workmen.

Any question arising out of this agreement shall, failing settlement, be dealt with in accordance with 'Provisions for Avoiding Disputes'.

Chapter 8

The Shipbuilding Lockout 1923

In 1922 the shipbuilding employers requested that the unions should conclude with them a national agreement on overtime and nightshift working. Discussions on the subject had been held intermittently since the introduction of the shorter working week at the end of the war. The Boilermakers' Society had taken the view that a national agreement would not be advantageous because it would tend to worsen rather than to improve the arrangements existing in many yards. The Society preferred to maintain its local arrangements.

In the depressed conditions of 1922 the Society, together with other shipyard unions, could no longer defer negotiations. The employers pressed strongly for a national agreement. Eventually the unions agreed to meet the employers to discuss four main issues to form part of an overtime and nightshift agreement. These four issues were the regulation of overtime, how the overtime should be calculated, the rate of payment for overtime, and the definition and rate of payment for nightshift working.

LONG HISTORY

There had been a long history of negotiations in the industry on the regulation of overtime. The employers wanted to eliminate the banning of overtime as a weapon in industrial disputes. The Society, on the other hand, wanted to limit the amount of overtime worked in the industry. Consistent overtime was regarded as a threat to basic wage rates and claims for a shorter working week.

The first attempt to regulate overtime was in 1907. The Federa-

137

tion and the Society opened discussions on a number of contentious issues including overtime, wages and disputes procedure. Agreement was reached on wages and disputes procedure but there was no agreement on the regulation of overtime. Negotiations were conducted not only with the Boilermakers' Society but with other unions in the shipbuilding industry.

In 1911 the unions intimated to the Federation that they were not prepared to discuss the question of a general agreement on overtime and nightshift except in the context of a reduction in the length of the basic working week in federated firms. The Federation refused to take these two issues together and the negotiations broke down.

An agreement for a reduction in the basic working week was concluded in November 1918 and a forty-seven-hour week was introduced from 1 January 1919. This was, however, made subject to conditions and one of these conditions was that there should be further discussion about overtime and nightshift arrangements.

In these subsequent discussions it was agreed, largely in response to representations by the unions, that the matter should be remitted for district negotiations. These were not successful and in December 1922 the Employers' Federation and the unions appointed a special joint committee to consider whether agreement could be reached at national level. These further discussions soon ran into difficulties and the Boilermakers' Society withdrew their representative from the joint committee. The other unions continued the discussions and eventually an agreement was signed on 22 March 1923.

The new overtime and nightshift agreement was accepted by the Engineering and Shipbuilding Trades Federation only after prolonged debate. At various times the shipwrights, woodworkers and the AEU all expressed opposition to the agreement. The problem for the Boilermakers' Society was more far-reaching than for members of the other unions. Members of the Boilermakers' Society were overwhelmingly piece-workers whereas the general method of remuneration for other trades was by time rates. The effect of the agreement, said the Boilermakers' Society, was to reduce the overtime earnings of boilermakers. These earnings had hitherto been protected by many different local agreements.

The Boilermakers' Society refused to accept the national agreement and they were joined by certain other unions. The Society

138

wrote notifying its intention to withdraw from the Federation. A stoppage of work took place in the Tyne district and on 30 April 1923 the Shipbuilding Employers' Federation locked out all members of the Boilermakers' Society throughout Britain.

At the annual meeting of the Engineering and Shipbuilding Trades Federation which took place in May 1923 the Society was expelled from membership. The Society had already indicated its intention to take a ballot vote with a strong recommendation from the Executive Council in favour of disaffiliation. At the annual meeting, however, it was pointed out that one of the rules of the Federation stated that 'any Society having associated itself with any general movement and subsequently withdrawing without the consent of the emergency committee will be expelled from the Federation'. It was held that this rule applied to the action of the Boilermakers' Society in withdrawing from the negotiations on overtime and nightshift arrangements.

A PROLONGED STRUGGLE

The lockout had a very serious effect on the shipbuilding industry and aroused considerable public interest. Some nine weeks after the beginning of the lockout the General Council of the TUC issued a statement urging that immediate steps should be taken to secure a settlement. The General Council said that the continued effort of the Shipbuilding Employers' Federation to compel the boilermakers to adhere to the overtime agreement as the only condition on which they would withdraw lockout notices was indefensible. The General Council accepted the general principle that when a group of unions entered into collective negotiation with an employers' federation all unions party to the negotiation should be prepared to abide by the agreements collectively reached. They did, however, accept that in the shipbuilding dispute the negotiations appeared to the General Council to prejudice the interests of the boilermakers to a disproportionate extent in comparison with other trades. The General Council suggested that the dispute should be resolved by arbitration.

The support of the members for the Society's stand was overwhelming. Eight weeks after the beginning of the lockout the

History of the Boilermakers' Society

Society decided to take a ballot as to whether the agreement should be accepted. The agreement was rejected by 17,042 votes to 7,454. The Society then urged the Minister of Labour to appoint a court of inquiry into the dispute under the terms of the Industrial Courts Act. He declined to do so. The Society also asked for arbitration. This also was refused.

The Society introduced a levy of members to support the locked out workers in the shipbuilding industry. By 8,706 votes to 2,293 the members voted in favour of a levy of 1s per week.

The lockout eventually came to an end on 16 November with an agreed statement between the Employers' Federation and the Boilermakers' Society to the effect that federated establishments would, so far as work was available, be open to members of the Boilermakers' Society, and that the Federation would consider with the Society how far the operation of the terms of the national overtime and nightshift agreement revealed anomalies which needed correction. The agreed statement referred to 'special circumstances peculiar to members of the Society'. The statement went on to say that failing agreement points of difference were to be referred to the Industrial Court. The lockout had lasted for seven months. Although it could not be claimed that the Society had won all their demands they had certainly not been defeated. They had finally compelled the Shipbuilding Employers' Federation to accept that there should be negotiations on the special difficulties faced by piece-workers.

The General Council of the TUC also congratulated the Society on what they described as 'the successful termination of your prolonged dispute'. They expressed appreciation of the stand made by the Executive Council of the Society and of the support given by the membership.

PRIDE IN SOLIDARITY

In the annual report for 1923 the General Secretary claimed that the Boilermakers' Society had always been a fighting organisation. In the year 1923, he said, the Shipbuilding Employers' Federation had forced upon the Society the biggest dispute in its history. The old spirit of the boilermakers was still alive, he claimed, and they were prepared today as their fathers were ninety years previously when the Society was inaugurated to fight for reasonable wages and conditions of employment.

At the end of the lockout the Society issued a circular to all branches which indicated clearly the pride of the Executive Council in the struggle waged by the membership. The terms of the letter were as follows:

We were locked out by the Shipbuilding Employers' Federation on the 30th of April, and their gates were closed against us until Monday, the 26th November, a period of 30 weeks.

At the opening of the dispute it was confidentially stated by representatives of the employers, that about 3 weeks would be sufficient to force the boilermakers into submission, but as the weeks and the months passed people began to recognise something of the determination of the Boilermakers' Society.

The lack of employment and wages, and even the lack of bread in many cases, was insufficient to break the spirit of our members in their endeavour to secure what they believed to be their legitimate rights as workmen.

The lock-out by the employers was aggravated by the attitude adopted by a majority of the other trades in the Engineering & Shipbuilding Trades Federation. This attitude of the other trades was the chief obstruction to ourselves, and to everyone who made an endeavour to assist us in arriving at an honourable settlement.

Notwithstanding these difficulties, which were unique in the annals of trade unionism, your representatives have succeeded in obtaining a settlement, and although it is a compromise on our part, it is an honourable one, such as we were able to recommend, in the circumstances, for acceptance.

Throughout the long period of the dispute not a single member of ours was guilty of disloyalty, and we have closed the dispute as we began, solid to the last man.

The Executive Council felt it their duty in notifying the close of this dispute to pay a tribute of honour and respect to our members who suffered through these months and upheld the proudest traditions of their Society.

We feel convinced that this struggle, in spite of its cost

financially and in sacrifice to the members, will yet yield its fruits worthy of the effort.

INDUSTRIAL COURT

Discussions between the Federation and the Society on the outstanding points of difference following the lockout took place during the early months of 1924. No agreement was reached. In accordance with the agreement made at the conclusion of the lockout the issues were referred to the Industrial Court. The court sat in London on 30 April and 1 May 1924.

At the Industrial Court the Boilermakers' Society argued that the national agreement negotiated by the Federation of Engineering and Shipbuilding Trades with the SEF was made by unions representing principally time working trades. The conditions of piece-workers were essentially different from those of time workers.

For many years the Boilermakers' Society had made district agreements or had established recognised practices with employers on overtime arrangements and payments. The national agreement, said the Society, purported to cancel these district agreements and customs, although the unions' signatories to the national agreement were not party to them and had little knowledge of their provisions.

The Society made a number of detailed criticisms of the new national agreement. They pointed out that the first clause, dealing with the regulation of overtime, provided in effect for unlimited overtime. Overtime on new work was expressly limited to thirty hours in any four weeks but this number could be extended by 'special arrangement'. The Boilermakers' Society wanted a more definite commitment for the limitation of overtime.

The clauses relating to payment for overtime were particularly objectionable to the Boilermakers' Society. Time workers were to receive an overtime premium of 50 per cent on plain time rates. Piece-workers, on the other hand, were to be given an allowance of only 25 per cent of the average hourly piece-work earnings. Piece-workers, it was said, earned substantially more than time workers and this lower overtime premium payment in percentage terms was intended to redress an imbalance which would otherwise occur. The employers argued that an overtime allowance should be regarded as an allowance for inconvenience and accordingly no differentiation should be made in the amount as between time workers and piece-workers. The employers said that they would have preferred to give both the piece-workers and the time workers an equivalent allowance on the time rate but some of the unions signatory to the national agreement had urged that the piece-workers' allowance should be given in the form of a percentage. This was, of course, totally unacceptable to the Boilermakers' Society.

AWARD

In its award the Industrial Court did not accept the argument of the Boilermakers' Society on the regulation of overtime, but they did agree that the percentage figures for overtime premiums for piece-workers should be increased. The evidence, they said, had revealed anomalies which needed correction and that there were special circumstances peculiar to members of the Boilermakers' Society. The figure of 25 per cent as the premium for normal overtime was increased to $33\frac{1}{3}$ per cent. Corresponding increases were awarded for overtime payments for Sundays and nightshift working.

Thus the outcome of the shipbuilding lockout and the subsequent Industrial Court award largely vindicated the stand taken by the Boilermakers' Society. A new national agreement on overtime and nightshift working was concluded between the Shipbuilding Employers' Federation and the Society on 12 July 1924. The agreement stated that:

The parties are agreed that systematic overtime is to be deprecated as a method of production, and no workman shall be required by the employer – unless by special arrangement – to work more than 30 hours' overtime in any four weeks. In the following cases, however, viz. ship-repairing, launches, trial trips, work subject to tidal considerations, breakdown work, plant installation and plant repairs, agreed urgency and emergency, and linking-up dayshift and nightshift, there shall not be any restriction of overtime.

The premium rates awarded by the Industrial Court were embodied in the agreement.

FINANCES

The national disputes in 1922 and 1923, together with heavy unemployment, had left the Society in a very poor financial state. At the end of 1923 the general fund had an overdraft of £102,000. By the spring of 1924 this overdraft had increased to nearly £120,000. There were still substantial funds available for superannuation so that the net balance at the end of 1923 amounted to £241,000. In 1923 the expenditure of the Society exceeded its income by no less than £180,000. More than £155,000 had been paid during the year in dispute benefit, £96,000 in unemployment benefit, nearly £50,000 in sickness benefit and nearly £70,000 in superannuation benefit. In contrast, members' contributions amounted to only £135,000. Other sources of income included unemployment benefit refunds from the Ministry of Labour and dispute grants from the General Federation of Trade Unions.

The financial situation of the Society had been worsening for a number of years. In 1920 the total balance had been £834,000, representing about £8 per member. In 1921 expenditure exceeded income by £232,000, in 1922 by a further £179,000, and this was followed in 1923 by an excess of expenditure over income of £180,000.

Three alternative propositions to remedy the financial situation were put to the membership. The first was that contributions should be increased. First class members, it was suggested, should pay an increased contribution of 6d per week. The second proposal was that all benefits should be reduced or in some cases suspended. The third proposal was that members' contributions should be increased by a smaller amount than under the first proposal and that unemployment benefit should be reduced by one half. The second and third proposals were heavily defeated in a ballot vote and the first proposal was carried by 3,735 to 1,617. The effect was to increase the contributions of first class members to 2s a week. This increase took effect from Monday 29 September 1924.

Chapter 9

Political Action 1922-1924

The major industrial disputes in which the Society was engaged in 1922 and 1923 appear to have sharpened the political interest of many members. At the 1922 November General Election a member of the Society, David Williams, was elected as Member of Parliament for Swansea. He was not at the time of his election a sponsored candidate. The Executive Council decided shortly afterwards to submit to a ballot of the membership a proposal that David Williams should be accepted as a sponsored candidate and that a financial allowance of £50 each three months should be made to him. The Executive Committee explained that without some financial assistance it would be impossible for David Williams to maintain his home in Swansea, find accommodation in London and meet the heavy travelling and postal expenses which his responsibilities as an MP made inevitable. The sum of £50 each three months was already being paid to Alfred Short, who had been re-elected to Parliament for Wednesbury as a Labour candidate sponsored by the Boilermakers' Society.

By 6,771 votes to 860 the membership supported the proposal to adopt David Williams as a boilermakers' MP and to make a grant to him of £50 each three months. By a similarly large majority they agreed to make a grant of £70 towards the election expenses of another member of the Society who had fought as an unsponsored Labour candidate. He was Joseph Gibbins who was unsuccessful but polled over 10,000 votes against a shipowner in the West Toxteth division of Liverpool. Four other unsuccessful candidates were sponsored by the Society in the November 1922 General Election. In this election the Labour Party increased its total vote

145

to nearly 4¼ million from 2,385,000 in the previous General Election in December 1918.

John Hill welcomed these developments. In writing in the monthly report about the membership ballot figures he said 'I believe this is the biggest majority vote we have ever had in favour of Labour representation. It is a clear indication of the growth of a new political consciousness amongst our members'.

COMMUNIST AFFILIATION?

The Boilermakers' Society played a prominent part in the debates at the annual conference of the Labour Party between 1922 and 1924 on the relationship between the Labour Party and the Communist Party. The 1922 annual report of the Labour Party contained a lengthy section on an application for affiliation received from the Communist Party. The substance of the report was that the aims and methods of the Communist Party were very different from those of the Labour Party. The Labour Party was committed to bringing about social change by winning a parliamentary majority. The Communist Party, on the other hand, was committed to revolutionary struggle for the dictatorship of the proletariat and the establishment of a Soviet system of power. The Communist Party, it was pointed out, endorsed and was bound by the policy statements of the Communist International. These statements made it clear that Communists should participate in Parliament for the purpose of using it as a platform, but that their ultimate intention was to destroy Parliament, as part of the machinery of the bourgeois state.

Harry Pollitt, on behalf of the Boilermakers' Society, moved the reference back of this section of the report at the 1922 Labour Party conference. He urged that discussions should be held with the Communist Party. The Labour Party, he argued, was by its constitution a combination of working class parties and trade unions. The proper place for the Communist Party was inside the labour movement. He acknowledged that Communist candidates were opposing Labour candidates in elections but said that this could be the subject of negotiations. He suggested that the Labour Party should put to the Communist Party the question 'Will you, or will

146

you not, abide by the constitution of the Labour Party?' The reference back was seconded by the AEU, but was nevertheless overwhelmingly defeated. The voting was 3,086,000 to 261,000.

At the 1923 Labour Party conference Pollitt again spoke on behalf of the Boilermakers' Society in a debate on Communist affiliation. Barrow Labour Party moved an amendment to the report of the National Executive Committee to the effect that the Communist Party should be accepted into affiliation. The amendment was defeated by 2,880,000 votes to 366,000. At the 1924 Labour Party conference, when Pollitt again spoke on behalf of the Society, the affiliation of the Communist Party was rejected by 3,185,000 votes to 193,000. It was also decided by 2,456,000 to 654,000 votes that Communist Party members should not be endorsed as Labour candidates. In addition it was decided by 1,804,000 votes to 1,540,000 that members of the Communist Party should not be eligible for membership of the Labour Party.

Despite the defeat at the Labour Party conferences of the proposal for Communist affiliation, with which Harry Pollitt was identified and for which he acted as spokesman for the Boilermakers' Society, he continued to command wide popularity within the Society. In 1923, 1924 and 1925 he topped the poll in the branch ballots for the election of delegates to the TUC, the annual conference of the Labour Party and the annual conference of the General Federation of Trade Unions.

At the beginning of 1924 Pollitt was nominated for the Boilermakers' Society panel of parliamentary candidates. In his election address he said that he stood 'for the overthrow of capitalistic society, and for the establishment at the earliest possible moment of a workers' commonwealth, with all power invested in the hands of the workers' government'. He also put forward an immediate programme of demands. They included a capital levy, a minimum wage, a six-hour working day and full work or maintenance for the unemployed. He said that he was a member of the Executive Committee of the Communist Party of Great Britain, but he pledged himself to accept the constitution of the Labour Party. Pollitt was elected at the top of the poll for the electoral district in which he stood, which embraced most of southern England and South Wales. He received more than twice as many votes as the next candidate. Another communist, Aitken Ferguson, was elected to the parliamentary panel from the Scottish electoral district. He had a narrow victory in a second ballot over Mr T. Irwin.

Aitken Ferguson, a Glasgow boilermaker and former member of the Clyde Workers' Committee, was at the centre of another controversy. Though a Communist, he was nominated by the Boilermakers' Society to stand as Labour candidate for Kelvingrove in 1923. He was adopted as Labour candidate but he did not receive national endorsement. Nevertheless he polled well in the election and was only narrowly defeated. The following year he was again nominated by the Boilermakers' Society as Labour candidate for Kelvingrove and he gained strong support within the local labour movement. There was much discussion nationally about whether the Labour Party should permit him to stand as Labour candidate. In the outcome he did, but on this occasion he was defeated in the election by a larger majority.

POLLITT – A NEW CONTROVERSY

The report of the 1924 Labour Party conference, published in the monthly report of the Society, recorded the decisions of the conference to reject the affiliation of the Communist Party and to affirm that no member of the Communist Party should be eligible for membership of the Labour Party or for endorsement as a Labour candidate for Parliament or any local authority. Delegates Alfred Cooper and John Hill, who were the signatories to this published report, drew the attention of members to these decisions and said that they were of considerable importance to the Society in view of the fact that two of the Society's parliamentary candidates were Communists, namely Harry Pollitt and Aitken Ferguson. The boilermakers' delegates said that the Labour Party conference decisions made it impossible for the Society to sponsor them as Labour candidates and it would be necessary for members 'to reconsider the question of parliamentary candidates in the divisions in which these two brothers were elected'. Notwithstanding this invitation to the membership not to nominate Pollitt and Ferguson, Pollitt received more nominations for the next Labour Party conference than any other candidate in the Society.

Throughout this period Pollitt was a regular correspondent to the columns of the monthly journal, writing on a wide range of issues. He advocated the amalgamation of unions engaged in similar industries. The objective, he said, must be one union for each industry. He argued for the recognition of the Soviet Government in Russia. British workers, he said, should continue to demonstrate their solidarity with the working class of the Soviet Union. The development of trade between the two countries would help employment in the engineering and shipbuilding industries. In 1925 Pollitt was scathing in his criticism of one of Britain's leading shipping lines which had decided to place orders for new ships with German yards. The workers of all countries, he urged, should unite and not permit the capitalists to play off worker against worker. A single trade union international could fight capitalism effectively and prevent the workers of each country from being set against each other, either in a wages war or in a repetition of the imperialist war of 1914–18.

In 1925 Harry Pollitt was again nominated for a vacancy on the Executive Council of the Society. His nomination was supported by a number of branches and, in accordance with normal practice, a committee in support of his nomination published an appeal in the monthly report. The appeal recalled that Pollitt had entered the Society in January 1912 at the age of 21 years and had been active since that time. He had been a shop steward, district representative, secretary of the London District Committee and, for the previous four years, had represented the Society at the TUC, the Labour Party conference and the General Federation of Trade Unions. His supporting committee said that Pollitt was one of the best known men in the working class movement and his abilities as a speaker, debater, writer and organiser were unquestioned.

A number of branches protested to the Executive Council that Pollitt was ineligible to stand as a candidate for the Executive Council. The rules stated that 'none but past and present officers who have held office for a period of at least three years shall be eligible for the position of councilman'. It was held that Pollitt did not satisfy this requirement.

A LABOUR GOVERNMENT

As a result of a General Election in December 1923 a Labour Government took office for the first time in British history. It was a minority government dependent heavily upon Liberal support. At the General Election the Conservative Party had received more than 5½ million votes, the Labour Party more than 4,400,000 and the Liberal Party more than 4,300,000. Five members of the parliamentary panel of the Boilermakers' Society contested the election as sponsored candidates and two were successful. They were Albert Short, who was elected for Wednesbury, and W. H. Egan, who was elected for Birkenhead West. J. M. Airlie, S. E. Walters and M. H. Connolly were unsuccessful. Candidates sponsored by the Boilermakers' Society received automatic financial assistance from the Society's political fund. Two other members of the Society, including David Williams, who was successful, also fought the election though not as sponsored candidates of the Boilermakers' Society. In May 1924 the two boilermakers' MPs were joined by a third, Joe Gibbins, who was elected at a by-election for the West Toxteth division of Liverpool. This represented a Labour gain.

The minority Labour Government did not last very long. In the early autumn of 1924 when the Labour Government was discussing the 'recognition' of the Soviet Government in Russia and trade arrangements with the Soviet Union a 'red scare' was created by the press. Newspapers and Conservative and many Liberal MPs were strongly opposed to any negotiation with the Soviet Government. A Communist journalist, J. R. Campbell, who was editing the *Workers' Weekly*, was prosecuted on a charge of inciting troops to sedition. Later the charge was dropped. This was the cause of the immediate fall of the Government. The Conservatives and their allies alleged that 'extremists' had exerted pressure on the Government. In the following General Election an alleged letter was produced by the Foreign Office which was said to have been sent by Zinoviev on behalf of the Communist International to the British Communist Party giving instructions for subversion. The publication of this alleged letter, whilst the Prime Minister was still nominally Foreign Secretary, embarrassed the Labour movement throughout Britain and gave the Conservatives the opportunity they wanted. As always a 'red scare' of this kind played into the hands of political reactionaries. The letter was a forgery but the Labour leadership at the time were equivocal in their attitude. In the General Election Labour lost over forty seats and the Conservatives gained substantially, both from Labour and even more from the Liberals.

In the 1924 General Election six members of the Boilermakers' Society stood as Labour candidates. Three were members of the Society's panel and three stood independently of the panel. Of the six candidates four were successful. They included A. Short, Wednesbury; M. Connolly, Newcastle; D. Williams, Swansea; and J. Gibbins, West Toxteth, Liverpool. W. H. Egan lost his seat. In writing about the election the General Secretary, John Hill, was in no doubt that the outcome had been determined primarily by 'the red plot'. He noted that despite its defeat the national vote for the Labour Party was more than a million higher in October 1924 than in December 1923 when a Labour Government had been elected.

Chapter 10

Continuing Problems of Trade and Employment

Trade picked up in the summer of 1924. Members in various parts of the country secured wage increases and national claims were submitted to the Shipbuilding Employers' Federation and to the Engineering Employers' Federation. The claim for wage increases in the shipbuilding industry did not lead to an immediate settlement. The two sides agreed, however, to refer the claim to the Industrial Court. The Court's decision was announced in June 1924. A wage increase of 7s per week was awarded to be paid in two instalments. The first instalment took effect in June and the second in September 1924.

DEPRESSION IN SHIPBUILDING

The revival in trade was short-lived. Throughout 1925 more than 20,000 members of the Society were unemployed. The most serious depression of all was in shipbuilding. The Society suggested to the Government that the industry should be subsidised. It claimed that if one quarter of the money paid out in unemployment benefit to unemployed shipbuilding workers were used as a subsidy it would restore prosperity to the industry. This proposal was supported by a meeting of mayors and deputy mayors from towns in the north east of England. At this meeting a resolution was adopted urging the Government to introduce a shipbuilding subsidy 'on the

152

understanding that for all new tonnage so assisted an equivalent amount of old tonnage will be scrapped'.

In October 1925 the Society decided to write to the Prime Minister in support of its 'scrap and rebuild' scheme for shipbuilding. The letter pointed out that, on average, during the previous five years one third of the men employed in the shipbuilding industry had been unemployed. It was suggested that a grant of 50s per ton on each ton of shipping constructed beyond current average output from each yard, up to a maximum of 50 per cent increase, would require a subsidy of £1½ million per annum. This expenditure of £1½ million in subsidies would save more than £5 million in unemployment benefit.

The Prime Minister rejected the subsidy scheme put forward by the Boilermakers' Society. In the Government's view it would have been wrong to divert the unemployment fund into industrial subsidies. The Government also felt that there were objections to the granting of subsidies to particular industries and that the grant of a subsidy could seldom prove more than a temporary relief. The Government also referred to difficulties arising from competition between subsidised and unsubsidised ships.

The Society sent a further letter to the Prime Minister dated 13 November 1925 reiterating their point of view. The Society felt that whilst the Government had set out various difficulties they had offered no alternative.

SHIPBUILDING INQUIRY

In August 1925 a joint committee of the Shipbuilding Employers' Federation and the shipyard unions published a report on foreign competition and working conditions. The committee was established in the spring of 1925 on the initiative of the Shipbuilding Employers' Federation. This followed an announcement in March 1925 that a British shipping firm, Furness Withy and Company, had placed an order in Germany for five large motor ships. The shipbuilding employers wrote to the shipbuilding unions on 17 March stating that the placing of this contract provided a vivid illustration 'of the severe continental competition which this country is experiencing'. They suggested that the employers and the unions should jointly consider the situation.

The unions responded to this invitation and a conference was held in London on 27 March 1925. The employers then proposed that a joint committee should be established to investigate conditions bearing on the shipbuilding and shiprepairing industry, and that attention should be given to the machinery for the avoidance of disputes. They further suggested that an index should be established whereby future fluctuations in wages could be regulated in accordance with the ability of the industry to pay. The unions considered this statement and at a meeting of the executives of all the unions held on 24 April it was agreed to establish a joint committee with power 'to inquire into the whole of the facts submitted from all sides and report'. Mr John Hill represented the Boilermakers' Society on the joint committee. The committee conducted its inquiries with the help of the Board of Trade and the Ministry of Labour.

In the early stages of the inquiry the attention of the committee was directed to the hours of work being worked in Germany. Although nominally the hours were eight per day, there were many German yards in which, by agreement between employers and workers, the regular hours of work were fifty-four per week, with overtime rates being paid only after fifty-four hours. Similarly in Holland, although by statute the hours of the basic working week were forty-eight, the hours in shipyards had been increased to fifty-four. A review was also made of demarcation problems, overtime rates, piece-work rates, payment-by-results and financial information relating to firms in the shipbuilding industry.

A detailed study was also made of the prices quoted for the motor ships required by Furness Withy and Company Limited. The accepted German price was £153,000, whereas the lowest British tender was £213,000. The lowest British tender made no allowances, however, for certain indirect charges such as rates, management expenses and directors' fees. Nor was any allowance made for any return on capital. The employers said that the margin of difference between British and German prices for the Furness Withy contract was quite abnormal and did not represent accurately the usual margin between British and foreign tenders.

The report said that British wages exceeded Hamburg wages by 47–56 per cent for skilled workers. Based on hourly rates alone British wages were some 69–79 per cent higher than wages in

154

Hamburg for skilled workers. Similarly, overtime rates were lower in Germany than in the United Kingdom. The report served to illustrate the difficulties under which the British shipbuilding industry was operating. Wages and conditions were at a much lower level in Germany than in the United Kingdom.

AT THE TUC

The reports of the Boilermakers' Society delegations to the 1924 and 1925 Congresses of the TUC both commented on the militancy and progressive nature of the decisions taken by the delegates. The hand of Harry Pollitt was clearly discernible in the drafting of these reports. The report of the 1924 Congress said that there was one great theme running through it and that was the absolute need for the unification of the trade union movement both nationally and internationally. Important discussions took place on a resolution dealing with trade union organisation by industry, and on a resolution designed to give increased power to the General Council. Relations between the International Federation of Trade Unions and the Red International of Labour Unions were also debated. A workers' charter was adopted including demands for a minimum wage, forty-four-hour week, measures for dealing with unemployment and the provision of better housing, improved educational schemes, increased compensation to workers injured at work, and pensions for all at 60 years of age. John Hill, the General Secretary of the Society, spoke on behalf of the General Council of the TUC on a resolution stating that in the event of war a special TUC should be convened to declare a general strike. This resolution was carried.

At the 1924 Congress there was a fraternal delegate from the Soviet trade unions. He addressed the Congress and the Boilermakers' Society reported that the reception was magnificent. The speech by Tomsky, the leader of the Russian delegation, was said by the Boilermakers' delegates to be the best speech that the TUC had yet heard from a fraternal delegate. The 1924 Congress, said the Society's delegation, 'marked a new stage on the road of the workers in their fight for emancipation from capitalism'.

A similarly favourable report was given by the boilermakers' delegation on the proceedings of the 1925 TUC. The President of the 1925 Congress was Mr A. B. Swales of the Amalgamated Engineering Union. The keynote of his speech, said the boiler-makers' delegates, was 'the necessity for closer unity of all trade union organisations in order to defeat the efforts of the capitalists and prepare the way for the real fight against the whole capitalist system'. The Congress did not grant increased powers to the General Council but agreed that a report should be prepared to strengthen the power of the General Council. Proposals for trade union amalgamation were approved and the Congress pledged itself to do all in its power to bring about the formation of an all-inclusive international trade union movement.

The boilermakers' delegates reported that by a large majority the Congress had repudiated the Dawes' Plan which, they said, had been mainly responsible for forcing down the wages and working conditions of German workers and thus putting in the hands of the capitalists of Britain a weapon with which they sought to force down the standards of British workers. Congress registered its opposition to reparations and indemnities which injured not only the working class of the countries which had to pay them but also the workers of the countries which received them.

The Congress also carried a resolution expressing opposition to imperialism and expressing determination to assist workers in the various countries of the British Empire to fight for their economic and political freedom. The boilermakers' delegates said that the Congress listened to fraternal speeches from delegates from America, Canada and the International Federation of Trade Unions but it was significant that the warmest reception of all was given to the delegate of the Russian trade union movement.

INTERNAL PROBLEMS

In 1924 three members of the old Light Platers' and Sheet Iron Workers' Society, which had amalgamated with the Boilermakers' Society in 1919, took legal action to recover some of the funds which belonged to the Sheet Iron Workers' Society at the time of the amalgamation. They did not succeed in their action, though the Boilermakers' Society acknowledged that the amalgamation had not been carried out strictly in accordance with the law. At the time the Boilermakers' Society did not believe that it was necessary to conduct a ballot and to secure a majority before an amalgamation could take place. When the amalgamation took place the Light Platers' and Sheet Iron Workers' Society had a membership of 1,383 in comparison with a membership of the Boilermakers' Society of 100,628. The funds of the Light Platers' and Sheet Iron Workers' Society amounted to £8,469, which was approximately one hundredth of the funds then possessed by the Boilermakers' Society.

Despite the increase in contributions which had been made in 1924 the Society was not able to balance its income and expenditure either in 1924 or 1925. In 1924 there was a deficit of nearly £89,000 and in 1925, even after a full year at the increased level of contributions, the deficit was over £9,000. In addition to normal items of expenditure the Society had to meet heavy overdraft charges. The situation was made worse by the decline in membership. In 1924 the membership stood at 82,432 of whom 3,666 were superannuated. In 1925 it had dropped to 74,287 and the number of superannuated members had risen to 4,206. The 1925 annual report of the Society said that during the previous five years the number of employees in the shipbuilding industry had declined from 300,000 to 150,000. The Society estimated that some 50,000 members had been thrown out of employment during this period.

Chapter 11

The General Strike
and its Aftermath

The General Strike took place in May 1926. In reality it was not a general strike; the majority of workers were not called to strike by their unions and remained at work for the duration of the dispute. The total number of workers involved in the stoppage was about two million. They included transport workers, railwaymen, iron and steel workers and printers. Other workers were held 'in reserve'. Engineering workers were called out in the very final stage of the strike, but before many of them had received the call the strike had been brought to an end by the General Council of the TUC.

The General Strike was, nevertheless, of great significance in the history of trade unionism. It was regarded by the Government of the day as a challenge to the social order. It was seen by millions of citizens as a struggle centred on an economic issue concerning not only the miners but the standard of living of many other industrial workers. It represented a turning point in post-war British history. On the one hand stood the trade union movement, with its support for the miners in their resistance to demands for wage reductions and longer hours of work. On the other, stood the Government and, behind it, most of Britain's employers, determined that economic realism, as they saw it, should prevail, that miners' pay should not continue to be maintained at its existing level and that the power of trade unionism to resist this attack should be broken. The Government prepared carefully for the

158

mining struggle of 1926. The trade unions made very few preparations.

The General Strike of 1926 was defeated. But it was not defeated by any failure on the part of rank and file trade union members to respond to the strike call made to them. Indeed they responded in a manner which surprised even the most optimistic of their leaders. They showed great determination in their support for the miners. They were defeated because the strike was called off by the TUC General Council in exchange for hints – which proved to be worthless – that concessions would be made.

The TUC leaders terminated the strike because they were not prepared to carry through to its conclusion the course on which they had embarked. The General Strike represented a release of power which frightened them even more than it frightened those who were in Government. When the strike ended there was great dismay and even disbelief among many of the rank and file. They felt that they had been misled. They had been encouraged to take up the challenge on behalf of the miners and were then let down by some of the leaders who had issued the strike call.

A TURNING POINT

The election of a Conservative Government towards the end of 1924 marked a turning point in post-war industrial relations. The collapse of the post-war boom and the subsequent depression led employers in the coal industry to demand wage reductions and longer working hours. The economic situation was made worse by the extraction of reparations from Germany. The reparations reduced the demand for British goods. Moreover, German economic recovery was assisted by the Dawes Loan from the USA. The newly-elected Conservative Government was sympathetic to the employers. The miners were regarded as the advance guard of the trade union and labour movement. If sacrifices could be imposed on the miners the resistance of workers everywhere could be overcome.

In 1925 the coalowners gave notice to the miners demanding lower wages, longer hours and reversion from a national agreement to district agreements. The owners argued that only by cutting

159

production costs could they remain competitive in a shrinking market. The miners rejected the owners' demands and pointed out that the coalowners had failed to organise the industry effectively. Investment had been neglected. Reduced wages, they said, would worsen the economic depression because it would have the effect of reducing the level of demand.

The miners were supported by railwaymen and other transport unions who said that in the event of a lockout in the mining industry they would impose an embargo on the movement of coal. This firm expression of support secured the result desired by the unions. The Government agreed to provide a subsidy for nine months and to appoint a Royal Commission to investigate the industry. The unions regarded this step as a victory and the day on which the Government made its announcement became known as 'Red Friday'.

The unions were, however, too optimistic. The Government saw these moves only as a temporary retreat. The real challenge was yet to come and the Government immediately started to prepare for the challenge. An Organisation for the Maintenance of Supplies was set up and a skeleton arrangement was introduced to divide the country into ten areas each under a Civil Commissioner who was to have extensive powers. In contrast, the unions made virtually no preparation for a struggle which was clearly impending.

The Royal Commission – known as the Samuel Commission – which had been appointed to investigate the coal industry did not include anyone with Labour sympathies. Its report was published early in 1926. It recommended that colliery amalgamations should be encouraged, that coal royalties should be bought out, but that the ownership of the industry should remain unchanged. It also recommended that wages should be reduced.

The miners rejected the recommendations on wages and in the subsequent negotiations the owners remained adamant in their demands. The talks broke down and the owners posted lockout notices to enforce their demands. The TUC attempted to bring about a settlement but they too were unable to persuade either the owners or the Government to change their policy.

TUC SUPPORT

Working-class opinion in Britain was strongly sympathetic to the miners' cause. Other trade unionists rightly recognised that if the miners were defeated an employers' offensive would be launched against wages and conditions in many other industries. The TUC convened a conference of trade union executives and by an overwhelming majority authority was given to the General Council to organise a General Strike. The voting was:

For	3,653,529
Awaiting instructions	319,000
Against	49,911

The strike began from midnight Monday 3 May 1926. The response from the first group of workers to be called out was overwhelming. The problem was more to restrain other workers from joining the strike than to persuade those called upon to participate. This remained so throughout the nine days of the General Strike.

The Government used extensive powers to try to break the strike. All official means of publicity were employed to give the impression, first, that the strike was a challenge to constitutional authority and illegal and, secondly, that the response to the strike call by workers was half-hearted. Strike breaking by volunteers was encouraged. The Government failed to make any significant impression on the strike or on the mood of the strikers.

DEFEAT

The strike was eventually called off when the TUC General Council decided, against the opposition of the miners, to accept a private memorandum prepared by Sir Herbert Samuel, the chairman of the Royal Commission, which the General Council interpreted as offering a compromise solution to the dispute. The General Council were, in fact, seeking a way to bring the strike to an end. Samuel's private memorandum carried no authority from either the Government or the coalowners. Nevertheless, the General Council terminated the General Strike and the miners were left to continue their struggle unaided. The battle went on for a further seven months with very great hardship in the coalfields. The miners were driven into defeat.

BOILERMAKERS IN THE GENERAL STRIKE

In the months before the General Strike the Boilermakers' Society was already seriously weakened by high unemployment. Nearly 38 per cent of all shipbuilding workers were out of a job. Financially the Society was in a serious plight. The mood of the membership was not particularly sympathetic to measures which might make even further calls on the depleted funds of the Society. In 1925 an attempt was made, largely on the initiative of Ernest Bevin and the Transport and General Workers' Union, to form an Industrial Alliance between a number of unions. The purpose of the alliance was to provide increased industrial strength to the participating unions. On a ballot vote the members of the Boilermakers' Society rejected the proposal to join the Industrial Alliance. The proposal was defeated by 3,822 votes to 1,949. At that time the attention of the members of the Society was directed mainly towards the inquiry being conducted jointly by the employers and unions into the problems of the shipbuilding and shiprepairing industries, including the possibility of introducing new machinery for resolving disputes.

Despite its financial problems the Boilermakers' Society expressed its support for the miners, and at the conference of trade union executive committees held immediately before the General Strike voted in favour of giving authority to the General Council to organise the strike. When the strike call came the Society's members employed on the railways and in the steel industry were immediately affected. The rules of the Society required that a ballot should be held before members were called out in a dispute. To get round this difficulty the Executive Council issued a circular which contained the following paragraph:

The rules do not authorise the Executive Council to call members out on dispute without a ballot vote, but as the General Council

162

have advised the suspension of work in railway repair shops and steel works our members may, if they so desire, decide their course of action in co-operation with the members of all other unions having members employed in railway workshops or steel works.

Members employed by colliery companies were already locked out. Altogether the number of members who were directly affected in coal, railways and steel and who responded to the call, was 10,441. There were very few cases indeed of members not withdrawing their labour in these industries.

NO DISPUTE BENEFIT

In their letter urging members employed in the steel industry and on the railways to respond to the strike call of the TUC, the Executive Council stated that because of the lack of funds it would not be possible to pay dispute benefit. It was explained, however, that members who contributed to the levy of the General Federation of Trade Unions might be eligible for dispute benefit of 5s per week, 'always provided that the funds of the GFTU . . . will be sufficient for the emergency'.

This reference to the possible payment of dispute benefit by the GFTU was the beginning of a sad sequence of events. The Management Committee of the Federation decided not to accede to the request for payment except in the case of 291 members employed at collieries. This left more than 10,000 members in the steel industry and on the railways without benefit. The Executive Council of the Boilermakers' Society expressed regret at this decision and informed the Federation that they did not accept it. They stated that they would raise the issue at the annual meeting of the GFTU.

The annual meeting of the GFTU took place in July 1926 in Dover. On behalf of the Boilermakers' Society John Hill moved a motion calling for the payment of dispute benefit to members of affiliated organisations employed in collieries, steel works and transport who took part in the General Strike. The motion was opposed by the Management Committee of the Federation who argued that under the rules only those directly involved in a dispute about pay and conditions were eligible for benefit. Entitlement did not extend to workers who came out on sympathetic strike. The Boilermakers' motion was lost by forty-four votes to six.

TUC GENERAL COUNCIL DEFENDED

In the June 1926 issue of the monthly report the General Secretary, John Hill, defended the decision of the TUC General Council to end the General Strike. He said that members would expect him 'to clear up the mystery of the calling off of the General Strike'. He started his explanation by saying that the object of the strike was to defend the miners against a reduction of wages or an increase in hours. In deciding upon the strike the unions of the TUC had borne in mind the statement of the Prime Minister that not only the miners' wages but all wages must be reduced.

John Hill emphasised that the conference of trade unions which gave authority for the calling of the General Strike left the conduct of the strike in the hands of the General Council of the TUC. He said that a small sub-committee of the General Council had met the Prime Minister immediately before the strike and a basis of settlement concerning miners' wages and hours was reached. Mr Baldwin had then gone to meet his Cabinet colleagues but they had not endorsed his action. Leadership had been assumed by Mr Churchill who was reported to have said that a little blood-letting would be a good thing. The majority of the Cabinet, said John Hill, were with Mr Churchill, preferring blood rather than peace. Thus ended the strenuous but sincere efforts on the part of the TUC to avoid a lockout of the miners and a sympathetic strike.

After the General Strike started the TUC tried, according to John Hill, to get negotiations reopened and the negotiating committee reported to the full General Council that 'they had received definite assurances that if the strike was called off temporary financial provision would be made by the Government to enable the miners to resume work on the old conditions, and negotiations with the miners would be at once resumed on the basis of the Commission's report, [ie the Samuel Commission]'. It was on this assurance, said John Hill, that the TUC General Council unanimously decided to call off the strike. Subsequently the TUC 'were let down as the conditions afterwards submitted by the Prime Minister were not in accordance with the definite assurances given to the TUC'.

The letter sent by the TUC General Council on 12 May 1926 to all affiliated unions calling off the strike was in the following terms:

The General Council, through the magnificent support and solidarity of the trade union movement, has obtained assurances that a settlement of the mining problem can be secured which justifies them in bringing the general stoppage to an end.

Conversations have been proceeding between the General Council representatives and Sir Herbert Samuel, Chairman of the Coal Commission, who returned from Italy for the express purpose of offering his services to try to effect a settlement of the differences in the coal mining industry.

The Government had declared that under no circumstances could negotiations take place until the General Strike had been terminated but the General Council feel as a result of the conversations with Sir Herbert Samuel and the proposals which are embodied in the correspondence and documents which are enclosed, that sufficient assurances had been obtained as to the lines upon which a settlement could be reached to justify them in terminating the General Strike.

The General Council accordingly decided at their meeting today to terminate the general stoppage, in order that negotiations could be resumed to secure a settlement in the coal mining industry, free and unfettered from either strike or lock-out.

The General Council considered the practicability of securing a resumption of work by the members in dispute at a uniform time and date, but it was felt, having regard to the varied circumstances and practices in each industry, that it would be better for each Executive Council itself to make arrangements for the resumption of work of its own members. The following telegram was dispatched to you today:

General Council TUC have today declared General Strike terminated. Please instruct your members as to resuming work as soon as arrangements can be made. Letter follows.

Pugh, Citrine

Throughout the negotiations and during the whole of the stoppage, the General Council have declared that they have been fighting to protect the miners against an intolerable degradation of their standard of life and working conditions. It was with this object, and with this object alone, that the General Council assumed the grave responsibility of calling upon its affiliated organisations to unite in strike action to enforce the cancellation of the lock-out notices and the withdrawal of the new wages scale posted in the mining districts. No attack was at any time contemplated upon the established political institutions of the country, and it is a testimony to the loyalty and discipline of the Movement that disorders have been practically unknown.

The unions that have maintained so resolutely and unitedly their generous and ungrudging support of the miners can be satisfied that an honourable understanding has been reached.

The General Council accept the consequences of their decision with a full sense of their responsibility, not only to their own membership, but to the nation at large. They have endeavoured throughout the crisis to conduct their case as industrial disputes have always been conducted by the British trades unions, without violence or aggression. The General Council feel in taking the last steps to bring the crisis to an end that the trade union movement has given a demonstration to the world of discipline, unity and loyalty without parallel in the history of industrial disputes.

Yours fraternally

Arthur Pugh, Chairman
Walter M. Citrine, Acting Secretary

In the July issue of the monthly report the Boilermakers' MPs, D. Williams, J. Gibbins, M. Connolly and A. Short, said that 'the Government had no policy unless it be one, as events have proved, to support the coalowners in their cruel, brutal and vicious attempt to force the miners, through starvation to accept lower wages and longer hours'. The MPs went on to say:

The mining industry is not in a state of bankruptcy; enormous profits have been made, and millions have been paid in royalties to people who render no useful service to the state. The chaotic

condition of the industry is due to inefficiency, lack of organisation and maladministration on the part of the coal owners, who
now desire – and the Tory Government support them – to make
the miners pay for their folly and gross neglect.

WORSENED CONDITIONS

Information that the General Strike had been terminated by the
General Council of the TUC was received at the head office of the
Boilermakers' Society in the early afternoon of 12 May. Telegrams
were sent immediately to branches informing them of the decision
of the TUC and advising members to present themselves for work
on the following morning. Within hours telegrams were being
received in reply from branches stating that where members had
presented themselves for work the employers had not allowed them
to start or were seeking to impose terms of re-employment which
were much worse than those in existence before the strike. Many
members refused to accept new terms and conditions of employment and were therefore still in dispute with their employers.

The General Secretary of the Society got in touch with the
TUC and advised them of the information being received from
branches. He drew particular attention to information being
received from branches with members employed by railway companies. The railway companies indicated that they were prepared
to re-employ only a certain number of men who had been on
strike and only on new conditions of employment.

In the meanwhile the Executive Council of the Boilermakers'
Society sent further telegrams to branches with members employed
by railway companies urging all members to stand firm in support of
existing conditions of employment. The telegrams said that where
the companies were seeking to impose worsened conditions the
members should not return to work. Where conditions were unchanged members should resume work. In cases where employment
was being refused the members were urged to send a deputation to
the employers to find out the reasons for the action.

The experience of the Boilermakers' Society was typical of the
experience of trade unionists in many industries when they presented
themselves for work. The TUC received messages from many unions

167

of attempts by employers to enforce worsened conditions for the resumption of work. A telegram was sent from the TUC to affiliated unions confirming that reports were being received that some employers were attempting to 'enforce humiliating terms as conditions of resumption'. The General Council of the TUC said that it was imperative that agreements, understandings and conditions existing before the dispute should be maintained. It was to prove of little avail. Attacks were made upon active members in many firms and conditions of employment were worsened.

On the railways the unions tried to persuade the employers to accept a resumption of work on conditions existing before the dispute. They failed in this effort. On 14 May terms of settlement were concluded between the railway companies, the National Union of Railwaymen, the Associated Society of Locomotive Engineers and Firemen and the Railway Clerks' Association which were humiliating in the extreme. One of the clauses of settlement said that the trade unions 'admit that in calling the strike they committed a wrongful act against the companies and agree that the companies do not by reinstatement surrender their legal rights to claim damages arising out of the strike from strikers and others responsible'.

In further clauses the railway unions undertook 'not again to instruct their members to strike without previous negotiations with the companies, to give no support of any kind to their members who take any unauthorised action, and not to encourage supervisory employees . . . to take part in any strike'. The railway companies also said that as a condition for the return to work it might be necessary for them to remove certain employees to other positions. The companies said that they would notify the unions within one week of the names of men whom they proposed to transfer.

The Boilermakers' Society protested to the three railway unions about the terms of settlement which they had accepted. In particular, the Society objected to the failure of the railway unions to consult them or any of the other craft unions before accepting the terms of settlement. The action of the railway unions, said the Society, 'was hardly in accordance with the usual concerted action between trade unions'. Nevertheless, the Society advised members to resume work but to report to the district delegate or the Executive Council any objectionable conditions which the companies might seek to impose or any refusal to re-employ members who had been on strike.

DRASTIC ECONOMIES

The high level of unemployment, together with the payment of benefit to many members involved in the General Strike, led to a serious worsening in the financial position of the Society. Early in September 1926 a circular was sent to all branches stating that the Society had overdrawn its bank account to the extent of £173,600. The bank had stated that unless the Society reduced its expenditure any further withdrawals would be stopped. To meet this desperate situation the Executive Council proposed that all benefits and salaries, including the salaries of full-time officials should be reduced by an average 15 per cent. The effect of these proposed savings would be to reduce expenditure by more than £31,000 per annum. Increased subscriptions were already being paid.

The proposals of the Executive Council to reduce all benefits and salaries were put to the membership in a ballot. They were rejected by 6,450 votes to 5,887. From comments made at branch meetings and from correspondence received by the Executive Council it was clear that the main objection was to the proposed cut in superannuation benefit. Despite the rejection of the proposals by ballot the Executive Council said that the situation was so serious that they had no alternative but to implement the cuts in expenditure with the exception of the reduction in superannuation benefit. The cuts took effect from Thursday 30 September 1926.

At the beginning of 1927 the Boilermakers' Society ceased to administer the payment of state unemployment benefit to its members. It was no longer able to satisfy the statutory conditions that a trade union administering state benefit must also pay unemployment benefit from its own funds. The payment of unemployment benefit from the Society's funds had been suspended for many months. The Ministry of Labour had on a number of occasions drawn the attention of the Society to the statutory conditions and, finally, stated that permission to administer state benefit would cease on 19 January 1927.

Sections of the press seized upon the financial difficulties of the

169

Society to make strong attacks against its policy and its administration. The General Secretary said that the press 'had laid violent hands' on the financial problem and had so distorted it as to 'create a considerable amount of suspicion and distrust'. At this period the Society was distributing some £30,000 each week in benefits through the branches. Press speculation about the stability of the Society and attacks upon its policy and administration inevitably caused concern and apprehension among many members. The General Secretary pointed out in reply to these attacks that the difficulties had arisen not through strikes but primarily through unemployment and lockouts by employers. The press, he said, was being assiduously used to discredit trade unionism.

John Hill conducted a vigorous defence of the administration of the Society. He recalled that in the last full year for which figures were available, 1925, the income of the Society from all sources had been £1,543,721. Benefits paid to members had amounted to £1,305,469. Thus 84 per cent of the total income had been distributed to members in benefits. Of the remaining income more than £20,000 had been spent on the administration of state unemployment benefit. John Hill also reminded members that the full-time officials of the Society had accepted three successive reductions in wages. The first two reductions were each of 10 per cent, and the third reduction introduced in September 1926 was of 15 per cent.

JOINT WORKING ARRANGEMENTS

Difficulties which had arisen in the railway industry regarding trade union recruitment, including numerous inter-union disputes between the NUR and the craft unions, led to further discussions about a new agreement between the NUR and the craft unions on trade union membership. Discussions also took place with the railway companies for a new negotiating procedure agreement. In the summer of 1926 draft agreements were put to the membership.

The draft agreement on trade union membership said that the membership of the unions, parties to the agreement, should be regarded as inviolate. The purpose was to eliminate the poaching of members by one union from another. Each union undertook to make inquiries about existing membership, if any, when receiving applications for new membership. The unions also undertook to work towards the unification of contributions as a means of eliminating union competition. A further clause in the draft said that it was in the interests of all railway shopmen that national negotiations should be conducted jointly by all the unions. Each craft union was, however, to maintain its right to negotiate individually on craft questions.

The draft agreement between the railway companies and the unions representing railway shop employees stated that the object was to 'afford full facilities for the discussion and settlement of all questions relating to the rates of pay and general conditions of employment'. Matters of management and discipline, it was said, would 'continue to be dealt with as at present'. The draft agreement provided for the establishment of shop committees, works committees and departmental line committees, and specified the way in which they should be elected. The draft also included a negotiating procedure for dealing with matters raised either by individual employees or by groups of employees.

The proposed agreement with the railway companies on negotiating procedure was submitted to a ballot of members of the Society employed in railway workshops. It was rejected by 512 to 338. The Boilermakers' Society thus did not become a party to the new agreement affecting railway shopmen. The tradition was still strong among members of the Society that all negotiating procedure agreements were to be regarded with suspicion because their effect was to limit the freedom of the rank and file to take immediate action on unresolved grievances.

An even more serious rejection of joint working arrangements took place in the shipbuilding industry. Following the decision of the Boilermakers' Society to leave the Engineering and Shipbuilding Trades Federation the Society conducted negotiations with other principal shipbuilding unions with a view to developing co-operation. At the beginning of 1926 a draft constitution was drawn up for a shipbuilding trades committee composed of the Boilermakers' Society, the woodworkers, the shipwrights, the plumbers, the Electrical Trades Union and the National Society of Painters. The substance of the draft was contained in the first rule which stated that there should be joint action on issues of common con-

171

cern including changes in working hours, conditions and wages and trade union organisation.

This draft was commended by the Executive Council to the membership. They said that the Society had found it necessary from time to time to take joint action with other trade unions on certain general questions. They also pointed out that the Society was associated with similar unions in other areas of employment including the Royal Dockyards and the railways. The Executive Council emphasised that the new shipbuilding trades committee had been established for consultative purposes and that its functions would be limited. Despite this support from the Executive Council the membership failed to give a decisive majority for the draft. The voting figures were 1,149 in favour of the draft and 1,136 against. The Executive Council decided that this very small majority was unsatisfactory and that the question should again be submitted to a ballot vote. They reaffirmed their support for the draft agreement. It was to no avail. The members voted against the Society being associated with the shipbuilding trades committee by a majority of 359. The voting was 2,087 in favour and 2,246 against.

SHIPBUILDING AGREEMENT REJECTED

In the meantime the Engineering and Shipbuilding Trades Federation had drawn up and concluded a negotiating procedure agreement with the Shipbuilding Employers' Federation. The Federation repeatedly requested the Boilermakers' Society to accept the same agreement or a similar agreement. In February 1927 the Executive Council agreed to recommend to the membership that the Society should sign the agreement. John Hill said that the agreement provided 'opportunities for the application of the spirit of justice and fair play in all questions of difference'. A vital point in the agreement was that if a 'failure to agree' were reached at a central conference between the Federation and the Society, there should be a further stage in the procedure. The disputed issue was to be referred to a general conference consisting of representatives of the Federation and of five other unions who were parties to the agreement.

Despite the support of the Executive Council for the new draft

172

agreement it was rejected on a ballot vote of the membership by 3,257 to 1,439. The Executive Council felt that this vote was unsatisfactory because of the low number of members who had participated in the ballot. In a statement to the membership they pointed out that other trades had already accepted the agreement and previous experience had shown that the isolation of the Boilermakers' Society was 'very far from satisfactory'. The Executive Council also complained about a circular which had been issued by the South Coast District Committee criticising the draft agreement. The Executive Council said that the circular contained statements which were untrue and unfair and had confused the minds of members. They had decided therefore to take a further vote on the draft. The Executive Council also wrote to all branches complaining of interference by the Minority Movement which they described as a 'Communist organisation'. The Minority Movement, with which Harry Pollitt was prominently associated, was urging members to attend branch meetings and to vote against the proposed shipbuilding agreement. On the second ballot the proposed agreement was again rejected, though this time with a rather narrower majority. The voting was 2,660 against the draft agreement and 1,911 in favour.

Two points in the draft agreement swung the vote. The first was the provision for a general conference, including other unions, as a final stage in the negotiating procedure. Some members felt that this put the interests of boilermakers into the hands of representatives of other trade unions. The second was that the draft did not provide for the speedy resolution of piece-work disputes at yard level. Many members felt that it would be to the continued advantage of boilermakers to retain an unwritten procedure in shipyards. Under such an arrangement the membership had more freedom to take strike action on unresolved piece-work disputes.

NEW LEGISLATION

After the General Strike the Conservative Government introduced new legal proposals to curtail trade union rights. These proposals were eventually passed by Parliament and placed on the statute book as the Trade Disputes and Trade Unions Act 1927. The Act said that a strike was illegal if it had any object other than or in addition to the furtherance of a trade dispute within the trade or industry in which the strikers were engaged. It also declared illegal any strike 'designed or calculated to coerce the Government either directly or by inflicting hardship upon the community'. Any person instigating or inciting others to take part in or act in furtherance of a strike declared by the Act to be illegal was liable to imprisonment for up to two years.

Another clause in the Act declared it unlawful for one or more persons to picket 'in such numbers or otherwise in such manner as to be calculated to intimidate' anyone, or to obstruct the entrance to a place of work or to lead to a breach of the peace. This clause widened the area of legal liability for pickets and introduced a concept of 'intimidation' which appeared to eliminate any appeal to objectivity. It depended solely on the state of mind of the complainant.

Other clauses in the Act changed 'contracting-out' to 'contracting-in' for contributions to trade union political funds, prohibited civil servants from belonging to unions with members outside the civil service and prohibited civil service unions from belonging to federations (such as the TUC) which included unions not based on the civil service. The Act also made it unlawful for any local or other public authority to make it a condition of employment that an employee should be a member of a trade union.

The trade union movement conducted a campaign against this proposed legislation when it was being debated, but the Conservative majority was sufficient to ensure its passage through Parliament. In a letter issued to all branches the Executive Council of the Boilermakers' Society said that every trade unionist should be mobilised to fight what it described as this anti-trade union measure. Rights which the unions had exercised for more than 100 years, said the Executive Council, would be suspended. Trade unionists engaged in industrial disputes might unwittingly render themselves liable to fines or to imprisonment for up to two years. The measure, said the Executive Council, had been hailed with satisfaction by employers all over the country.

In July 1927 the General Secretary, John Hill, condemned the Government's proposals in the strongest possible words. He said that though the Bill might become law it would be the most glaring example in British history of the difference between law and justice. John Hill described the Bill as a 'class attack' on the workers. He predicted that it would lead to a 'retaliatory class consciousness' in the minds of workers and the time would come when the Bill would be swept from the statute book. John Hill concluded his attack by quoting from a speech from James Maxton MP about the part played by the Attorney General in steering the Bill through the House of Commons:

> The right hon. gentleman has prostituted his high parliamentary ability; he has prostituted his profound legal knowledge; he has prostituted his high oratorical skill on behalf of a body of rich men, who have never known what it was to lack one single thing of the material things of life; men who have all the advantages of education, men who have had all the advantages of social standing, men who have had all the advantages of wealth, and he has presented to them his skill and denied to common working people the merest, barest existence. Not merely that, he has used his skill to deny them the right to struggle for something better. I say that this is political blackguardism, that this is political treachery, and I say that the right hon. gentleman, the Attorney-General, is a blackguard and a liar.

The Executive Council of the Boilermakers' Society issued a number of statements to the branches on the campaign against the Government's Bill. They urged branches to hold special meetings on the subject but regretfully pointed out that because of the desperate financial position of the Society no expenses of any kind could be charged against funds. Many branches sent resolutions to Members of Parliament and to the Prime Minister. The Executive Council itself wrote to the Prime Minister urging that the measure should be withdrawn. These efforts were unsuccessful. The repeal of the Act had to wait for nearly another twenty years. It was finally repealed in 1946 by the first majority Labour Government.

1927

At the beginning of 1927 John Hill was re-elected as General Secretary of the Society. On the first ballot he received 4,212 votes against a combined vote for two other candidates of 2,266. In his election address John Hill concentrated entirely on the need to preserve the funds of the Society and to observe economy in its administration. He said that during the previous year branch costs had been cut by 10 per cent, district costs by 18½ per cent and head office costs by 39 per cent.

Towards the end of 1926 trade improved and unemployment fell throughout 1927. At the end of 1926 nearly 30,000 members of the Boilermakers' Society were out of work. A year later the figure was just over 11,000. With the revival in trade national wage claims were submitted both to the Engineering Employers' Federation and the Shipbuilding Employers' Federation. The negotiations in engineering finally led to a settlement for a 2s per week increase, restricted to plain time workers. The increase took effect from 1 August 1927. The proposed settlement was rejected by the members of the Boilermakers' Society by 2,900 votes to 2,423 but was accepted by the unions collectively within the Engineering Joint Trades Wages Movement by 82,531 votes to 42,154. The settlement was for a period of six months only. At the end of this period wages were again to be reviewed.

In shipbuilding the negotiations dragged on until the summer of 1928 when the employers agreed to an increase of 3s per week for men employed on plain time work. The increase was paid in two instalments of 1s 6d per week; the first was paid from 1 July 1928 and the second from 1 September 1928. The increase did not apply to ship repair workers on the Thames, Bristol Channel, the Mersey and Manchester, where wages were higher.

The membership continued to decline after the General Strike. Between 1925 and 1926 the membership fell from 74,287 to 68,830. In 1927 there was a further loss of 523 members and in 1928 a further 2,206 members. Membership had fallen every year since 1920. Towards the end of 1927 the Executive Council issued a statement to the membership suggesting that there should be a reduction in the number of full-time district delegates. They recalled that in 1919, when the membership of the Society was more than 100,000 it had been decided, as a result of appeals from branches, to increase the number of district delegates. Six additional delegates had subsequently been authorised and had been elected.

In 1924 the General Council of the Society considered the possibility of reducing the number of district delegates but eventually decided to retain all delegates in the belief that it might be possible to increase the membership. Subsequently a letter was sent to all district delegates stating that while the size of the membership hardly justified the retention of the existing full-time organising staff it was hoped that the membership would increase. Since 1924, however, the membership had continued to decline. The Executive Council reminded the membership that a number of measures had been taken to reduce administrative costs but they had not been sufficient to overcome the serious financial difficulty in which the Society found itself. A number of branches had suggested a reduction in the number of district delegates.

This proposal by the Executive Council was strongly opposed by a number of district committees including Barrow, Tees and Hartlepool, Clyde, East of Scotland, Mersey and Yorkshire. This strong opposition in the districts was reflected in the result of the ballot vote. By 3,940 votes to 2,164 the members voted not to reduce the number of district delegates.

Chapter 12

Exclusion of Minority Movement Supporters

The division of opinion within the trade union movement about the conduct of the General Strike was reflected in the Boilermakers' Society in a wide split between, on the one hand, John Hill and the elected leadership and, on the other, the supporters of the Minority Movement represented, above all others, by Harry Pollitt. This led finally to the exclusion from eligibility to hold office in the Society of all Communists and Minority Movement supporters.

It will be recalled that at its 1924 annual conference the Labour Party had rejected by 3,185,000 votes to 193,000 the application for the affiliation of the Communist Party. It had also been decided by 2,456,000 votes to 654,000 votes that 'no Communist Party member shall be eligible for endorsement as a Labour candidate for Parliament or any local authority', and by 1,804,000 votes to 1,540,000 votes that 'no member of the Communist Party shall be eligible for membership of the Labour Party'. This still left open the eligibility of individual Communists as delegates to the Labour Party conference from affiliated trade unions. This was of particular relevance to the Boilermakers' Society because of the role of Harry Pollitt. Pollitt was regularly elected to the delegation of the Boilermakers' Society to the Labour Party conference and he was also a well-known member of the Communist Party. Indeed Pollitt was second only to Tom Mann as Britain's most widely-known Communist.

THE ROLE OF POLLITT

At the 1925 Labour Party conference the National Executive Committee of the Party made two recommendations. The first was that no member of the Communist Party should be eligible to become a member of any individual section of any affiliated local Labour party, or be entitled to remain a member. The second recommendation from the NEC was 'that in its opinion affiliated trade unions can only act consistently with the decision of the annual conference in its relation to communists by appealing to their members when electing delegates to national or local Labour Party conferences or meetings to refrain from nominating or electing known members of non-affiliated political parties, including communists'. At the 1925 annual conference of the Labour Party Harry Pollitt moved the reference back of the first of these two recommendations of the National Executive Committee. He argued that the Labour Party was a broad organisation open to socialists of different approaches. Communists should not be excluded and the unions had the right to decide for themselves who their delegates should be. The reference back was seconded by Aitken Ferguson, also a member of the Boilermakers' Society, but who represented the Glasgow Trades and Labour Council at the Labour Party conference. One of the main speeches against Pollitt's view was made by Ernest Bevin. He said that the basic standpoint of the Communists could not be reconciled 'with the basis of evolutionary democracy that the Labour Party represented'. The reference back was defeated by 2,870,000 to 321,000.

In 1926 Harry Pollitt was again elected at the top of the poll in the ballot for the delegation of the Boilermakers' Society to the Labour Party conference. At the 1926 conference Pollitt moved the reference back of the section of the report of the National Executive Committee dealing with relations with the Communist Party. The NEC reported that thirteen local Labour parties had been disaffiliated because they had failed to operate the decisions of the previous Labour Party conference regarding members of the Communist Party. Pollitt's right to be a delegate was challenged but the chairman of the conference confirmed that Pollitt was a duly appointed delegate of the Boilermakers' Society. Pollitt pro-

179

ceeded to make his case against the NEC's decision and pointed out that the ILP had always organised within the Labour Party. The disaffiliation of local parties was a step towards the disunity of the workers' movement. The reference back was defeated by 3,414,000 to 209,000.

A report of the 1926 Labour Party conference did not appear in the Boilermakers' Journal. Pollitt did not accept the draft prepared by the General Secretary, John Hill, and the General Secretary in turn did not accept a draft prepared by Harry Pollitt. This was an indication of the gulf that had opened between them and their respective points of view.

The notice calling for nominations for representatives to attend the annual conference of the Labour Party in 1927 drew attention to the decision of the Labour Party advising affiliated trade unions not to nominate or elect known members of other political parties including Communists. The Executive Council of the Boilermakers' Society asked branch officials to pay strict attention to the instructions received from the Labour Party. They would thus, they said, 'avoid difficulties which might otherwise arise after nominations have been made'. Despite this appeal from the Executive Council Harry Pollitt was again elected at the top of the poll for the Labour Party conference delegation. Aitken Ferguson, another Communist, came third in the poll and was only narrowly defeated for the Society's two rank and file representatives.

Pollitt was also elected as one of the Society's delegates to the 1927 TUC. He drafted a report on the Congress but it was rejected by his fellow delegates John Hill and John Porter. John Hill's draft was in turn rejected by Pollitt but was, nevertheless, published in the Society's journal over the signatures of Hill and Porter. The report contained a strong attack on the views of Harry Pollitt. It said that members may have gained the impression that the only questions of importance discussed at the Congress were the relations between the TUC and the Russian trade unions and the relations between the TUC and the Minority Movement. Unfortunately, said John Hill and John Porter, these questions had been forced unduly on the attention of Congress and the immediate issues of wages and conditions of workers in Britain received less than their proper share of time and attention. The report then turned to the relationship between the TUC and the Russian

unions. It said that the Russians had not refrained from inter-
fering in British trade union affairs and had never ceased to say
publicly that the British unions were making a 'mess of their own
business'.

On the relations between the TUC and the Minority Movement
the report of John Hill and John Porter referred specifically to the
role of Harry Pollitt. The Minority Movement, they said, had been
established by the Red International of Labour Unions but it was
difficult to say how it was financed because no balance sheets were
published. Its energies, they alleged, were largely devoted to attacking British trade union leaders, and they referred to a manifesto of
the Minority Movement which, they claimed, said that the
General Council of the TUC was in some way associated with the
capitalists in preparing for war on Russia. Hill and Porter said
that 'this is a wicked accusation'.

In the report from Hill and Porter there were then the following
three paragraphs:

At the Congress the fullest opportunity was given to the representatives of the Minority Movement to attack the decision of
the General Council and defend their own attitude, but by
large majorities on each division on the question, the work of the
General Council, and their decisions were endorsed.

Through all the debates on Russia and the Minority Movement, our position as a Society was a subject of considerable
comment, for although Brother Porter and the General Secretary
are in no way associated with the Minority Movement, or the
Communist Party, neither of them could say that Brother Pollitt
did not represent our members, as the members, well knowing
Brother Pollitt to be a communist, and also secretary and principal organiser of the Minority Movement, year after year elect
him, by large majorities as their representative.

We have made this reference to the Minority Movement as it
is our duty here to give the members a report, so that they will
fully realise all that is involved in sending communists to
represent them.

In the final paragraph of their report John Hill and John Porter
said that Pollitt had spoken more frequently than any other dele-

gate to Congress and though he had spoken well his speeches 'were chiefly as a representative of the Minority Movement and in favour of the Russian point of view as against our own'. John Hill and John Porter said that this had created division amongst the boilermakers' representatives which considerably nullified the usefulness of the Society's votes at the Congress.

Pollitt replied to this attack on his point of view but it was not published. He circulated his reply privately by post. It was sent to every branch of the Society. In it he pointed out that his Communist views had always been known to those who voted for him since he was first elected in 1921 as a boilermakers' representative to the GFTU, the TUC and the Labour Party. He criticised what he described as the betrayal of the General Strike, the break with the Soviet trade union movement and the agreement of TUC leaders to industrial peace proposals. He asked whether boilermakers wanted him to support policies that received praise from enemies of the working class. As he saw it, his duty as a delegate was to make a contribution to debates at the Labour Party and the TUC not from the point of view of a particular section but from the standpoint of the working class movement as a whole.

In his letter Pollitt said that every time he had been nominated for any full-time official position in the Society he had been disqualied on some pretext or other. To the amazement of the Executive Council the members of the Society had continued to vote for him whenever they had a chance to do so. '. . . they have found that for six years boilermakers prefer an honest fighter (even though they may not agree with all his opinions) to a deaf-and-dumb delegate who goes to national conferences for a holiday at a good rate of pay.' Pollitt said that in 1926 he sent many articles to the Boilermakers' journal but every one of them had been rejected. Other members who supported his views had also had their contributions rejected.

EXCLUSION

Early in 1928 the Executive Council of the Society decided 'that no known Communist can be eligible for nomination as a representative to the Labour Party or to the Trades Union Congress'. By

placing a ban on Communists being nominated for the TUC delegation the Executive Council were going further than the decisions
of the Labour Party conference in relation to Communists. The
Executive Council justified their ban by stating that from time to
time they received letters from branches protesting against Communists representing the Boilermakers' Society at the Labour Party
and the TUC. The Communist Party, said the Executive Council,
was opposed to the industrial methods of the Boilermakers' Society
and it was opposed to constitutional parliamentary methods. 'The
policy of communists is to change the whole industrial and social
system by violent revolution. The Party takes its policy and its
orders from a committee of dictators in Russia who also finance
the propaganda of communists in this country.'

The Executive Council said that they could not deny members
of the Society their right to their political opinions, but members
who were Communists were also members of an organisation
whose purpose was to destroy the organisation of the Boilermakers'
Society and trade unionism generally and also to destroy and nullify
the Society's political efforts.

This decision was directed first and foremost against Harry Pollitt
and the views he represented. Harry Pollitt had been consistently
elected to delegations from the Boilermakers' Society to the Labour
Party and the TUC – usually at the top of the poll – and there
appeared to be no way in which his opponents within the Society
could secure his defeat by electoral means. They therefore resorted
to denying him and other members of the Communist Party the
right to stand for election to the delegations of the Society.

On 26 May 1928 Aitken Ferguson, a member of one of the
Glasgow branches, lodged an appeal against the decision of the
Executive Council. He appealed on the grounds that the decision
was 'unjustifiable, anti-working class, and contrary to the customs,
rules and usages of our Society'.

The Executive Council issued a long statement replying to Aitken
Ferguson's appeal and calling for its rejection by the members. The
Executive Council pointed out that Aitken Ferguson was a leader
of both the Communist Party and the Minority Movement in
Glasgow and they said that the Communists had seriously weakened
the labour movement in that city. The Executive Council claimed
that the Minority Movement was endeavouring to undermine the

183

constitution of the Boilermakers' Society. They quoted from a manifesto of the Minority Movement which said that for the first time in the history of the TUC an organised opposition had arisen which 'raises unreservedly the banner of revolutionary working-class politics in British trade unionism'. The Executive Council also alleged that members of various unions, including members of the Boilermakers' Society, had been invited to Moscow and a number of them – again including boilermakers – had been appointed full-time paid agents of the Soviet Communist Party with secret orders to discredit trade union officers. The Executive Council also said that the Communist Party was opposed to the objects of the Boilermakers' Society industrially and sought to improve wages and conditions not by negotiation but by armed revolution.

In a later statement published to the membership, the Executive Council said that the whole of the forces of Communism had been rallied to support Aitken Ferguson's appeal. Communist publications urging members to vote in favour of the appeal were being sold at branch meetings. This, said the Executive Council, was in direct violation of the rules of the Society. The Executive Council published their lengthy statement calling for the rejection of Aitken Ferguson's appeal in two successive issues of the monthly journal.

The wording on the ballot paper was not restricted to a simple 'yes' or 'no' to Aitken Ferguson's appeal as was customary in ballots on individual appeals. It was:

For Brother A. Ferguson's appeal and communist representation.
Against Brother A. Ferguson's appeal and communist representation.

Those who supported Aitken Ferguson's appeal argued that the issue before the membership was not that of communism or communist representation but 'whether members of the Society who are in full benefit and fulfil every trade union qualification in accordance with the rules are to be discriminated against and penalised because of their political opinions'.

Aitken Ferguson's appeal was rejected by 5,011 votes to 1,520. The Executive Council declared that members by their votes had made a decision of fundamental importance. The Communist attempt to create chaos in the Society, said the Executive Council, was the most serious and the most subtle with which they had had to deal. They interpreted the vote as meaning that in future no Communist would be eligible to apply for any office in the Society. Very shortly afterwards four Communists, including Aitken Ferguson and Harry Pollitt, were disqualified from being nominated for the TUC delegation.

Almost immediately following the rejection of Aitken Ferguson's appeal Harry Pollitt was also disqualified from standing for election to the Executive Council of the Society. He was nominated by the London number 11 and by Southampton number 2 branches but, in the words of the official notice, he was disqualified because he was a known Communist. In 1928 the ban on Communists standing for election was extended to members 'connected with the Minority Movement'. Letters were sent to all branches nominating candidates for the TUC and Labour Party conference delegations inquiring whether their nominees were 'known Communists or connected with the Minority Movement'. The list of nominees was published in the monthly journal 'on the understanding that each candidate is not identified with the movements mentioned'.

In his autobiography *Serving My Time** Harry Pollitt recalled that following this ruling of the Executive Council he took 'the best legal advice in the country' and was informed that if he cared to challenge it in a court of law 'there was no doubt that the Executive Council would lose the case'. Pollitt was tempted to go to law but acknowledged that he was reluctant to take his case into a 'capitalist court'. In his autobiography he stated, 'I see now that I was mistaken'. He felt that he should have gone to law to defeat what he described as the 'unscrupulous tactics' of the Executive Council. Their chief concern, he alleged, was not so much to prevent him going to the Labour Party conference as to prevent him from standing for election to the Executive Council.

OTHER POLITICAL ISSUES

Despite the bitterness of the internal controversy regarding the role of Communists in the Boilermakers' Society, the Executive Council continued to press for expanded trade with Russia. In July

* Lawrence and Wishart, 1940.

1926 John Hill reported that Russia was willing to place orders for the building of ships in British shipyards but that Mr Winston Churchill was campaigning against trade with Russia. The indications were, said John Hill, that Churchill was preparing for another war with Russia. The capitalists were afraid that a workers' government in Russia might be a success and would thus encourage the bringing to power of a workers' government in Britain.

A year later when the British Government broke off trade relations with Russia the Society protested vigorously. It pointed out that the orders for machinery which Russia was placing with Britain, including orders for electrical equipment, textile machinery, railway material and machine tools, would now go to Germany. The four Members of Parliament of the Boilermakers' Society asked in their parliamentary report in the monthly journal: 'Having in mind our large army of unemployed and the precarious condition of our trade . . . what benefit shall be derived from this rupture?' Anglo–Soviet trade, said the MPs, provided employment and employment meant wages.

Another international issue to which the Boilermakers' Society gave attention during the period was the plight of trade unionists under fascist rule in Mussolini's Italy. An appeal published by the Society reported that active trade unionists had been deported from the Italian mainland to an inhospitable island off the Italian coast. On this island the trade unionists had been subject to humiliation, privation and moral torture. The appeal ended with a call for international solidarity.

Chapter 13

The Mond-Turner Discussions

In the period following the General Strike there was much comment from politicians and newspapers in favour of industrial peace and the elimination of conflict in industry. According to the main exponents of this view the change was to take place not on the basis of a fundamental transformation in the social system and economic order but through discussion and harmony between employers and unions. It was a point of view favoured by the Prime Minister, Mr Stanley Baldwin, though it was hardly consistent with the steps taken by the then Conservative Government to place legislation on the statute book which the unions regarded as harmful to the interests of the trade union movement and of working people. Nor was it consistent with the continuing victimisation of many trade unionists who had played an active role in the General Strike. Nor, indeed, was it consistent with a continuing high level of unemployment.

TUC INITIATIVE

At the 1927 Edinburgh TUC the President, Mr George Hicks of the Building Trade Workers, responded to these suggestions for industrial peace by pointing out that practically nothing had yet been done, beyond collective bargaining on wages and conditions, to establish effective machinery of joint consultation between representative organisations entitled to speak for industry. He argued that a direct exchange of practical views between organised employers and organised labour would be of far greater significance than suggestions which had been made in some newspapers for a spectacular national conference where government and others could discuss a vague aspiration towards 'industrial peace'. Mr Hicks felt that it was important that the trade union movement should frame a coherent policy on practical lines and should not be debarred from entering into discussions with organised employers by allegations that some essential principles of trade unionism were being surrendered.

Shortly after the 1927 Congress of the TUC the National Confederation of Employers' Organisations issued a statement which was generally regarded as a reply to the address given by the President of the TUC. The employers said that discussion of the problems of industry could best be carried out in individual industries through existing joint machinery. Some few weeks later, however, a number of prominent industrialists, led by Sir Alfred Mond (later Lord Melchett), invited the General Council to a conference to discuss questions relating to the entire field of industrial reorganisation and industrial relations.

The letter from Sir Alfred Mond and his colleagues said:

As there appears to us, after investigation, to be no single existing organisation of employers which can take the initiative in inviting discussions to cover the entire field of industrial reorganisation and industrial relations, we desire, as a representative group of employers, to extend to the General Council of the Trades Union Congress an invitation to meet us to consider questions relating to these matters.

The letter went on to say that industrial prosperity could be fully attained only by a full and frank determination to increase the competitiveness of British industry in world markets. Among the supporters of this initiative were a number of prominent employers, including, for example, Sir Herbert Austin of the motor car industry, Sir Arthur Dorman and Sir Robert Hadfield of the steel industry, Lord Londonderry of the coal-mining industry, Sir Josiah Stamp of the railways, Lord Ashfield of the transport industry and Mr S. Courtauld of the synthetic fibre and textile industry.

The General Council decide to accept the invitation received from Sir Alfred Mond and his colleagues though it was recognised that the employers represented only themselves as industrialists and were not official representatives of employers' organisations. The TUC General Council agreed to enter into discussions 'without prejudice' on the understanding that the discussions would not trespass on the function of existing machinery between trade unions and employers. A preliminary conference was held with Sir Alfred Mond and his colleagues to explore the possible scope of further talks. Towards the end of January 1928 a special session of the General Council decided by a large majority to continue the discussions.

INTERIM REPORT

An interim joint report of the Mond-Turner discussions (they were called Mond–Turner after Sir Alfred Mond and Sir Ben Turner, who by now was the TUC Chairman) was adopted in July 1928. Ten joint meetings had been held and agreement had been reached on statements on trade union recognition, victimisation, the gold reserve and its relations with industry, new conciliation machinery in industrial relations, and industrial rationalisation.

The statement on trade union recognition said that it was in the interests of all concerned in industry that full recognition should be given to bona fide trade unions for the discussion and negotiation of all questions of working conditions, including wages, hours and other matters of common interest in the trade or industry concerned. The statement concluded by asserting that negotiations between employers and workers were facilitated by workers being members of a trade union and by employers being members of an employers' organisation.

The statement on victimisation said that one of the causes of friction and unrest was 'what is generally described as victimisation as applied either to workers or employers'. It went on to say that it was 'most undesirable that any workman should be dismissed or otherwise penalised on account of his membership of a union, on account of his official position in a union or on account of any legitimate trade union activities . . .' The statement said that, without expressing any view upon the events of the 1926 General Strike, it deprecated the penalisation of any worker for any part played in those events. It expressed the hope that the pre-1926 position would

189

be restored. It also urged that appeal machinery should be provided for the investigation and review of any alleged penalisation of a worker because of his trade union membership or activity.

The statement on industrial conciliation called for the formation of a National Industrial Council including representatives of the TUC and of the employers' organisations. The three main functions of the Council were to be consultation on industrial progress, the appointment of joint conciliation boards for the prevention of industrial disputes and the establishment of machinery for continuous investigation into industrial problems. A scheme for conciliation was outlined in the statement.

The statement on rationalisation welcomed the tendency for individual units within industry to be grouped into larger units 'in so far as it leads to improvements in the efficiency of industrial production . . . and to the raising of the standard of living'. The statement endorsed resolutions on industrial rationalisation adopted by the 1927 World Economic Conference held in Geneva. Rationalisation was defined as 'the methods of technique and of organisation designed to secure the minimum waste of either effort or material. It includes the scientific organisation of labour, standardisation both of material and of products, simplification of processes and improvements in the system of transport and marketing'. The statement recognised that certain measures of rationalisation might tend to displace labour or to modify in undesirable ways the conditions of work. Safeguards were therefore necessary to ensure that the interests of workers did not suffer by the adoption of such measures.

THE BOILERMAKERS' RESPONSE

When the proposal for discussions with the TUC was first put forward between Sir Alfred Mond and his colleagues it was given a warm welcome by John Hill in the journal of the Boilermakers' Society. He said that he would gladly consider with employers such questions as the organisation of industry, the security and status of workers and compulsory investigation into potential disputes. He not only preferred negotiations to other methods of resolving disputes but would ask for compulsory arbitration when negotiations failed. He referred to the criticisms which were being directed towards the proposed discussions and acknowledged that trade unionists had reason to be critical and even suspicious. They had been let down previously. He felt, however, that on this occasion there was no justifiable reason for the adverse criticism.

In the summer of 1928 John Hill answered the criticism that the trade union leaders should not have joined in the discussions with Sir Alfred Mond and his colleagues. He said that the capitalist press hailed the discussions as the road to the millenium whereas the Communist press had condemned them as the road to hell. James Maxton, the ILP leader, had joined A. J. Cook, the General Secretary of the Miners' Federation, in a campaign against the Mond–Turner discussions. By what authority, asked John Hill, did the Communist Party, A. J. Cook and James Maxton tell the trade union leaders not to meet the employers? Every day trade union members called upon their leaders to meet employers on wages, hours and many other issues of concern to them at work. John Hill said that he wanted to put the membership on guard against the growing misrepresentation of capitalists who wanted a 'peace of subjection' and the misrepresentation of Communists whose first object was to create revolution.

In August, immediately before the 1928 Congress of the TUC, John Hill again returned to the subject of the Mond–Turner discussions. He drew particular attention to the statements which had been issued on trade union recognition and provisions for the prevention of industrial disputes. He pointed out that the participants in the Mond–Turner discussions had agreed that the TUC was the body possessing the necessary authority to negotiate on general policy questions on behalf of workers. He also emphasised that the statement issued by the Mond–Turner conference called for the full recognition of unions affiliated to Congress.

In another statement John Hill confirmed that as a member of the General Council of the TUC he had voted for the acceptance of Sir Alfred Mond's invitation to joint discussions. Moreover, he favoured continuing the Mond–Turner discussions.

GENERAL COUNCIL POLICY

The report of the General Council to the 1928 Congress on the Mond–Turner discussions drew attention to the existence of severe unemployment, the decline in the standard of living of certain sections of the working class and the gravity of the economic situation in coal, iron and steel production, shipbuilding, engineering, cotton textiles and other industries. The General Council was convinced that if it had failed to explore any and every means by which improvement could be secured it would be unworthy to hold office.

The General Council argued that there were three possible lines of policy open to the trade union movement. The first was to say that the unions would do everything possible to bring the industrial machine to a standstill in the hope of creating a revolutionary situation. The second course was to stand aside and to tell employers to get on with their job but without trade union participation or influence. The third course was for the trade union movement to say boldly that not only was it concerned with the prosperity of industry but that it was going to have a voice as to the way industry was conducted. In this way it could influence developments. The General Council said that the trade union movement had decisively rejected as futile the first course. The objection to the second course was that it was entirely inconsistent with the modern demand for a completely altered status for the workers in industry. The third course was the one that the trade union movement should follow.

The General Council recounted the history of the discussions with Sir Alfred Mond and his colleagues. They reported that the constitutional right of the General Council of the TUC to enter into such discussions had been challenged by the Amalgamated Engineering Union. The General Council had rejected the challenge of the AEU and had pointed out that the General Council had discretion to act on behalf of Congress on all general issues where the interests of the organised working class movement were concerned. They also revealed that within the General Council a move had been made to discontinue the discussions with Sir Alfred Mond and his colleagues. This move had been defeated.

The report of the General Council outlined the discussions which

192

had taken place with the employers and concluded by giving the full text of the statements on trade union recognition, victimisation, the proposed national industrial council, the prevention of industrial disputes, rationalisation and the gold reserve.

Support for the General Council's policy was urged in a speech by the General Secretary of the TUC, Walter Citrine. He pointed out that there was no single employers' organisation in Britain which was able to deal with the range of questions involved both in industrial relations and industrial organisation. Sir Alfred Mond and his colleagues were willing to discuss these questions with the trade union movement. World trade unionism, said Citrine, stood for the voice of the worker in the administration and control of industry. To talk about exercising control without meeting the employers to discuss that control was a figment of the imagination. Trade unionists could not await the breakdown of capitalism before they began to exercise control. Citrine was supported in speeches by, amongst others, J. R. Clynes of the General and Municipal Workers, Ernest Bevin of the Transport and General Workers' Union and J. H. Thomas of the railwaymen.

Opposition to the General Council was voiced both on constitutional and on policy grounds. Delegates from the AEU argued that constitutionally the General Council had no power to commit affiliated unions in the kind of discussions which they had been having with Sir Alfred Mond and his colleagues. The main case against the Mond–Turner discussions was, however, made by Mr A. J. Cook, the General Secretary of the Miners' Federation. He challenged the statement of the General Council where they had described three possible lines of policy open to the trade union movement. He said that no intelligent trade unionist had ever suggested that the unions should do everything possible to bring the industrial machine to a standstill as a means of bringing about the downfall of capitalism. Nor had responsible trade unionists ever argued that the unions should stand aside and not seek to influence the conduct of industry. The trade union movement was engaged in a struggle with the employing class. That conflict had not been eliminated. The development of new techniques in industry had led to greater concentration of power in fewer hands. A. J. Cook did not believe that there was any possibility that the Mond–Turner discussions would give real control to the working class. He pointed out that some of the employers involved in the discussions were men who had strongly opposed trade union claims and objectives. He appealed to the delegates not to have 'alliances with the enemy'.

In the debate A. J. Cook was followed immediately by Herbert Smith, the President of the Miners' Federation, who revealed that the miners' delegation had decided to support the General Council. At the end of the debate the General Council's report on the Mond–Turner discussions was adopted by 3,075,000 votes to 566,000. The delegation of the Boilermakers' Society voted with the majority. They did, however, vote with the minority on a proposal from the AEU that the whole matter of the Mond–Turner discussions should be referred to affiliated unions for consideration. This was defeated by 2,921,000 votes to 768,000.

In its published report on the Congress debate on the Mond–Turner discussions the Boilermakers' delegation said:

> By this vote we settled the question of the 'class war' between employers and employees. For the 'class war' we have now substituted co-operation. The success of this new principle will depend on each side placing all their cards on the table. For this purpose we shall require statutory authority to investigate all the facts relative to a claim from either side before the dispute takes place.

This was an example of the kind of illusion which could be created by the Mond–Turner discussions and against which the critics had warned.

THE MINORITY MOVEMENT

The acute nature of the controversy in the trade union movement about the conduct of the General Strike and the subsequent Mond–Turner discussions found reflection not only in the Boilermakers' Society but also within the wider trade union movement. At the 1928 Congress a resolution was carried which instructed the General Council to inquire into 'the proceedings and methods of disruptive elements within the trade union movement . . . and to submit a

194

report, with recommendations, to the affiliated organisations'. This resolution expressed the concern, and indeed hostility, of most trade union leaders towards the activity of the Minority Movement, of which the secretary was Harry Pollitt. Pollitt retained this position until August 1929 when he became the General Secretary of the Communist Party. He was followed as secretary of the Minority Movement by Arthur Horner who, years later, was to become the General Secretary of the National Union of Mineworkers.

Only days before the opening of the 1928 TUC the Minority Movement had held its fifth annual conference at Shoreditch Town Hall, London. The Minority Movement was an unofficial organisation but its conference was attended by nearly 850 delegates, including eight members of the Boilermakers' Society. The national committee of the Minority Movement presented a report which said that the most significant change in the trade union movement during the previous year was 'the definite attempt and failure of the reactionary trade union bureaucracy to smash the workers now organised under the banner and leadership of the National Minority Movement'. The report said that year after year promises of a trade revival had been made by bankers, businessmen and reformist trade union leaders. Yet the decline of capitalism in Britain continued. The report attacked what it described as the policy of class collaboration represented by the Mond–Turner conferences. It emphasised the importance of local trades councils and called for their affiliation to the Minority Movement.

The report also attacked capitalist industrial rationalisation which it said had led to a rapid increase in unemployment. It called for the fullest support to be given to the National Unemployed Workers' Movement which, it claimed, the General Council of the TUC had tried to smash. The report deplored the attacks on the Minority Movement by union leaders and referred to the General Council and trade union executives as 'the agents of the capitalist class in the trade union movement'.

Various sectional conference reports, drawn up by delegates from different sections of industry, were also presented to the full conference. One such report was from boilermakers associated with the Minority Movement.

It made a number of proposals and called for 'a strong militant group inside the Society to press the policy of the Minority Movement as an alternative to the present reactionary policy of the Executive Committee'. It urged members to write to the journal and to extend its circulation. It urged also that there should be a rank-and-file conference of the Boilermakers' Society and that consideration should be given to the replacement of a full-time by a part-time Executive Council. The list of proposals also urged that the head office of the Society should be moved to London, that all members should enjoy equal rights within the union and that there should be 'one union for the industry'.

When the General Council of the TUC presented the report of its inquiry into disruption to the 1929 TUC it said that the investigation into the activities of the Communist International, the Red International of Labour Unions, the Communist Party and the National Minority Movement had left no doubt 'that these organisations deliberately exercised a disruptive influence inside the trade union movement'. They pointed out that the initiative in setting up the National Minority Movement was taken by the British Bureau of the RILU. The Minority Movement was sponsored by the Communist Party. The report said that the National Unemployed Workers' Movement had also been sponsored by the Communists. The leader of this movement was a Communist, Mr Walter Hannington (many years later to become a full-time official of the Amalgamated Engineering Union). The NUWM, the General Council pointed out, was promoting hunger marches which, according to one NUWM spokesman, were directed 'against the solid front of reformist sabotage'.

Another part of the report prepared by the General Council summarised evidence submitted by affiliated unions. A number of unions complained that the policy of the Minority Movement was to discredit executives and officials of trade unions. Disruption also took the form of intervention in disputes and in union negotiations. Unofficial strikes had been promoted.

The report of the General Council concluded by saying that the Minority Movement appeared to have done 'most serious harm in the affairs of those unions who have not thought it advisable in the early stages to check communist activity in their branches and districts'. The reference back of the General Council's report was moved but was defeated.

The period during which Pollitt served as the General Secretary of the Minority Movement, 1924–9, was one which left its mark on British trade unionism both positively and negatively. On the one hand, the Minority Movement sought to stimulate workers to fight back against the offensive of employers once the post-war boom had ended. It sought to extend consciousness that unemployment was caused by capitalism and that trade unionism had to be linked to political action for changing the social system. It called for strengthening the powers of the General Council of the TUC so that it could give leadership as a 'general staff' of labour. It supported industrial unionism and encouraged trade union amalgamation for this purpose. It emphasised the very important role of trades councils and campaigned for international solidarity.

On the other hand, it often acted as though it were an alternative trade union centre to the TUC. Its criticisms of the elected leaders and executives of unions were frequently made in extravagant language. Its various sections brought out their own publications, and those who were influenced by the Minority Movement were sometimes called upon to support and to act upon policies which were different from or even in opposition to the official policies of their unions. Inevitably they were accused of disruption.

Pollitt's own summary of the role of the Minority Movement was:

> On looking back, it seems to me now that one of the chief weaknesses of the M. M., as it was popularly called, was that it tended to create the impression that it was a separate and rival body to the trade unions and to the Trades Union Congress, although this was never its true aim. But in preparing the material for this book, I have had to go over all the documents and publications of the Minority Movement, and I can state without the slightest hesitation that, despite mistakes and weaknesses, it did a great deal of good work inside the trade unions.

Pollitt's verdict was probably more generous than the Minority Movement deserved. The existence of one trade union national centre has always been of great value to British trade unionism. Given the need to maintain this unity there could be no acceptable basis for the permanent existence of a national centre providing an alternative leadership. This was a formula for disruption. This is not to say that the Minority Movement was wrong in everything that it said. Many of its criticisms were justified, but others were not. Nearly always its criticisms were levelled in terms which were designed to evoke maximum hostility from trade union executive committees and officials. Its policies were seen as a reflection of the interests of the Soviet Government and the 'line' of the Communist International. The Minority Movement had to be brought to an end. It came nowhere near winning majority support among even active trade unionists and, indeed, it served in many ways as an example of the folly of sectarianism.

FURTHER DISCUSSIONS

The Mond–Turner discussions continued through 1929. A joint report on unemployment was adopted which urged that industrial rationalisation should be pressed forward as rapidly as possible and that the unions should be consulted, particularly in dealing with labour displacement. It was suggested that where possible displaced workers should be assisted from a labour reserve fund to be set up out of profits. The recommendations called for the encouragement of emigration and the augmentation of pensions for workers aged 65 and over, who ceased work. The report asked that consideration should be given to raising the school leaving age.

At the beginning of 1929 the National Confederation of Employers' Organisations and the Federation of British Industries responded to the Mond–Turner suggestion that a National Industrial Council should be established. The two employers' organisations invited the TUC to meet them with a view to exploring the suggestion. The TUC responded to this invitation and a joint conference took place in April 1929. Eventually, towards the end of 1929, a scheme of consultation and co-operation was agreed between the TUC and the two employers' organisations. The scheme envisaged that the three organisations would be able to discuss a wide range of subjects of mutual interest to employers and workpeople including unemployment, taxation, international trade and labour questions.

At the 1929 TUC a further effort was made to bring the Mond–Turner discussions to an end. The National Amalgamated Furnishing Trades Association moved a motion declaring opposition 'to the false cry of industrial peace and to the policy of collaboration with the enemies of labour, who are vigorously and ruthlessly attacking the standard of living of the working class at the very time they are conferring with the General Council . . .' The motion was seconded by the Amalgamated Engineering Union and supported in the debate by the Associated Society of Locomotive Engineers and Firemen. It was opposed by the two general workers' unions and by the General Council. The resolution was defeated.

In their published report on the 1929 Congress the delegation of the Boilermakers' Society said that there was a feeling among the delegates that after two years of the Mond–Turner discussions 'it was about time that the employers were putting their joint decisions with us into practice in the industries which they represented'. The delegation said that a pledge was given by the General Council to press this question on the employers concerned as a test of their sincerity to carry out their pledges.

INDUSTRIAL REALITIES

In the hard reality of industrial relations at the level of the workplace the Mond–Turner discussions found little reflection. Attacks were still being made on workers' conditions, there were many cases of victimisation, every improvement had to be fought for and unemployment still stalked the scene. There was no indication that the rank-and-file membership felt there had been any change.

In 1929, for example, further efforts were made by the Executive Council of the Boilermakers' Society to persuade the membership to endorse a draft negotiating procedure agreement for the shipbuilding industry. In a statement published in February 1929 the Executive Council said that they had pointed out to the Shipbuilding Employers' Federation the unsatisfactory nature of the procedure in the existing agreement with other trade unions for dealing with piece-work questions and that the employers had been finally persuaded to introduce two supplementary clauses to meet the grievances of boilermakers. The first clause provided for arbitration at the request of either party where there had been a failure to agree on a piece-work issue at a local conference. The issue had to be of such a nature that it affected only the yard or dock where it had arisen, or concerned the interpretation of a district price list. The other new clause stated that when the parties failed to settle a local piece-work issue, arrangements should be made, where-ever possible 'for a temporary price to be paid pending settlement of the question'.

Despite the support given by the Executive Council to these additional clauses the members refused to endorse the draft agreement. It was rejected by 2,272 votes to 2,209. The Executive Council described this as a most unsatisfactory result because of the narrowness of the vote and decided to re-submit it to the membership. On the second vote the majority against the proposed agreement rose to 346. The vote was 2,906 against the agreement and 2,560 for it.

Some few months later in August 1929 the Shipbuilding Employers' Federation wrote to the Boilermakers' Society to express concern at the repeated rejection by the membership of the proposed negotiating procedure agreement. They recalled that as long ago as 1918, at the time of the introduction of the forty-seven-hour week, the Boilermakers' Society, together with other unions, had undertaken to enter into a new procedure agreement. After a very long delay an agreement had been reached with the Federation of Engineering and Shipbuilding Trades towards the end of 1926. The remaining craft unions not affiliated to the FEST, with the exception of the Boilermakers' Society, had signed similar agreements in June 1927. The Executive Council of the Boiler-makers' Society had commended this agreement to the membership but on two occasions in 1927 it had been rejected.

The Shipbuilding Employers' Federation further recalled that at the request of the Executive Council of the Society they had agreed to two supplementary clauses in an attempt to meet the criticism of the draft which had been voiced by piece-workers in the Society. Two further ballot votes had then been taken and again on both occasions the draft had been rejected. The Shipbuilding Employers' Federation said that they could not accept the position as being in any way satisfactory. They gave notice therefore that the procedure agreement, together with the supplementary clauses, would be regarded by the Federation as applying to members from 1 November 1929.

This threat from the employers served only to increase the strength of opposition among the membership. On a further ballot the size of the majority against the draft agreement increased very substantially. The number of votes against the draft agreement was 3,604. The number in favour was 1,483.

Towards the end of 1929 the Boilermakers' Society asked the Shipbuilding Employers' Federation to join with them in ensuring that overtime was strictly limited. Complaints had been received from most districts that overtime was being worked and that the overtime agreement with the Shipbuilding Employers' Federation was being used not as a means of limiting overtime but as a means of compelling members to work overtime. Many of the complaints were in respect of repair work, but there were also a number which spoke of excessive overtime on new work. The Executive Council of the Society asked the Federation to amend the agreement to provide for stricter control.

At the conference to discuss this request from the Society the Federation was reminded that the first words in the overtime agreement were 'The parties are agreed that systematic overtime is to be deprecated as a method of production'. Nevertheless, argued the Society's representatives, overtime was both systematic and excessive. The employers did not agree to the suggested amendment but assured the Society that they were anxious to avoid overtime. They said that the statement in the existing agreement deprecating systematic overtime would be observed both in letter and spirit. Following the conference the Executive Council asked all district delegates, stewards and members to pay strict attention to the need to control overtime.

In 1928 the railway companies sought to reduce the wages of all railway workers. Negotiations were conducted with the three railway unions, the National Union of Railwaymen, the Amalgamated Society of Locomotive Engineers and Firemen and the Railway Clerks' Association and agreement was reached for a 2½ per cent reduction in pay.

The Boilermakers' Society protested strongly about this agreement. They said that the railway companies and the three railway unions had no authority to reach agreement about the wages of railway shopmen without the participation of the Boilermakers' Society. There was no doubt that the Society were constitutionally right in their protest. This was acknowledged both by the companies and by the railway unions.

Eventually it was agreed that a negotiating committee representing all railway shopmen would meet the companies on 10 August 1928. A small concession was secured in these discussions relating to the pay of shopmen employed on the Great Central and Cheshire lines. It was pointed out that pay reductions had already taken place on these two lines. All other unions agreed to accept the new arrangements for a 2½ per cent pay reduction and finally the Boilermakers' Society decided reluctantly to fall into line. It was accepted that the agreement could be terminated at the end of twelve months.

In engineering the negotiations on a national claim submitted by the unions proved abortive. The negotiations extended over many months but the employers adhered to their stand that the industry could not afford to pay higher wages.

The membership of the Society continued to decline. In 1929 the Society's overdraft at the bank was nearly £150,000. The General Council of the Society were convened to consider proposals to restore the finances of the Society. Various propositions were made and were accepted by the membership but in August 1929 the Executive Council sent a letter to all branches stating that the proposals approved by the membership were insufficient. The Executive Council therefore took into their own hands the decision to reduce benefits. The main effect was to reduce both sickness and superannuation benefits. From 1 October 1929 no member was entitled to apply for superannuation benefit unless he had been a member for at least forty years. This proved to be only the first stage in a scaling down of benefits necessitated by the worsening economic situation and growing unemployment among the membership.

Chapter 14

The Second Labour Government and the Depression

At the General Election held in May 1929 there were six members of the Boilermakers' Society who stood as Labour candidates. Four of them, A. Short at Wednesbury, M. H. Connolly at Newcastle East, T. Irwin at Montrose and W. H. Egan at Birkenhead West, stood as members of the Society's parliamentary panel. J. Gibbins at West Toxteth, Liverpool and David Williams at Swansea East stood independently but the Society gave them some limited financial support.

Four of the candidates won seats. They were A. Short, W. H. Egan, J. Gibbins and D. Williams. The victory of W. H. Egan at Birkenhead West represented a Labour gain. The defeat of M. H. Connolly at Newcastle East represented a Labour loss. The results were as follows:

Birkenhead, West

W. H. Egan (Lab)	15,634
E. Nuttall (C)	13,410
R. P. Fletcher (L)	4,946
Labour majority	2,224

Liverpool, West Toxteth

J. Gibbins (Lab)	19,988
G. Watson (C)	16,309
Labour majority	3,679

Montrose Burghs

Sir R. Hutchison (L)	11,715
T. Irwin (Lab)	9,381
Liberal majority	2,334

Newcastle-on-Tyne, East

Sir R. Aske (L)	17,856
M. H. Connolly (Lab)	16,921
Liberal majority	935

Swansea, East

D. Williams (Lab)	16,665
A. Hopkins (L)	9,825
P. Jones (C)	3,003
Labour majority	6,840

Wednesbury

A. Short (Lab)	22,420
H. Rubin (C)	17,089
J. H. Stockdale (L)	5,249
Labour majority	5,331

Mr A. Short was subsequently appointed a member of the Government as Under Secretary for Home Affairs.

At the 1929 General Election there was a very big increase in the Labour vote. With a total poll of nearly 8,400,000 Labour secured nearly 3 million more votes than at the 1924 General Election. Labour emerged from the 1929 election as the largest single party with 288 seats in Parliament. This was not sufficient, however, to give them an absolute majority. The Conservatives won 260 seats and the Liberals 59. Labour formed its second minority Government with Ramsay Macdonald as Prime Minister.

BOILERMAKERS' VIEWS

Immediately before the election the four members of the boiler-makers' parliamentary panel issued an appeal to members of the Society to vote Labour. They recalled that the Tory Government had obtained office at the previous General Election in October 1924 as a result of 'a fraudulent conspiracy'. They had issued a scare about a so-called 'red letter' issued by the head of the Communist International, Zinoviev. The boilermakers' candidates said that the first task of the new Parliament would be to fight unemployment. Under the Tories the army of unemployed had steadily increased. Unemployment benefit had been reduced and the power of Parliament had been used to enrich the wealthy at the expense of the poor.

Shortly after the election of the Labour Government the Society decided to put its views on unemployment before the President of the Board of Trade. The President met representatives of the Executive Council, together with the boilermakers' Members of Parliament, on 24 July. The delegation was led by John Hill.

The delegation urged the Government to encourage the building of both cargo vessels and fast passenger ships. Britain, they said, was being overtaken by other countries and foreign owners were being subsidised by their governments. Orders for new fishing vessels were also at a very low level. Between 1910 and 1914 789 trawlers had been built whereas in the five years 1924–9 only fifty fishing vessels had been completed. The delegation pointed out that during the previous fifteen years the increase in foreign merchant shipping amounted to 75 per cent whereas the increase in British merchant shipping was only about 6 per cent. The boilermakers' representatives also urged the Government to seek a trade agreement with Russia. Russia needed ships, machinery, bridges and locomotives and in return could offer timber, flax and grain.

The boilermakers' delegation reported that the President of the Board of Trade had given them a most attentive reception. The Executive Council asked branches to forward resolutions in support of the Society's policies to all Members of Parliament, whether Labour, Liberal or Conservative.

By the end of 1929 the boilermakers' Members of Parliament reported that an encouraging start had been made in implementing Labour's programme even though the Government did not command an overall majority in the House of Commons. A new Unemployment Insurance Bill had been introduced which provided for improved benefits and abolished some of the harsher conditions of existing legislation affecting unemployed workers. New factory legislation was being prepared, pensions were being granted to an additional 500,000 widows, and schemes were being launched to reduce unemployment.

Nevertheless, because it could not command an overall majority, the Labour Government was severely restricted in what it could do. In addition some of its leaders were timid in putting forward bold solutions. In the spring of 1930 the Chancellor of the Exchequer, Philip Snowden, said in a debate on unemployment that there had been an organised conspiracy against the Government ever since it had come into office. It had been the deliberate policy of certain interests, he said, to create uncertainty. The Federation of British Industries, for example, had issued 'the most alarming manifesto, full of pessimism and calculated to increase whatever feeling of despondency there might be'. Mr Snowden accused the FBI of making inaccurate statements. Ominously the figures for unemployment continued to rise.

WAGES AND UNEMPLOYMENT

The efforts of the engineering unions to secure a wage increase were unsuccessful. The employers insisted that trade prospects were extremely uncertain and they pointed to the rising trend of unemployment. In the spring of 1930 the unions asked the Prime

Minister to set up an inquiry into the claim for an increase in engineering wages. The Government did not dismiss this request from the unions but found it impossible to secure the co-operation of the employers to an inquiry.

On the railways the unions were more successful. In May 1930 they secured the restoration of a 2½ per cent wages cut which had previously been imposed. They also secured an undertaking that wages would again be considered towards the end of the year.

Unfortunately towards the end of the summer a new problem arose affecting engineering workers on the railways. The London and North Eastern Railway, which ran services covering some of the areas affected by rising unemployment decided on a campaign of economies. According to the Executive Council of the Boiler-makers' Society about 15 per cent of the membership of the Society in railway workshops were discharged or given notice. The Society made strong representations to the LNER and suggested that the normal 'wastage' of employees through death, old age, illness and other causes would be sufficient to bring about a reduc-tion in numbers. The Society also pressed for a shorter working week or for periodic layoffs as an alternative to unemployment. The representations of the Society were of little avail.

The continued growth in unemployment prompted the Society to place a motion on the subject on the agenda for the 1930 TUC. The motion said that the capitalist system had failed to find employ-ment for all able bodied workers. It regretted that the efforts of the Government were inadequate to deal effectively with the evils of unemployment. It concluded by saying that it was the duty of the Government to take emergency measures to offer employment on trade union rates and conditions to 'the surplus able-bodied workers which capitalism fails to employ'. Two other motions were sub-mitted by the Society for the 1930 TUC. One called for an im-mediate effort to obtain the reduction of working hours to forty-four per week and the other called for the restriction of overtime.

The motion on unemployment was moved by John Hill. He drew attention to the failings of the capitalist system and the existence of mass unemployment. He said that it was the duty of the Govern-ment to take measures to provide employment at trade union rates to the unemployed workers. The resolution was carried without opposition. The motion calling for a reduction in hours of work

207

was composited with similar motions submitted by other unions. The composite motion was moved by the General and Municipal Workers' Union and seconded by M. H. Connolly on behalf of the Boilermakers' Society. The motion was carried. The motion on the restriction of overtime was also composited in the general motion calling for a reduction of working hours.

In 1930 a report on family allowances was published from a special joint committee appointed by the TUC and the Labour Party. One of the members of the committee was John Hill. The majority report, to which John Hill was a signatory, recommended that family allowances should be paid out of public funds in respect of each child from birth to school leaving age, that the allowance should be paid direct to the mother, that the allowance should be paid for all children and that the allowances should be paid through the Post Office.

A minority report, submitted by three of the trade unionists on the joint committee, felt that the limited funds available for social expenditure should be concentrated on improving the social services. They were particularly concerned that a school medical service should be developed, that more should be spent on housing and that milk should be provided for children as a means of eliminating turberculosis. The advocacy of family allowances by the majority on the joint committee foreshadowed the introduction many years later of this important development of social policy.

By the end of 1930 the General Secretary, John Hill, was complaining in the monthly journal of a 'massed attack on wages'. World capitalists, he said, had sent out the slogan 'wages must come down'. In the industrial countries of the world at least twenty million were unemployed. John Hill said that this was a crazy system. How was it possible to promote employment by reducing the purchasing power of consumers? Particular concern was expressed by the General Secretary at the proposal of the railway companies to reduce railway shopmen's wages by 10 per cent by the end of 1930.

The numbers of unemployed members of the Boilermakers' Society had by this time risen to more than 20,000. Membership was also declining. Between 1929 and 1930 it fell from 64,568 to 61,992. In shipbuilding unemployment rose particularly sharply. The average number of unemployed shipbuilding workers in 1930 was over

63,000, representing more than 30 per cent of the workers in the industry.

In 1931 wage reductions and demands from the employers for new reductions were reported every month. Early in the year the Engineering Employers' Federation told the unions that because of the conditions of British engineering workers they were unable to compete internationally. They proposed that the normal working week should be increased from forty-seven to forty-eight hours, that overtime rates should be reduced, that the premium rates for nightshifts and for double dayshift or three-shift working should be cut and that standard piece-work earnings should be reduced from time-and-a-third to time-and-a-quarter. These demands evoked numerous resolutions from branches calling for resistance. The unions were strongly opposed to the employers' claims but the ever-rising level of unemployment left them with little alternative but to negotiate the best terms they could get.

In June 1931 the engineering unions, including the Boilermakers' Society, agreed to recommend a series of measures designed to reduce manufacturing costs. The overtime rate for the first two hours worked per day was reduced to time-and-a-quarter and the nightshift rate reduced to time-and-one-sixth. Reductions were also introduced in the rates for double dayshift and three-shift working. The normal rate for a piece-worker of average ability was reduced from time-and-a-third to time-and-a-quarter. The agreed memorandum stated:

All systems of payment by results will be subject to the following conditions:

No piece-work prices, bonus or basis times once established may be altered except for the following reasons:

(1) A mistake in the calculation on either side, or
(2) The material, means or method of production, or the quantities are changed, or
(3) A mutual arrangement has been come to between the employer and the worker in the same way as a new price is arranged.

The Executive Council of the Boilermakers' Society wanted the recommendations to be submitted to a ballot vote of the entire membership of the engineering unions. The employers would not agree to postpone the implementation date, 6 July 1931, to enable a ballot on the recommendations to be held. Despite this opposition the Boilermakers' Society pressed their proposal. It did not find support from other unions. The Society felt in the circumstances that they had no practical alternative but to accept the recommendations. They pointed out to the membership that though the recommendations represented a worsening of conditions, they were not as drastic as at first proposed by the employers.

In shipbuilding the employers also pressed for wage reductions. In June 1931 they proposed that the wages of all plain time workers should be reduced to the national uniform time rate except that, unless agreed in local negotiations, no worker should suffer a reduction of more than 2s 6d per week. Further consideration would then be given locally to any higher rates of pay, 'having regard to the desirability of wiping out as early as possible the excesses which at present exist'. For piece-workers it was proposed that the 7s bonus should be withdrawn and that certain other bonuses should be abolished.

The unions made sustained efforts to secure a modification of the employers' proposals. A series of national conferences were held at which the union representatives offered to go some way to meet the employers' demands. At a final conference held in August 1931 the employers refused to amend the proposed reductions but agreed to implement them not in one but in two stages. The first half of the cuts was to be introduced in October 1931 and the second half in January 1932.

The unions unanimously rejected the employers' demands, but the employers then stated that the new conditions would be enforced with or without agreement. The unions refused to accept this ultimatum but lacked the strength to resist. By this time more than half the workers in shipbuilding and shiprepairing were unemployed. There was not a single union that had the money to pay dispute benefit. The unions decided to advise their members not to accept the new conditions by formal agreement but to remain at work under protest. In describing the new enforced conditions John Hill said that they were more serious than any previous wage reductions in the history of the industry. They not only provided for wage cuts but they cut 'right across district customs and district agreements'.

In the districts, despite the advice given by the Executive Council, there was much local resistance to wage cutting. The Executive Council reported that there was a series of large and small disputes. The most serious was in London.

LONDON SHIP REPAIR DISPUTE

In the spring of 1931 the London ship repair employers demanded that the pay of boilermakers should be reduced by 10s to 12s per week. This was in addition to the demand for wage reductions being formulated at that time by the shipbuilding employers nationally. The London members rejected the demand of the London employers and were finally locked out.

The dispute lasted for about seven weeks and was bitterly fought. The London District Committee reported that the struggle had been made more acute by a decision of the authorities that men sacked twelve days before the dispute should not be allowed unemployment benefit. An appeal was lodged with the Court of Referees and the claim of the men was allowed. The Insurance Officer then appealed and during the delay no benefit was paid. The London District Committee reported that some 300 members were affected by this ruling. The public assistance committee were notified by employers that work was available for members prepared to accept a 10s to 12s per week reduction. Members were refused relief or, according to the London District Committee, directed to the alternative of the workhouse. The committee said 'The whole of these drawbacks are causing untold distress amongst our members'.

The London boilermakers did not win their dispute with the ship repair employers but their strong resistance to the proposed wage cuts helped to stop the full attack on their wages and conditions. The leadership of the London boilermakers included among their number a group of supporters of the Minority Movement including Harry Pollitt. Two other prominent members who later were elected to national office in the Society were Ted Hill (later to become General Secretary) and Alf Whitney (later to become a member of the Executive Council).

One outcome of the London dispute was the defeat of J. T.

Husband in the election for district delegate. J. T. Husband had held office for fifteen years. Among the candidates who opposed him were Ted Hill and Alf Whitney. In his election address Ted Hill said that it was time that the London district was reorganised. The members employed on shiprepairing he said had suffered untold agony. Many honest and fearless members found themselves un-employed rather than tolerate 'the iniquitous systems and tech-niques adopted by the employers'. Ted Hill himself had been victim-ised. He also called for a strong system of shop stewards to strengthen the workshop organisation of boilermakers. Ted Hill was the president of the East Ham branch and the committee acting on his behalf said he was a fearless advocate of the members' interests. During the ship repair dispute he had acted as secretary of the dispute committee.

Alf Whitney's election address also called for the strengthening of the role of shop stewards in the Boilermakers' Society. He called for greater class consciousness among the membership and said that in all discussions on working conditions the last word should rest with the members affected.

In the first ballot for the election of the London district delegate both Ted Hill and Alf Whitney received more votes than J. T. Husband. In the second ballot Ted Hill had a narrow majority over Alf Whitney. He was elected by 320 votes against 302.

Following his defeat J. T. Husband sent a dignified letter to the monthly journal thanking members who had supported him both in the election and during his fifteen years as a full-time official. He said that he had no desire to criticise other members but to those who had thought fit to turn him down 'I desire to say most emphatically that I have no regret or apology to offer for the part I took in the last dispute'. He appealed to the London membership to give full support to their branch officers and their full-time officials. In a statement on the outcome of the election Ted Hill said that the election had been fought in a clean manner and he expressed his appreciation for the attitude of the defeated candi-dates. Alf Whitney, in a similarly dignified statement, pledged his loyal support to Ted Hill and his continued allegiance to the Society.

FURTHER CUTS

The members employed in railway workshops also suffered wage reduction in 1931. In March the wages of traffic employees (i.e. not employees in workshops) receiving more than £2 a week were reduced by 2½ per cent on the first 40s and 5 per cent on any amount over 40s per week. Overtime rates were reduced from time-and-a-quarter to time-and-one-eighth and nightshift premiums were also cut. Later in the same month, March 1931, agreement was reached between the railway companies and the Boilermakers' Society on an application by the employers for wage cuts. The deduction, which took effect at the end of March 1931, was 4⅙ per cent. This was submitted to a ballot vote of the branches with members employed in railway workshops and was confirmed by 424 votes to 228. The reduction was not to operate 'so as to reduce the earnings of any adult male employee below £2 per week'.

The heavy unemployment of the period and the declining membership worsened the financial position of the Society. In 1929 the members had accepted by vote a proposal that the number of district delegates should be reduced by six. Six additional delegates had been elected in 1919 when the membership was much higher. The intention was that these six posts should be terminated from the end of January 1930. During the final weeks of 1929, however, numerous appeals were received from branches calling for a reconsideration of the decision. At that time the Executive Council thought that the finances of the Society might improve because of a revival in trade. They also called for a reduction in arrears of subscriptions. They agreed to take another ballot among the members regarding the six district delegates. The result of the ballot was announced in June 1930. It showed a majority for the retention of the additional district delegates appointed in 1919.

One year later, by which time the depression in trade had deepened, the Executive Council issued a special statement indicating that if existing conditions continued the superannuation reserve fund of the Society would be exhausted by the end of the year. Alternative proposals were suggested to the membership to bring the Society's expenditure into balance with its income. These proposals provided for a reduction in superannuation benefit and a narrowing of the eligibility for benefit. It was proposed also to withdraw one of the scales of sickness benefit. By ballot vote the members accepted one of the proposals, the effect of which was to reduce by 1s per week the superannuation benefit for members who had been drawing benefit for less than five years. Members who had been drawing benefit for between five years and ten years had their benefits reduced as follows:

$$
\begin{array}{ll}
8s & \text{to } 3s\ 6d \\
7s & \text{to } 3s \\
6s & \text{to } 2s\ 6d \\
5s\ 6d & \text{to } 2s\ 3d
\end{array}
$$

Members who had been drawing benefit for more than ten years had it reduced to 2s per week. One of the scales of sickness benefit was totally withdrawn.

In the autumn of 1931 approximately 60 per cent of the total membership of the Society were either unemployed or drawing superannuation or sickness benefit. In the annual report for 1931 it was stated that thousands of members of the Society had not worked a single day during the year. Membership declined from 61,992 to 58,041. Total income during the year amounted to just over £87,000, but £88,000 was paid in superannuation benefit alone. Sickness benefit amounted to more than £23,000 and funeral benefit to nearly £13,000. Thus benefit payments substantially exceeded income. In addition the Society still had to meet the salaries of the full-time officials and office staff, organising and negotiating expenses, rents and rates, and branch and district expenditure.

ORGANISATION

In November 1930 the Assistant General Secretary of the Society, John Barker, died suddenly from a heart attack. He was 60 years of age. He joined the Society in 1891 and served as a branch official and district secretary. In 1908 he was elected Assistant General Secretary and remained in that post until his death. He served for a number of years as a Labour representative on the Newcastle City Council and he was appointed a Justice of the Peace in 1927.

214

John Hill said of him that he was a very conscientious and loyal officer of the Society.

The election for a new Assistant General Secretary went to a second ballot when M. H. Connolly narrowly defeated J. S. Holmes. The voting was 4,284 for Connolly and 3,950 for Holmes. Martin Connolly joined the Society in August 1898 and held office at every level. He served as full-time district delegate and was for a short period a member of the Executive Council in 1917–18. For four and a half years between 1924 and 1929 he was a Labour Member of Parliament. After his defeat he had returned to the shipbuilding industry.

In 1930 the Society found itself in conflict with the Constructional Engineering Union. For some time the Society had been seeking to improve its organisation among men employed on structural steel work. In this organising drive the Boilermakers' Society were frequently in competition with the CEU.

On 29 March 1930 the Society sent a letter to all district delegates stating that the CEU was formerly part of the Iron and Steel Trades Confederation but it had now become a separate organisation. It had secured direct affiliation with the TUC. The Boilermakers' Society said that the CEU did not restrict their membership to craftsmen. The Society felt that it was much more able than the CEU to represent skilled men employed on structural steel work. From returns made by district delegates the Society claimed to have nearly 2,700 members employed on structural steel work in 102 firms. It was acknowledged, however, that these figures were incomplete. CEU subscriptions were considerably lower than those of the Boilermakers' Society. District delegates were asked to give particular attention to the organisation of structural steel workers.

FALL OF THE LABOUR GOVERNMENT

The origin of the economic slump of the early 1930s could be traced back for many years. After the ending of the First World War, capitalism had emerged as a very unstable system. There was first a boom, then a depression and later a period of relative stabilisation. In 1929 the boom in stock market prices in the United

States collapsed. This foreshadowed a deepening economic crisis. It was most severe in the United States and Germany. In the United States industrial production fell to about half its level at the height of the boom, and in Germany many millions became unemployed.

Events moved quickly in Britain. In the summer of 1931 British financial institutions were reported to be heavily involved in a currency crisis in some European countries. The TUC said that London finance houses had made loans to Germany which could not be repaid on short notice. The funds lent to Germany had been borrowed by British finance houses in France and America. It was felt that British credit might be affected. The withdrawal of foreign balances from London was said to be endangering the British economy. The Bank of England raised the bank rate in an effort to stop the withdrawal of these foreign balances. At the same time pressure was building up from financial and business interests for drastic economies in public expenditure. These cuts, it was argued, were essential to maintain foreign confidence in British currency.

In the middle of August representatives of the General Council of the TUC met the Prime Minister and other members of the Labour Government to discuss the situation. The Prime Minister and his colleagues gave the TUC an indication of the kind of policy which the Government were wanting to pursue. They said that economies would have to be made, including the raising of unemployment insurance contributions, the restriction of insurance benefits to twenty-six weeks in the year, the reduction of the pay of teachers, police and members of the armed forces and the reduction of public expenditure on roads.

The TUC representatives did not like what they heard from the Government. The General Council discussed the situation and, according to the report which they subsequently placed before the 1931 Congress, 'They felt that the Government's policy was on entirely wrong lines'. The cutting of wages, salaries and the social services, and the reduction of grants for public work would still further aggravate unemployment. There was the further factor that the pay of public service workers including, for example, teachers, was subject to negotiating arrangements. The Governments proposals, if implemented, would render the existing negotiating machinery ineffective. The General Council said that the

216

Government's approach to the problem would 'lead to the accentuation of our economic difficulties'.

The TUC put forward a number of alternative proposals. They suggested that the existing method of collecting unemployment insurance contributions from worker, employer and the state should be replaced by a graduated levy upon profits and incomes. It was further suggested that new taxes should be introduced on unearned income and upon fixed interest securities. The fall in the price level, it was pointed out, had greatly enhanced the real value of such holdings. The TUC sent a deputation to the Cabinet to convey their views. In addition to the economic arguments which they advanced they emphasised that any limitation of unemployment benefit would impose great hardship on working class families.

On 21 August the Prime Minister, Mr Ramsay MacDonald, sent a letter to the TUC stating that the proposals of the General Council would not reduce Government expenditure but would substantially increase it. The letter rejected the General Council's proposals. The final sentence of the Prime Minister's letter read 'As you know nothing gives me greater regret than to disagree with old industrial friends, but I really personally find it absolutely impossible to overlook dread realities as I am afraid you are doing'.

Within a few days the Labour Government had resigned and a number of its leading members, including the Prime Minister and Chancellor of the Exchequer, had joined with Conservatives and Liberals to form a so-called National Government. On Wednesday 26 August 1931 there was a joint meeting of the General Council of the TUC, the Executive Committee of the Labour Party and representatives of the Parliamentary Labour Party. A resolution was passed stating that they were unanimously of the opinion that the new Government should be vigorously opposed in parliament and by the labour movement throughout the country. They expressed their approval of the action taken by a number of Labour ministers who had not given their support to the new Government.

On 27 August the TUC, the Labour Party and the Parliamentary Labour Party issued a manifesto stating that the labour movement repudiated all responsibility for the new coalition Government. The new Government, the manifesto said, was determined to attack the standard of living of the workers in order to meet a situation caused by a policy pursued by private banking interests in the control of which the public had no part. The manifesto went on to say that the Government's proposals to economise at the expense of the public were not only unjust but economically unsound. They would increase unemployment and aggravate the basic problem underlying the crisis by reducing the consuming power of the masses. Cuts in wages and salaries and in national and local services would lead to attempts to enforce similar cuts in industry generally. The manifesto ended by saying that the forces of labour emphatically rejected the view that the national interest could only be secured by the impoverishment of the workers.

The Society's delegation to the 1931 Congress of the TUC strongly supported the policy of the General Council. The delegation's report stated: 'The Bristol TUC of 1931 will stand out in history as the occasion on which organised workers made a stand against the new phase of plutocracy, i.e., "Government by the Banks".' The delegation asserted that the Labour Government, despite the defection of its leaders, had been destroyed because the majority of the Cabinet had not accepted the demand of the bankers that the 'dole' to unemployed workers should be cut as a first step to a serious reduction of all wages and working class standards.

CUTS AND MORE CUTS

The new coalition Government, made up of a minority of defecting Labour leaders, some Liberals and all Conservatives, lost no time in carrying out its policy of economy. An emergency budget was introduced which increased income tax and imposed heavier duties on beer and tobacco. The pay of teachers, civil servants, the armed forces and other public sector employees was cut.

In an atmosphere of crisis and impending collapse created by politicians, newspapers, bankers and industrialists, the new Government enjoyed support from a majority of the public. Among millions of workers who had voted Labour there was disillusionment that leaders in whom they had placed their confidence had gone over to an alliance with the Tories. To the millions who had supported the Conservatives the events of 1931 seemed to confirm the allegation that Labour was incapable of governing and that reliance had to be placed on the 'representatives of business'.

218

Even so the economy measures introduced by the new Government soon met resistance. The most dramatic challenge came, unexpectedly, from the lower ranks of the Royal Navy. In the middle of September the fleet at Invergordon went on strike. The signal for strike action was passed from one ship to another by the organised and disciplined cheering of the men. The men produced an appeal to the Admiralty to 'amend the drastic cuts in pay which have been inflicted on the lowest paid men of the lower decks'.

The Invergordon mutiny stunned the ruling circles of Britain. The unthinkable had occurred. The men of the senior service had mutinied on a pay issue. The Government retreated. The pay cuts were modified and there was a promise of no victimisation. Subsequently, however, this promise was broken and a number of the leaders of the strike were dismissed from the Royal Navy. Some of them remained active in the labour movement for years afterwards.

The teachers also resisted. They claimed that the pay cuts to be imposed upon them were more severe than on other public sector workers. Street demonstrations were held and there was intensive lobbying of Members of Parliament. As in their response to the Invergordon mutiny, the Government retreated and announced that pay reductions throughout the public services would not exceed 10 per cent. Though these expressions of resistance were significant and succeeded in bringing about some modification of proposals, they did not change the strategic direction of Government policy. The majority of the public was overwhelmed by a wave of propaganda in favour of economies.

GENERAL ELECTION 1931

The coalition Government, which described itself as a National Government, resolved to appeal to the country for a mandate for its policies. A General Election was fixed for 27 October. Five members of the Boilermakers' Society stood as Labour candidates. They were A. Short, MP, W. H. Egan, MP, J. Gibbins, MP, D. Williams, MP, and T. Irwin. Short, Egan, Gibbins and Williams defended their existing seats at Wednesbury, Birkenhead West, West Toxteth and Swansea East. T. Irwin stood for Greenock.

An appeal for support for Labour was published by the Boilermakers' Society. The appeal pointed out that the Labour Government which took office in 1929 lacked a parliamentary majority. Because of its lack of a majority Labour had been attacked from outside by financial and business interests. The formation of a National Government, said the statement issued by the Society, marked the inception of a general attack on the wages and conditions of workers. Labour was now at its greatest testing time. Never before had it been so essential for the workers to have faith in their own ability and power to manage in government.

In a report to the membership the boilermakers' Members of Parliament W. Egan, J. Gibbins, A. Short and D. Williams listed some of the measures which the Labour Government had introduced. They pointed out that about half a million more people, including widows and orphans, had been made eligible for pensions. Some of the more onerous conditions relating to the payment of unemployment benefit had been removed. Between 100,000 and 150,000 persons had been transferred from poor law relief to unemployment benefit. Work had been initiated by the Government to promote employment. Legislation had been introduced for slum clearance and rehousing. Miners' hours had been reduced by half an hour per day and legislation had been introduced for minimum wages in road passenger transport. Increased provision had been made for education. The distribution of taxation had been changed 'to place the burden on those whose shoulders were broad enough to carry it'. The boilermakers' MPs said that the Labour Government had brought to its tasks courage and sympathetic understanding of the needs and aspirations of the worker.

The General Election was conducted in an atmosphere described by the boilermakers' General Secretary, John Hill, as one of terror. 'Simple men and women were terrorised by notes in their pay envelopes stating that the works would close if a Labour Government were elected.' On the eve of the poll statements were made that workers' money in savings banks had been wrongfully used by the Labour Government and this, said John Hill, had stupified and stunned many working men and women. The result of the General Election was an overwhelming majority for the new coalition. Within this coalition there was a very substantial majority of Conservatives. Of the five boilermakers who stood as Labour candidates only David Williams was elected at Swansea East. The other four candidates were defeated. The results were as follows:

Swansea East

David Williams (Lab)	17,126
P. D. Chalke (Nat Lib)	13,177
Labour majority	3,949

Wednesbury

Viscount Ednam (C)	25,000
Alfred Short (Lab)	20,842
Conservative majority	4,158

Birkenhead West

J. S. Allen (C)	22,336
W. H. Egan (Lab)	12,671
Conservative majority	9,665

Liverpool West Toxteth

T. C. Wilson (C)	20,613
J. Gibbins (Lab)	14,978
Conservative majority	5,635

Greenock

Sir G. Collins (Lib)	18,013
T. Irwin (Lab)	10,850
A. Ferguson (Communist)	6,440
Liberal majority	7,163

In Greenock Tom Irwin had to face not only a Liberal candidate, who was elected, but also another boilermaker, Aitken Ferguson, who stood as a Communist.

As a result of the 1931 General Election the Labour Party were reduced to a mere fifty-two representatives in Parliament. In contrast the National Government could depend upon the support of 554 MPs of whom 473 were Conservatives. Despite this over-whelming majority in terms of seats, Labour still managed to secure some 30 per cent of the total vote. In fact their vote in 1931 of nearly 6,650,000, though smaller than their vote of 8,389,000 in 1929, was higher than their vote of 5,489,000 in 1924.

ATTACKING THE UNEMPLOYED

With their victory at the 1931 General Election the National Government went further in their attack on the unemployed. At that time about 2¾ million people were registered as unemployed. Unemployment insurance benefit was 17s per week for an adult man, 9s for his dependent wife and 2s for each child. Agricultural workers, domestic employees and salaried workers earning more than £250 per year were not in the unemployment insurance scheme. Just before the General Election it was proposed that unemployment benefit rates should be reduced to 15s 3d for an adult man and 8s for his dependent wife. Insurance contributions were also to be increased.

After the General Election the National Government introduced a new scheme which became widely known as the 'means test'. The period for which unemployment benefit could be drawn as of right was limited to twenty-six weeks. Those who were no longer eligible had to apply for 'transitional payments', and were made subject to a means test by the local public assistance committee. The amount which the applicant received could be reduced, depending upon any income received by other members of the household – sons or daughters, for example, who held a job – or upon the local scales of poor law relief. In general the scales of poor law relief were higher in Labour-controlled areas than in Conservative areas but they could not exceed, though they could be lower than, the unemployment insurance benefit scales. Within weeks of the

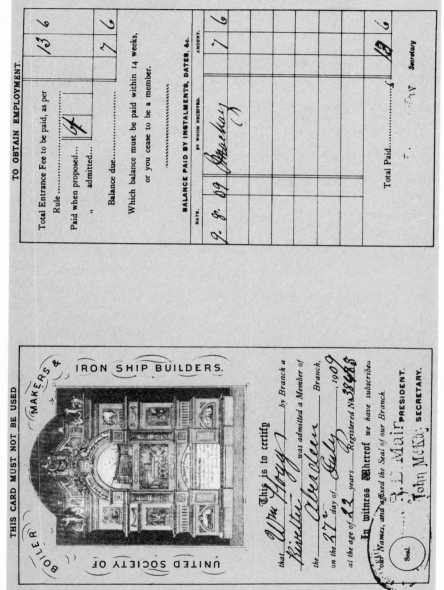

7 The card of the Boilermakers' Society.

21st May,   31.

The Rt: Hon: J. Ramsay MacDonald,
     Prime Minister,
          10. Downing Street,
               Whitehall,
                    LONDON.

My Dear Prime Minister,

Your letter of 18th instant arrived
here in my absence from home.

I appreciate your kind wish to honour
me with the offer of a Title, and I find
it hard to refuse you, as at all times of
your life, and in all circumstances, you
have been the ablest champion of the
common people at Home and Abroad.

My acceptance of a Title would not
help you in the hard and heavy work you

are now responsible for, and, as
for myself, my position is as it was in
1917, when I was offered the Title of
'Companion of Honour'.

The acceptance of a Title might
be misunderstood and thus render my
work less useful amongst those whom
I serve.

I, therefore, ask you that I
be excused.

Faithfully yours,

(signed) John Hill

8 Exchange of correspondence when John Hill, General Secretary of the
Boilermakers' Society, declined to become a Companion of Honour.

The Hillocks,
Lossiemouth.

10, Downing Street,
Whitehall.

May 27th 1931.

<u>VERY PRIVATE AND CONFIDENTIAL</u>

My dear John,

       I am sure you will not misunderstand me
when I say that your refusal of the Honour does my
heart good. I wish to heaven that was the spirit of
all our people. I made the offer to you because I
hold you personally in the very highest esteem and
believe I can understand what a hard uphill work you
have had to do, especially during the last few years.
I wished to let you know that some of us, although
we may be absorbed in the midst of work, have not
forgotten you and that our feelings for you are just
the same as ever. Still, I must say, that it goes
against my grain when good democrats of the Labour
School do not only accept but actually run over each
other to ask for these things. The safest thing for
you to do would be to burn this letter, unless you
can keep it under lock and key for the next fifty years,
when neither you nor I will care what people publish
about us.

       With kindest regards,

         Believe me, Yours very sincerely,

           Ramsay MacDonald

John Hill, Esq.

                                        July,   3rd,

The Secretary of the
        Order of Companions of Honour,
            Buckingham Palace,
            LONDON, S.W..

Sir,

        I beg to acknowledge receipt of your

favour of 30th ultimo, and thank you for the

honour it is intended to confer upon me.

        I have always felt that I am a citizen

of no mean Country, and my endeavour has been

to serve my Country by the efficient discharge

of my duties of citizenship.

        My work lies amongst my own class, and

I recognise that whatever I can do for their

betterment is of National service.

        I hope to continue that work, and the

acceptance of any title might cause me to be

misunderstood, and render my work less useful.

        I therefore respectfully ask to be

excused.

                            Faithfully yours,

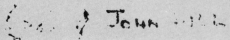

introduction of the new scheme nearly a million unemployed workers were on the 'means test'.

John Hill described the new arrangements in the following words:

> The dole is not only reduced in amount, but after 26 weeks' benefit the registered unemployed are sent to the poor law authorities to be further reduced or cut off altogether. Already thousands of self-respecting men have forfeited their claim rather than suffer the poor law destitution test which many of these committees are making their standard for a continuance of any benefit.

Industrial depression, mass unemployment and the means test had become the hallmarks of the economic crisis of British capitalism.

Chapter 15

The Depth of the Depression

The years of the depression in the early 1930s imposed great hardship on the members of the Boilermakers' Society and on the Society itself. John Hill said that 1931 had been a year of wage reductions and of humiliation and degradation for many wage earners. Of the year 1932 he said that it was the worst in the history of the Society. At least half the membership were unemployed.

The decline in membership continued throughout the first half of the 1930s. In 1930 the membership was nearly 62,000. By the end of 1935 it had declined to 49,719. At the height of the depression more than 28,000 members were unemployed. Another 2,500 were on superannuation benefit and more than 1,100 were on sickness benefit. Thus about 60 per cent of the membership were not at work. At the end of 1932 the superannuation fund was in deficit. Some ten years earlier the balance in the fund had amounted to more than £300,000. Superannuation benefit was once again reduced from the end of March 1932. Members who had received benefit for less than five years had their benefit reduced by 2s per week. Members who had received benefit for more than five years ceased to receive any benefit at all.

WAGE CUTS

The years of the depression were years of wage reductions for engineering, shipbuilding and shiprepairing workers. From January

224

1932 the Engineering Employers' Federation called for cuts in bonus payments introduced towards the end of the First World War. The Boilermakers' Society argued strongly against the employers' demands and pointed out that the last reductions had taken place only a few months earlier. The employers, however, were insistent and the negotiations led to a 'failure to agree'. In a circular to the membership the Executive Council said that unemployment was so serious that they had no other alternative but to recommend members to remain at work under protest. The employers gave no indication of when their demands would be enforced but it was soon learnt that reductions of about 5 per cent in net earnings were being introduced immediately.

Within a few weeks new demands were being made by the Shipbuilding Employers' Federation, even though wage reductions had been introduced from the beginning of January 1932. At a conference held on 25 February 1932 the employers said that there was a large number of excessive allowances paid both to time workers and to piece-workers which were no longer justified. The Federation said that they would be approaching individual unions or groups of unions at local level with a view to eliminating these allowances. The employers also called for a reduction of the national overtime rates. They had new proposals, they said, to place before the unions. Finally they called for the immediate consideration of measures to bring about greater interchangeability between classes of workers within the industry.

Further discussions took place on these suggestions from the Shipbuilding Employers' Federation when it was agreed that the question of 'excessive allowances' was essentially a local matter to be resolved by negotiations at district and yard level. The unions felt they had no alternative but to agree to set up a joint committee to examine the existing overtime and nightshift agreement. In these negotiations the employers pressed for a reduction in the premium rate for the first two hours of overtime each day from time-and-a-half to time-and-a-quarter. They urged that the nightshift rate should be reduced from time-and-a-third to time-and-a-sixth. The unions countered with a proposal that there should be much stricter control of overtime. The existing agreement provided for overtime up to a limit of thirty hours in any four weeks but it permitted a wide range of exceptions. The unions sought to reduce and to tighten the exceptions. They also urged that the limit of thirty hours should be reduced to twenty-four hours. The employers replied that it was impossible for them to accept any of the amendments proposed by the unions. The negotiations continued through the autumn of 1932 and by the end of the year they were suspended. The unions made no gain in these negotiations but equally they had succeeded in resisting any worsening of conditions. This was an achievement in the depressed conditions of 1932.

Reports were received every month by the Society of wage reductions in different shipyards and repair shops. In October 1932 the General Secretary said that successive wage reductions had meant that the pay of many members had been reduced by a half since 1920. He pointed out that trade had never improved as a result of wage reductions. He referred also to the pressure for wage cuts on the railways. In the railway workshops wages had been reduced by 2½ per cent in August 1928 and by a further 10d in the pound from March 1931. Companies were now pressing for a further 10 per cent reduction.

FURTHER DECLINE IN SHIPBUILDING

In October 1932 the Society decided to draw public attention to the appalling state of the shipbuilding and shiprepairing industries. A statement, in the form of questions and answers, was published which pointed out that the number of persons described as employees of the shipbuilding industry had declined from 354,000 in 1922 to 195,000 in the autumn of 1932. The number of registered unemployed was some 116,000 or 59·8 per cent of the total. Even those in employment were working only half the normal hours because of short-time arrangements.

The Society pointed out that of nearly 20 million gross tons of British shipping only 8 million tons were under 10 years old. Three-and-a-half million gross tons of British shipping were over 20 years old and 2 million tons were fit only for scrap. The Boilermakers' Society again put forward proposals for a 'scrap and build' scheme. The Government, it was suggested, should buy these scrap ships and break them up, thus giving immediate employment to hundreds of men. The tonnage should then be replaced by 1 million tons of new ships built with extended credit guaranteed by the Government at not more than 2 per cent interest. The building of 1 million gross tons, it was argued, would give employment to 100,00 men directly for twelve months or more and would indirectly give employment to a further 50,000. The employment of these 150,000 men would save a substantial sum in unemployment benefit.

In the annual report for 1932 John Hill called for a reduction in the hours of work and a limit on overtime. He urged that there should be a thirty-six-hour working week and an end to the existing overtime agreement. Overtime, he said, was limited only 'by sheer exhaustion'.

Throughout 1932 and 1933 the TUC continued to make representations to the Government to assist the shipbuilding industry. John Hill acted as the chairman of the TUC committee responsible for these representations. The TUC urged the Government to encourage the scrapping of old British tonnage. They pointed out that the German, Japanese and Italian governments had introduced schemes giving direct assistance for the disposal of old tonnage. The TUC also asked the Government to give financial assistance to the shipbuilding industry. This assistance, it suggested, should be given on condition that the materials used in ship construction should be of British manufacture.

In reply to the representations of the TUC the Government stated that they felt the keenest anxiety about the situation in the industry but argued that it would not be improved by the adoption of suggestions made by the TUC. The result, they said, would be to increase the existing glut of tonnage.

NATIONAL SHIPBUILDERS SECURITY LIMITED

In the meanwhile the shipbuilding employers were preparing their own scheme for the reorganisation of the industry. It had been launched by a company known as National Shipbuilders Security Limited. Its purpose was declared to be to assist the industry by the purchase of surplus building capacity. In order to reduce the capacity of the industry certain yards were purchased and their sites were restricted against further use for shipbuilding purposes.

Their equipment was scrapped. NSS Limited were also empowered to make payments to firms to contract not to build ships.

By the middle of 1933 the Boilermakers' Society were expressing indignation at the activities of NSS Ltd. NSS Ltd, they reported, were buying up shipyards under a deed which prevented them being used again for shipbuilding purposes for a period of forty years. Under this scheme twenty shipbuilding yards had been bought up and closed. These yards had 102 shipbuilding berths with an annual output capacity of over 700,000 tons. The result, said the Boilermakers' Society, was that certain towns whose prosperity depended on shipbuilding were in the direst poverty.

The activities of NSS Limited were highlighted in a book *The Town That Was Murdered* written by Ellen Wilkinson, MP*. The town referred to in the title of the book was the town for which she was the Member of Parliament, Jarrow. In her book she explained that the moving spirit behind the formation of NSS Ltd had been Sir James Lithgow, himself a leading shipbuilding employer. NSS, she said, had bought and scrapped one third of the British shipbuilding industry. Among the directors of NSS were men drawn from some of Britain's largest shipbuilding and engineering firms, including Vickers Armstrong, English Steel Corporation, Guest Keen and Baldwin, John Brown, Hawthorn Leslie, Colville, Harland and Wolff, Swan, Hunter and Wigham Richardson. The banks also had interests in NSS. Shipbuilding firms which joined NSS undertook to pay the company a levy of around 1 per cent of the contract price of all vessels built over a length of 300 feet.

Yards were closed in different parts of the country and Ellen Wilkinson alleged that some of the best sites in the world for shipbuilding purposes were being 'sterilised'. She drew attention to the fact that in the north east 72 per cent of shipbuilding workers were without a job. In Jarrow nearly three-quarters of the working population were out of work. Indeed, at the worst period, in the summer of 1932, no less than 80 per cent of the insured population of Jarrow were unemployed.

The big shipyard in Jarrow, known as Palmer's, was finally sold to NSS in 1934. Ellen Wilkinson said that the death warrant of the town had been signed. The reason for Jarrow's existence

* Gollancz, 1939.

had vanished overnight. She pointed out that Palmer's yard was not inefficient. It was one of the finest sites in the country. She said that NSS had been able to buy one of the six largest firms in the industry at a scrap price and had then closed it down, thus eliminating one of the strongest competitive firms. Palmer's was a financially weak company 'which had chained a derelict steel works to an efficient shipyard'. Financial weakness and not technical inefficiency, said Ellen Wilkinson, had decided the fate of the company.

WELDING

In the shipyards that were still working there was a new development which ultimately was profoundly to affect the membership of the Society. It was the development of the burning and welding of metal plates. In 1933 the Executive Council of the Society wrote to all districts and district delegates regarding the introduction of burning and welding machines in shipbuilding, boilerwork and on construction sites. The letter said that rapid developments were taking place in the use of oxy-acetylene and electric welding machines. The Executive Council wished to ensure that the machines were used under proper conditions. It was pointed out that their use was often dangerous and that poisonous gases were frequently produced in their operation. There had been many reports to the Society of members becoming ill after working on the new machines.

On 25 May 1933 the Shipbuilding Employers' Federation met the shipyard trade unions to discuss the use of electric welding in shipbuilding. They pointed out that considerable technical progress had been made in recent years and they felt that it was of importance that the development of welding in Britain should proceed as rapidly as possible. The employers argued that electric welding required a certain aptitude among the men who were doing it but it was nevertheless 'a simple, straightforward job, calling mainly for conscientious workmanship'. They emphasised that the cost of ship construction, including welding, was of the utmost importance to shipbuilders and ship owners.

The Federation put forward a number of points which they asked the unions to consider. They suggested that one workman should be employed on each arc and that a new class of workmen to be known as ship welders should be established. In the early stages of the development of electric welding the new class of ship welders would be recruited as far as possible from shipyard workers most suitable for the work, but not necessarily from men displaced by welding or from shipyard apprentices to other trades. Boys with no previous experience of shipyard work would normally be required to serve an apprenticeship of five years on ship welding but apprentices who had already served a part of their apprenticeship before taking up ship welding would be required to serve the balance of their apprenticeship period on welding. In no case would this be for less than two years on actual welding work. Men who had completed an apprenticeship to a shipyard trade and who were wanted for welding would be required to undertake training for a period of two years. Fully qualified ship welders were to be paid a plain time rate of £3 per week with lesser rates for trainees. In the initial stages all welding work on shipbuilding would be carried out on a time basis.

During the rest of the year there was a succession of conferences on the welding proposals of the Shipbuilding Employers' Federation. The proposals received a very hostile reception from the unions, particularly from the Boilermakers' Society. The Society replied to the Federation by stating that they saw their proposals as an attempt to reduce wages. In the past welding machines introduced on shipbuilding had been operated by members of the Boilermakers' Society and they saw no reason to create a new class of workmen.

Early in 1934 the shipyard unions held a conference to determine what action to take following the largely abortive negotiations on the employers' proposals on welding. At this conference all the unions reported that they were opposed to the creation of a new category of ship welders. They claimed that there was sufficient skilled labour available in the shipyards to meet all requirements for electric welding on new construction work. They supported the existing arrangements for the training of apprentices including instruction in welding. A resolution was carried in the following terms:

That the unions here represented pledge themselves to secure that the work to be welded be done by the class hitherto doing the

230

work. In the event of any member refusing to do the work of another trade being subject to discrimination by the employers all unions here represented pledge themselves to render support to such member in the fullest sense.

The Shipbuilding Employers' Federation, having put their welding proposals to the unions, regarded the negotiating procedure as completed and they told the unions that their scheme as originally submitted, subject to amendments which had been made during the course of negotiation, would stand. They had decided to implement their proposals. They indicated that notices would be posted to this effect in all federated establishments. The unions in the industry informed the Federation that their letter meant that wage reductions were being introduced. They rejected the ultimatum. The posting of notices, they said, would be met by the most strenuous opposition.

The shipbuilding unions remained determined and united in their opposition to the employers' proposals. In March 1934 the unions agreed that if and when any trainees or wage reductions were introduced the members of all unions would refuse to touch the work in dispute. The unions undertook to conduct the struggle yard by yard. Thus a direct national confrontation was avoided. It was left to individual employers to precipitate any disputes. Trade union members continued working normally so long as existing arrangements were maintained.

A national committee representing the unions was established to co-ordinate activity. It acted in close co-operation with joint committees established at district level. This resistance by the shipbuilding unions appears to have been successful. Difficulties were encountered in some yards but generally the unions were able to maintain established arrangements without wage reductions. The greater part of the welding work in the industry remained in the hands of members of the Boilermakers' Society.

COTTON DISPUTE

Some of the most significant struggles against wage cuts and the worsening of conditions in the great depression occurred, perhaps

231

unexpectedly because so many of the workers were women, in the cotton and woollen textile industries. In 1932 the employers in the cotton textile industry were seeking to cut wage rates and to require workers to operate more looms. The workers in the industry voted overwhelmingly to resist the employers' demands. Mass demonstrations of protest took place in many Lancashire towns.

A report of the dispute was given to the 1932 Trades Union Congress by Mr A. Naesmith of the Amalgamated Weavers' Association who said that he wanted to tell delegates in a plain, straightforward manner of the difficulties which the cotton unions faced and the magnificent response from the members of the textile unions in Lancashire. Their loyalty, he said, had inspired everyone with boundless hope. Because of the very severe depression in the industry and the loss of morale as a result of domestic suffering the union officials thought that the spirit of resistance among the workers might have been broken. But this was not so. The workers had responded in a most remarkable manner indicating that there was a limit to which the working class could be driven. In Lancashire there had been a deep-rooted human protest against intolerable industrial and economic circumstances.

Mr Naesmith said the cotton employers had displayed an acquisitiveness and greed that had been positively amazing. They had proposed a 30 per cent reduction in piece price lists. Cotton operatives working forty-eight hours a week were earning about 37–38s. Many of them were on short time and their wages varied between 17s and 22s per week. The employers were demanding reductions even on these rates of pay.

In the middle of September 1932 the Boilermakers' Society issued an appeal for financial assistance to the cotton workers. The appeal said the recent Congress of the TUC had regarded the attack by the employers on the cotton workers 'as the opening of another all-round attack on the wages and conditions of workers in all trades'. The crisis in the cotton industry, said the circular of the Boilermakers' Society, could not be solved by the starvation of the operatives. The circular pointed out that despite repeated appeals from successive governments, economists and the textile unions, the employers had refused to reorganise the industry. Instead they were seeking to force down the wages of the workers.

Towards the end of September, following intervention by the

Government, a settlement of the cotton dispute was reached. It provided for a wage cut of about 8 per cent, introduced the working of six looms per operative on some cloths and provided for the reinstatement of workers engaged in the dispute. Unfortunately the assurances given to the unions about the reinstatement of workers were not observed by many employers. Moreover even after the wage cuts imposed by the agreement further reductions were imposed in some mills. By 1933 the system of collective bargaining in the cotton industry and the effective observance of agreements had broken down. In 1934 a new law was passed by Parliament which gave legal effect to a wage list in the cotton weaving industry. The unions welcomed this measure of support but they complained that its effect was often to reduce still further wage rates on four-loom working though raising them on six-loom working.

In January 1933 the Boilermakers' Society passed to the cotton unions the sum of £52 3s collected among branch members. The TUC cotton solidarity fund raised in all more than £58,000. Vouchers for the purchase of food were issued to cotton workers. The value of these vouchers was generously supplemented by the Co-operative Wholesale Society.

PROTESTS

With so many of its members in the ranks of the unemployed the Boilermakers' Society frequently participated in protest demonstrations. The London District Committee reported, for example, in November 1932 that members had been demonstrating against 'the iniquitous means test'. The London District Committee said that it was necessary for all members to agitate and demonstrate for the abolition of the means test.

In his parliamentary report to the membership towards the end of 1932 David Williams, MP, said that since their period of office began the National Government had extracted £15 millions from the unemployed by the operation of the means test. They had reduced unemployment benefit and reduced the pay of many public sector workers. They had also reduced disability benefit to women

233

and were making cuts in the public health service and in maternity and child welfare.

In 1933 demonstrations against unemployment were held in many towns. Some of them were initiated by the official trade union movement and others by so-called unofficial bodies formed for the purpose of organising the unemployed. The March 1933 issue of the monthly report of the Society's journal carried a photograph showing many members of the Society, together with their branch banners, participating in a London demonstration sponsored by the TUC against unemployment. John Hill, in commenting on this demonstration, said that it was the biggest in British history. The demonstration, he said, was the spontaneous product of the workers against the callous indifference of a government towards the semi-starvation of three million unemployed workers and their dependants. At each of the demonstrations sponsored by the TUC resolutions were carried demanding the abolition of the means test, the introduction of national work schemes, a forty-hour week, and a trade agreement with the USSR. The London District Committee in reporting on the London demonstration said that there were three boilermakers' banners on display and about 200 members participated in a march held before the demonstration began in Hyde Park. TUC sponsored demonstrations were held in more than twenty cities.

Later in 1933 the TUC issued a policy statement on the reduction of unemployment. They called for the end of the economy campaign, adequate maintenance for the unemployed, the introduction of a forty-hour week and the provision of adequate credits for overseas trade.

In 1933 the Society tabled a motion for the TUC calling for legislation limiting overtime. The resolution was carried. Shortly afterwards the Society issued a circular to all branches drawing attention to the relationship between unemployment and hours of work. The circular pointed out that unions in engineering and shipbuilding had been pressing a claim for a forty-hour week and at the same time had sought the abolition of overtime or at the very least the reduction of overtime to the absolute minimum. This claim had not been successful. The employers, said the Executive Council, had claimed the right to determine when and how overtime would be worked and who would be selected to work it. The circular went on to emphasise that the employers were not solely to blame. Unfortunately there were some men in constant employment who were 'always grabbing overtime'. Overtime, said the circular, was bad for trade and bad for employment. The Executive Council called upon branch officers and shop stewards to co-operate with district delegates in pressing for the limitation of overtime.

The Boilermakers' Society supported a motion on unemployment and industrial recovery which was carried by the 1933 TUC. The successful resolution called for a forty-hour week and schemes of public works. It drew attention to the vigorous efforts being made by the newly-elected President of the United States, Franklin D. Roosevelt, to stimulate industry by means of an Industrial Recovery Act. This Act provided for public investment and sought to encourage trade union organisation in American industry.

NEW POLICIES IN THE USA

The efforts of President Roosevelt to bring about industrial recovery in the USA were warmly reported in the journal of the Boilermakers' Society. An outline of the industrial recovery plan was published. The United States Government, it was explained, proposed to spend 3½ thousand million dollars for public works to increase employment. Purchasing power was to be distributed through new employment and this in turn would be effective in starting again the wheels of other industries. Under a code of fair competition, employers would have to agree that their employees should have the right to join a trade union and to bargain collectively. The new President encouraged the reduction of hours of labour, the observance of minimum scales of pay and minimum standards of working conditions.

The journal of the Boilermakers' Society quoted with approval the statement made by President Roosevelt when he signed the Industrial Recovery Act:

In my inaugural I laid down the simple proposition that nobody is going to starve in this country. It seems to me to be equally plain that no business which depends for existence on paying less than living wages to its workers has any right to continue in this country. By business I mean the whole of commerce as well as the whole of industry; by workers I mean all workers – the white collar class as well as the man in overalls; and by living wages I mean more than a bare subsistence level – I mean the wages of decent living.

Throughout industry the change from starvation wages and starvation employment to living wages and sustained employment can in large part be made by an industrial covenant to which employers shall subscribe.

The journal of the Boilermakers' Society quoted from the American Federation of Labor that organised labour congratulated the President on his bold and statesmanlike declaration. Labour was more than glad to have its underlying principle of decent living wages upheld by the President of the USA and backed by the Industrial Recovery Act.

GERMAN FASCISM

Developments in the United States pleased and encouraged British trade unionists but developments in Germany filled them with apprehension for the future. In Germany Hitler came to power with the support of big business and with a policy designed to crush resistance from the workers' movement. The journal of the Boilermakers' Society said that Hitler and his Nazis had made no secret of their intention to exterminate 'all Marxist organisations', among which the Nazis included the trade unions, the Socialist Party and the Communist Party. Threats had been sent to party and trade union branches that if they continued to hold meetings the lives of their members would be in danger. It was estimated that within weeks of taking office the Nazis had been responsible for the deaths of more than 100 socialists and communists.

The Society's journal also quoted from the words of the president of the German Federation of Trade Unions. He said

The danger is now approaching when the workers are likely to be deprived of their lawful status in the nation. The recent official speeches on the radio . . . leave hardly any doubt that the forces to which the state has been delivered will have this for their objective. This cannot be otherwise regarded than as a challenge to the organised working class. The responsibility lies upon me before the future to say that this threatened struggle, if it is carried out with measures of force, must do the greatest harm to the people of Germany. Considering the determination of the German working class to maintain their freedom it would mean a struggle of life and death. The tragic consequences of such a conflict should make our present rulers pause.

A joint declaration issued by the TUC, Labour Party and the Parliamentary Labour Party said that in Germany dictatorship had usurped the place of democracy, and elected representatives had been imprisoned by triumphant reaction. Masses of working class electors – divided between communism and social democracy – had fallen victims to fascism.

WITHIN THE SOCIETY

The need in 1932 for economies in the Society to meet the financial deficit led to requests for the convening of the General Council. The proposal that the General Council should be called together was approved on a ballot vote of the membership by 2,143 to 956. The report of the General Council, suggesting substantial alterations to the rules, was published in the late spring of 1933. The recommendations of the General Council to bring about economies in the Society included the following:

- that the membership of the Executive Council should be reduced from five to four members;
- that the office of Assistant General Secretary should be suspended or abolished;
- that the number of district delegates should be reduced;
- that changes should be introduced in methods of remunerating district auditors and district delegates; and
- that there should be reductions in benefit payments.

Each proposed amendment was submitted to a vote of the membership. Unfortunately the outcome of the ballot made it impossible for the Executive Council to implement the decisions. At the beginning of 1934 the General Council issued a statement pointing out that the voting results 'altered the balance between contributions and benefits to such an extent that it was impossible to put them into practice'. The Society was expected to meet new liabilities on a reduced income. New amendments were therefore drawn up and submitted, not individually but as a comprehensive scheme, to another ballot of the membership. These further amendments to the rules were defeated by 3,740 votes to 1,411.

In May 1934 the Executive Council reiterated that it was financially impossible for them to operate the first set of amended rules as approved by the membership. They now submitted two alternative schemes, both of which were designed to bring the income and expenditure of the Society into balance. This time one of the alternative sets of proposals was approved on a very low vote by 1,413 votes to 355.

In November 1934 the Executive Council issued a full explanation of the new rules. They were to come into operation from 1 January 1935. From that date first class members' contributions were to be 1s 6d per week and first class members who were unemployed were to pay 4d per week. First class members were to be regarded as out of benefit when their arrears of contribution amounted to 12s. Second and third class members were to have an out-of-benefit limit of 10s and 6s respectively. Members who were not employed because of sickness were to be required to pay contributions at the same rate as unemployed members.

The reduction in the number of full-time officials was intended to be secured by not filling vacancies after the death or retirement of existing officials. It was not proposed that any of the officials should be dismissed. Two of the district delegates, one on the Tyne and one at Hartlepool, died fairly shortly afterwards. The vacancies were not filled. One of the Executive Council members, R. W. Lindsay, also resigned because of ill health and so this made it possible to avoid having to make a choice between the sitting Executive Council members.

In his letter of resignation R. W. Lindsay recalled that he had joined the Society as a member of Hartlepool No. 1 branch in 1882 and immediately became an active trade unionist. After a period as branch secretary in Sunderland he was elected to the Executive Council in 1896. During his period as a member of the Executive Council he served for eleven years as chairman and for six years as treasurer.

In December 1933 the Executive Council published a statement appealing for financial assistance to R. W. Lindsay. They pointed out that he had been a member of the Society for fifty-one years and had been a member of the Executive Council for thirty-seven years. There was no provision within the rules of the Boilermakers' Society for the payment of a pension to full-time officials. Unfortunately the appeal was issued at a time of economic depression and unemployment and was badly supported. In June of the following year it was recorded that the collection for R. W. Lindsay taken through the branches amounted to only £23 14s 6d.

One of the four remaining members of the Executive Council was J. S. Holmes who months earlier had defeated a sitting member J. Bell. The vote was keenly contested. J. S. Holmes received 1,396 and J. Bell 1,029. Although a majority of the branches supported J. Bell the vote for J. S. Holmes was very heavy in the Liverpool and Birkenhead branches. An appeal was lodged against the result and, after investigation, the Executive Council declared J. S. Holmes to be the winner. James Bell had been a member of the Executive Council for eighteen years.

The decision to convene the General Council for the purpose of drawing up amendments to the rules led to considerable controversy within the Society. In May 1932 the Executive Council reported that a number of members had been issuing circulars to branches calling for the setting up of a 'Central Council'. A number of branches complained to the Executive Council about these circulars and called for action against the members responsible. The EC said they had decided to expel the members concerned but they were not able at that stage to name all who were involved.

More than a year later the Executive Council took action against the authors of yet another unofficial circular. It was distributed from Belfast. The circular criticised both the Executive Council and the General Council for alleged failings in the administration and general conduct of the Society's business. The Executive

Council replied to the circular and called upon the members responsible to withdraw it and to apologise.

The Belfast members, who included a number of branch officers, refused to withdraw their allegations and continued to meet unofficially. They took the unprecedented step of advising members not to pay their contributions to the Society. Early in 1934 their action was supported by a group of members in Birkenhead. A further unconstitutional circular was issued to the branches. The Executive Council said that this new circular, with its accusation of a 'flagrant waste of our funds', was a deliberate attempt to disrupt the Society. The unconstitutional circular also contained the allegation that 'all the operations of the Executive Council seem to be shaded in a mist of falsehood and double dealing'.

The Executive Council pointed out that all the accounts of the Society were audited by a chartered accountant and that any member had the right to make an investigation at the general office. The Executive Council invited all the Belfast secretaries to discuss their grievances but this invitation was ignored.

Events then went from bad to worse when some of the Belfast branches approached officers of the AEU with a view to a mass transfer of membership. This was reported to the AEU Executive Council who in turn reported it to the Boilermakers' Society. The Executive Council of the AEU rejected all the overtures from the Belfast branches.

Two members from Belfast then went to Birkenhead and canvassed members to withhold their subscriptions. An advertisement also appeared in Belfast inviting contributions to newly-created breakaway branches. The Executive Council decided, in the light of these activities, to expel more than forty active members who were held to be responsible for this disruption in the Belfast and Birkenhead areas.

Shortly afterwards a number of the members who were due for expulsion sent letters of apology and regret to the Executive Council. The EC responded by acknowledging that the branch officers concerned were not intentionally guilty of disruption but thought that they were merely protesting against the payment of quota arrears. In the circumstances the Executive Council decided to reinstate them into membership.

The Executive Council then decided to take legal action against some of the remaining former members who had signed the un-constitutional circular calling for the disruption of the Society but who had not subsequently expressed regret for their action. In July 1934 a statement was issued under the authority of the High Court indicating that a further number of former members who had signed the unconstitutional circular had indicated that they wished to be regarded as loyal members of the Boilermakers' Society and that they did not intend to make any attempt to induce any branch or district to secede from the Society. The Society was able to contain the revolt in the Birkenhead area but it was less successful in Belfast. A breakaway organisation was established.

At the beginning of 1933 John Hill was re-elected for another term as General Secretary. He had two opponents in the ballot. The result was as follows:

J. Hill	4,004
W. J. Johnston	1,227
J. K. Marshall	156

One of the nominees, J. Miller, was declared ineligible as a candidate. The Executive Council said that his application was 'of a pronounced communistic character', and that the Society had already decided that Communists could not hold office.

TRADE UNION MEMBERSHIP

In September 1933 the Society gave publicity to a statement by the chairman of ICI, Sir Harry McGowan, reassuring employees that ICI were not opposed to trade union membership. In a notice issued to all members of the management staff Sir Harry McGowan said

I have recently become aware that considerable uneasiness exists in the trade union movement as to the attitude of ICI in its various works towards trade union membership, notwithstanding the frequent public declarations that have been made from time to time.

I therefore wish to emphasise again that membership by any

workers of any recognised trade union is not in any way contrary to the labour policy of this Company.

Suggestions have been made to me that in some ICI works a trade unionist is prejudiced in a subtle way and is made to feel that it would be better for him if he were not in his union. It must be recognised and accepted by every member of the supervisory staff that a worker has a real freedom to belong to his union if he wishes to do so, without the slightest prejudice to his employment or prospects with the Company.

In the autumn of 1933 the Society launched a recruitment campaign in the Royal Dockyards. Traditionally, some groups of workers in the Royal Dockyards, who in private shipyards would have been organised by the Boilermakers' Society, either remained unorganised or were within the sphere of influence of other unions. Moreover many Dockyard employees were 'established' industrial civil servants with security of employment and pension rights. To assist its recruitment campaign the Society created a special class of membership for men employed on ship construction in Royal Dockyards. The rate of contribution was 6d per week. They were not entitled to any of the provident benefits of the Society. This special arrangement was designed to encourage Royal Dockyard employees to join the Society. It was felt that men employed in Royal Dockyards were not attracted by provident benefits which were unsuited to their circumstances.

Chapter 16

A Slow Recovery

During 1934 there was a slow but steady improvement in trade. Nevertheless, there was a continued loss of membership. Membership declined by 530 to reduce the total figure to less than 50,000, of whom no fewer than 5,163 were retired. Just over 2,000 of this number were drawing superannuation benefit from the Society. The number of unemployed members at the end of 1934 was nearly 19,000 and another 700 members were drawing sickness benefit.

In 1935 trade continued to improve, and the decline in membership was almost halted. The loss on the year was 150. The number of unemployed members declined to about 14,000.

The improvement in trade enabled the Society to add to its financial reserves. In 1934 there was a net surplus on the year of just over £15,000 and in 1935 the net surplus was nearly £20,000. These were the best financial figures since 1920. Despite the improvement in trade approximately 40 per cent of all registered shipbuilding and shiprepairing workers were still unemployed at the end of 1935.

The slow improvement in shipbuilding was helped by a scrap and rebuild scheme introduced by the Government in 1934. Financial assistance was granted to British owners to enable them to build new tonnage or to modernise existing tonnage on condition that they scrapped not less than three times as much United Kingdom tonnage of the same general type. The scheme applied to United Kingdom tramp ships and general cargo liners. There were some exceptions. Financial assistance was given in the form of loans advanced or guaranteed by the Treasury. Shipowners were required to give assurances not to sell to foreign purchasers ships which had received assistance.

HOURS AND OVERTIME

With the revival in trade a new impetus was given to claims for a shorter working week and the strict control of overtime. The Society's annual report for 1934 said that the progressive introduction of new machinery during the year had increased productivity and thus further reduced the number of members employed per unit of work produced. The Society, said the annual report, had been pressing for the reduction of normal working hours and the abolition of all overtime except in cases where no alternative could possibly be arranged. The fight for a shorter working week, it urged, must continue. Whatever work was available would then be spread amongst unemployed members. By this method, said the annual report, long hours and unnecessary overtime simultaneous with mass unemployment would become a thing of the past.

The TUC also made representations to the Minister of Labour for a forty-hour week and the control of overtime. John Hill was one of the representatives of the TUC General Council who saw the Minister of Labour. They urged the Minister to institute a survey to find out how much overtime was worked in British industry. They also asked for the introduction of a Bill to reduce hours of labour and to limit overtime. John Hill reported that the Minister of Labour was unhelpful. The unions also sought to build up pressure in favour of a forty-hour week within the International Labour Organisation, the specialised agency of the League of Nations dealing with labour matters and representing governments, employers and trade unions throughout the world. The unions were not successful. John Hill reported that the strongest opponents of any international move towards a forty-hour week were the British Government and the British employers.

Claims for a forty-hour week were submitted both to the Engineering Employers' Federation and the Shipbuilding Employers' Federation in 1934. Both claims were rejected. Nevertheless the campaign continued. The 1934 TUC carried unanimously a resolution reaffirming support for the introduction of a shorter working week as a necessary means of eliminating unemployment. The resolution also protested against the attitude of the British Government in opposing at the ILO an international convention to limit the

244

hours of employment. The TUC urged all affiliated unions to continue their efforts towards securing a restriction of overtime and the introduction of a forty-hour working week without loss of pay. At the 1935 TUC the Boilermakers' Society submitted a resolution on the forty-hour week. This was composited with other motions and was carried.

WAGES

Efforts to increase wages were more successful than the campaign to reduce the working week. The first major step forward was made on the railways towards the end of September 1934. An agreement was reached that the reduction in pay of $4\frac{1}{6}$ per cent, which had been imposed in 1931 upon railwaymen and railway shopmen, including members of the Boilermakers' Society, should be replaced by a new arrangement. As from 1 October the deduction was to be reduced to $3\frac{1}{3}$ per cent and from 1 January 1935 to $2\frac{1}{2}$ per cent. The deductions were not to operate so as to reduce the earnings of any adult male employee below 40s per week.

In commenting on this improvement John Hill said that the outcome was disappointing. The reduction had first been imposed on the workers with the intention that it was to continue for one year only. In fact it had continued for three and a half years. John Hill accepted that the Boilermakers' Society was itself partly to blame for the lengthy negotiations. The Society has refused to be party to the joint negotiating machinery. He recalled that the Society's application for the complete ending of the deduction had been made more than six months earlier. He urged that in future it would be to the advantage of the Society to be associated with other unions in negotiations on general questions of wages, hours and conditions of employment.

In commenting on the outcome of the railway negotiations John Hill remarked on the 'extraordinary percentage of gross revenue which goes to capital in the form of interest and dividend'. He pointed out that in the previous year the gross receipts of the four big railway companies amounted to a total of just over £165 million. Out of this sum over £12¼ million had been paid in interest on loans and debentures, nearly £16 million as dividends on preference stock and over £2 million on dividends on ordinary stock. Thus more than £30 million was paid in interest and dividends in the course of one year. This was equal to 18½ per cent on the gross turnover of the four companies. He described the situation as a scandal and said it was one of the reasons why the nation should own the railways. Only in this way could there be an end to the exploitation of passengers and of the men employed on the railways.

Towards the end of 1934 the engineering unions decided to submit a claim for wage increases to the Engineering Employers' Federation. The claim was for 2d per hour, an equivalent increase in piece-rates and the restoration of the overtime and nightshift rates to the level existing before they were reduced in 1931. The discussions continued during the early part of 1935 and finally, at a joint conference held on 13 March, it was decided to appoint a small joint committee to complete negotiations. The employers indicated that they were prepared to consider granting an increase. In April 1935 recommended terms of agreement were reached. Time workers and piece-workers employed in federated engineering firms were to receive an additional 1s a week national bonus from Monday 13 May and a further 1s per week national bonus from Monday 15 July.

This recommendation was submitted to a joint conference of all the unions on 11 April. The boilermakers' delegates drew attention to the practice of the Society of submitting such questions to a ballot vote of the membership. The conference decided, however, that such a ballot was unnecessary. The delegates agreed to advise the Engineering Employers' Federation of their acceptance of the offer. In the circumstances the Executive Council of the Boilermakers' Society also accepted the offer.

In the shipbuilding industry the unions were less successful. Negotiations took place throughout 1935 but the employers adhered to their view that the industry was unable to afford an increase. The unions pointed out that since 1921 the employers had introduced successive reductions, the effect of which was to take from the workers the 32s 6d bonus received at the end of the war. They also took away a special 12½ per cent given to piece-workers and 7½ per cent to time workers, and eliminated other payments which were paid in various branches of the trade. Both sides in the negotiations referred to the steep decline in the industry. In 1921 the industry employed about 345,000 men whereas in 1935 it had no more than about 150,000. The unions referred to complaints which had been made from time to time by employers about the shortage of skilled men, and they

246

pointed to the wage increases which had been given in a number of other industries in 1935.

At a conference held late in December 1935 the Shipbuilding Employers' Federation acknowledged that there had been an increase in the number of orders received by the industry but they said that the orders had been taken without any increase in price. It would be necessary to work off these orders before considering a wage increase. They undertook to meet the unions again in 1936. The union representatives decided to refer the question to a meeting of Executive Council representatives of all unions to be held in January 1936. Thus by the end of 1935 the shipbuilding unions had still not secured a wage increase.

The negotiations for a national increase in pay in shipbuilding and ship repair, which began in 1935, followed a very bitterly fought dispute among London ship repair workers in the summer of 1934. It will be recalled that there had been a long dispute lasting approximately seventeen weeks in 1931 in London shiprepairing. Although the employers were not able to secure their full demands the workers had to resume work with a substantial pay reduction. In the summer of 1934 the River Thames Ship Repairers' Association proposed a further reduction in pay amounting in some cases to up to 10s 6d per week on day rates. It was proposed also that piece-work rates should be reduced.

The London District Committee of the Society conducted the dispute with great energy. Circulars were sent to every trade union in Britain. The district committee reported that except for about four members all the workers affected had responded to the call of the Society to resist the employers' demands. The outcome of the dispute was that the employers finally withdrew their drastic proposals. The London District Committee reported that never in the history of the port had there been a strike which left so much bitterness against the employers. The strike lasted for seven weeks.

There was also a major dispute on the Mersey. The origin of this dispute went back to April 1933 when revised arrangements affecting rates of pay for overtime and nightshift working were imposed on the members of the Boilermakers' Society. This revision also provided for the abolition of certain 'distance allowances' (i.e. walking time) together with various other conditions and was regarded by the Mersey District Committee as extremely detrimental to the interests of boilermakers. The revision of the agreement was accepted by all other trades but not by the Boilermakers' Society. The decision to reject the arrangements was taken at a mass meeting of boilermakers which had been preceded by resolutions from many Merseyside branches. Following the imposition of the new terms on the boiler-makers the district committee decided to place an embargo on all overtime and nightshift working. For some sixteen months this embargo was observed throughout the district.

During this period the employers made various attempts either to persuade or, according to the district committee, to intimidate members of the Boilermakers' Society into working overtime. These efforts were not successful. The employers then applied to the Labour Exchange for men for nightshift working, thereby, according to the district committee, 'turning the Labour Exchange into a blackleg institution for the purpose of forcing men to accept work which is in dispute'. The men refused to accept the work which had been declared 'black' by the district committee, with the result that several members of the Society were summoned before a court of referees as a test case for unemployment benefit. A decision was given against the members of the Society and the men concerned were disqualified from benefit.

The district committee said that they had no intention of capitulat-ing, despite these setbacks, though they made several attempts to negotiate a better agreement with the employers. According to the district committee they had been handicapped by the attitude of the full-time officials of some of the other unions, who had urged the employers not to grant to the boilermakers better terms than those embodied in the agreement with other unions.

The employers, frustrated in their failure to resolve the issue loc-ally, took the matter up with the Executive Council of the Boiler-makers' Society, and threatened a national lockout unless the issue was resolved. The Executive Council said they were not prepared to issue an instruction to the Mersey members to lift their embargo unless there was an improvement in the terms of the agreement accepted by the other unions. Further negotiations were held and a significant improvement was secured.

A new rate of pay of 19s 8½d per night was established. This, according to the Executive Council, was only 3¾d a night less than the original rate of pay existing before the agreement negotiated by the other unions. Many of the members in the Mersey district were, nevertheless, very reluctant to accept these terms. They could see no justification for any worsening of conditions.

Mass meetings of members were called but the Executive Council said that these meetings were unconstitutional because they were being convened without the authority of the Executive Council. Finally in January 1935 the Executive Council issued an instruction to the members in the Mersey district to work any necessary overtime 'when it is found to be the only practical method of completing the job'. Where there was doubt about the need for overtime the members were instructed to get in touch with the district delegate. The Executive Council said that the new agreement which they had negotiated was, in any case, intended only as a temporary arrangement until the whole of the terms of the overtime and nightshift agreement could be revised.

UNEMPLOYMENT – PROTESTS

In October 1933 the Government introduced a new Unemployment Bill. The Bill was in two parts. The first part dealt with the arrangements for the payment of benefit and provided for the introduction of compulsory instruction and training schemes. The second part dealt with the constitution and functions of an Unemployment Assistance Board. The main functions of the Board were to be the administration of the means test and the training and 'reconditioning' of the unemployed.

The trade union movement was strongly critical of the Bill. A manifesto was issued by the National Joint Council, representing the TUC, the Labour Party and the Parliamentary Labour Party, which said that the Bill failed to make unemployment insurance a really national scheme, and failed also to restore the cuts in unemployment benefit imposed two years earlier. In particular, the manifesto attacked the Unemployment Assistance Board which would be required to maintain the means test. Benefit would no longer be determined by public representatives but would be settled by officers of the Unemployment Assistance Board. The trade union movement conducted a campaign against the Bill and the TUC issued leaflets, speakers' notes and articles pointing out the failings of the new measure. Conferences and meetings were organised in many cities and towns. Resolutions strongly protesting against the provisions of the Bill were passed at trade union meetings in all parts of Britain. In February 1934 the National Unemployed Workers' Movement, which was not officially recognised by the TUC but acted as a left-wing independent organisation, organised a national hunger march. The marchers were greeted in Hyde Park, London, by a large demonstration consisting predominantly of individual trade unionists and supporters of the labour movement.

In the summer of 1934 the standard benefit rates for unemployment were restored to their former level, namely 17s for a single man, 26s for a married couple and 2s for each child. There were, however, a large number of unemployed workers who were on 'transitional payments' determined after a means test by a public assistance committee. These were men and women who had exhausted their normal benefit rights. Under the terms of the Unemployment Act the responsibility for these means-tested payments passed to the Unemployment Assistance Board. The new regulations began to operate early in 1935. It was found that in many areas the allowances made under the new arrangements were less than they had been under the previous scheme. The result was that there were many further meetings and demonstrations of protest. They were on an even wider and more extensive scale than before. The protests were effective and the Government retreated. New standstill arrangements were introduced which brought about some improvement but there was still no abandonment of the means test.

The Boilermakers' Society took an active part in the campaign of protest against the new measures on unemployment. A letter protesting against the provisions of the Unemployment Bill was sent to all Members of Parliament. Branches were also kept informed of developments and many of them sent resolutions to their respective MPs. John Hill said that the Unemployment Bill attacked not only the rights of the unemployed but undermined the wages and conditions of every employed worker. The unions should not allow the unemployed to be segregated from their fellow workers. He pointed out that the problem of unemployment was not insoluble. He went on: 'Russia, with the lowest development of any European country, is now proving that employment and wages can be found for a population of 165 million people.'

The London District Committee of the Society, as always in the forefront of any struggle, requested all members, especially those in receipt of transitional payments under the means test, to attend branch meetings and to press for changes. The District Committee said that the main object of the Unemployment Bill was to divide the workers and starve those who could not help themselves.

There was a contingent from the Boilermakers' Society in the mass demonstration in Hyde Park in February 1934 to meet the hunger marchers from the provinces. The London District Committee said that every credit should be given to those responsible for organising the hunger march and the accompanying demonstration. This was a reference to the National Unemployed Workers' Movement. Never before, it was claimed, had there been a more orderly demonstration. The report of the London District Committee went on:

> From all parts of the country came the hunger marchers, some haggard, some leg-weary, but full of enthusiasm. It was reminiscent of the Great War period but these stalwarts of the working class were not marching forward to destroy mankind as during the Great War, but to save their children and those unborn from the tortures of capitalism. This great working class demonstration was supported by every denomination of the working class movement; nobody asked of what party one belonged to and nobody cared. 'We are the working class' was the slogan, and it is about time we all realised this instead of slamming one another at every opportunity.

In the February 1935 issue of the monthly journal there was a full explanation of the provisions of the Unemployment Act 1934. It was pointed out that the unemployed worker who was not drawing unemployment insurance benefit as of right would be affected by the new regulations. Not less than one million unemployed workers, together with their dependants, would thus come under the new unemployment relief regulations framed by the Unemployment Assistance Board. These regulations provided for a means tested benefit. The means test required that an assessment should be made of household income so that the earnings of other members of the household were taken into account in assessing the benefit of any unemployed member of the household.

The revolt against the means test benefit regulations introduced

251

in 1935 was greeted enthusiastically by John Hill. He said that the published scales of benefit had aroused indignation in the hearts of every decent citizen. Public opinion, he claimed, was so hostile that the Government beat a humiliating retreat and temporarily increased benefits in all cases where they had been reduced.

For the 1935 Congress of the TUC the Boilermakers' Society submitted a motion urging that unemployment benefit should not be refused to any worker because of his participation in a trade dispute 'unless such worker is a direct disputant'. The motion also demanded the restoration of the provision in the 1924 Unemployment Insurance Act under which a worker did not lose benefit because of a stoppage of work if it could be shown that the stoppage was due to an employer contravening an agreement. This motion was composited with other motions and seconded at the Congress by John Hill on behalf of the Society.

In his speech John Hill spoke of the change of the provisions in the law as a result of legislation introduced by the Conservative Government. He explained that many disputes were forced upon workers by employers reducing wages and conditions in violation of long-standing agreements and customs. If the men stopped work to maintain their agreed rates there was no unemployment benefit for them. This, he said, was a powerful lever in the hands of employers to coerce men into acceptance of reduced wages and the scrapping of agreements honourably observed by the men. The motion was carried.

THE ADVANCE OF FASCISM

The coming to power of Hitler in Germany in the spring of 1933 was the most significant indication of the advance of fascism in the inter-war years. Big business supported fascism because it saw the strength of the working class movement and the civil liberties enjoyed by the workers as a major obstacle to the preservation of capitalism and the realisation of the objectives of the top financiers and industrialists. The crisis of the capitalist system in the early 1930s, with millions of unemployed workers, meant that in some countries the ruling circles could not continue to govern in the old way. As they saw it, the working class movement, including the trade unions and the political parties of the working class, had to be crushed, and dictatorship and the rule of terror against working class activists introduced. The minds of the people had to be diverted from their immediate economic problems of unemployment and pay towards racial hatred and a false patriotism designed to cover aggressive aims abroad.

John Hill gave a forthright warning of the danger of fascism in April 1934. In the monthly report of the Society he said:

From a trade unionist's point of view the world is in a dangerous state. Trade unionism, as we know it, had been wiped out of Germany, Italy and Austria. Trade union leaders who escaped the gallows suffered indescribable tortures. Others have been hounded into concentration camps and given opportunity to end their tortures by suicide. We are apt to look upon Hitler, Dolphus or Mussolini as prime agents in these brutalities, but they are only the instruments of capitalism which supplied arms and uniform and other support to maintain and equip illegal armies to hound to death law abiding trade unionists.

These are not the only countries where trade unionism is meeting similar attacks. Capitalism knows no country and no laws. Capitalism has neither a soul to be saved nor a body to be kicked.

We have evidence of attempts to establish a fascist dictatorship in this country. The trade unions of Great Britain are the only effective organisation to defend and enlarge democratic rights and liberties.

Throughout 1933 preparations were being made in Austria to crush the trade union and labour movement. In February 1934 armed attacks were made upon the social democrats, and orders were given in a number of towns to search workers' dwellings. In Vienna the workers conducted an heroic defence at the flats of the Karl Marx housing estate. Municipal dwellings were bombarded and trade unionists and socialists were shot. The struggle lasted for four days and ended with the defeat of the labour movement. The National Council of Labour in Britain issued a manifesto stating that Austria was in the grip of civil war and that the labour movement was resisting the attack of a ruthless dictatorship.

John Hill spoke of the murderous attack on trade unionists in Austria. He said that Vienna was one of the best governed cities in the world as far as civic amenities for the workers were concerned. It was governed by a majority of trade union and labour representatives. John Hill went on 'it was the success of the workers' government in Vienna which put fear into the minds of the reactionaries who exist in all countries and believe in force as the only law'. The new dictatorship, he explained, though described as fascism was, in reality, a new form of capitalism. Capitalism under democracy was coming to an end. He urged the members of the Boilermakers' Society to be aware of what was happening.

At the 1934 Congress of the TUC the delegates carried a resolution expressing unyielding opposition to fascism. The resolution affirmed profound abhorrence of the suppression of freedom and democracy, the nationalist and militarist tendencies, the racial intolerance, and the degradation of the status of women that were the characteristics of fascism. It drew the attention of workers everywhere to the fact that wherever fascism had been instituted trade unionism, co-operation and social democracy had been ruthlessly repressed and the standard of life of the workers had been degraded. Religious liberties and political freedom had been abolished and the methods of violence and savagery had dominated political and social life. The Boilermakers' Society printed the terms of this resolution in full in the monthly journal.

There was much discussion in the trade union and labour movement about how best to resist fascism. In international affairs it was increasingly recognised that fascism and its aggression could be halted only through collective security. This meant, above all, an alliance between Britain and France, Czechoslovakia and the USSR. Unfortunately there were many in the ruling circles of the democratic capitalist powers, including Britain and France, who did not favour effective collective security. Instead they had some sympathy with fascism as a political form of resistance to the strength of the workers' movement. In addition they considered that it might be possible to divert the aggressive ambitions of German fascism against the USSR. In this way they considered that they would not only avoid conflict for themselves, but would help to isolate and in the ultimate posssibly destroy the USSR.

John Hill warned the membership of Hitler's ambition. He said that Hitler said 'some very nice things to Britain' because he wanted Britain to stand neutral while he conducted a war of expansion against Russia. John Hill argued that the League of Nations was the only authority big enough to stop Hitler from waging a war against Russia.

PEACE BALLOT

In 1934 the League of Nations Union, a voluntary organisation in Britain which sought to support the existence of the League and the principles of collective security, decided to organise a ballot among the British people on the immediate issues affecting the preservation of peace. The ballot paper put five questions:

1 Should Great Britain remain a member of the League of Nations?
2 Are you in favour of an all round reduction of armaments by international agreement?
3 Are you in favour of the all round abolition of national military and naval aircraft by international agreement?
4 Should the manufacture and sale of armaments for private profit be prohibited by international agreement?
5 Do you consider that if a nation insists on attacking another the other nations should combine to compel it to stop by (a) economic and non-military measures, (b) if necessary, military measures?

Many organisations, including the Labour Party and the Trades Union Congress, agreed to sponsor the projected ballot. The refusal of the Conservative Party to join in the sponsorship was indicative of its attitude towards collective security.

The Boilermakers' Society welcomed the ballot and pointed out that the TUC was mobilising millions of trade unionists to participate and to help in the canvassing for completed ballot forms. The Society urged members to help in their own localities.

The ballot was an outstanding success. Over 11½ million votes were recorded. In some areas the percentage of the population who participated in the ballot was higher than the percentage recorded votes in the preceding General Election. The final results were published in June 1935. They showed an overwhelmingly affirmative vote in response to all five questions. The vote for Britain remaining a member of the League of Nations was over 11 million with only 356,000 against. The vote for the prohibition of the private manufacture of armaments was 10,417,000 in favour and 775,000 against. The vote in favour of economic sanctions against an aggressor was 10,027,000 with 635,000 against. The vote in favour of military measures, if necessary, against an aggressor was 6,784,000 with 2,351,000 against. The voting figures revealed that British public opinion was overwhelmingly in favour of collective security. They had shown awareness of the danger of fascism.

ABYSSINIA

The year 1935 brought a new example of fascist aggression and yet a further example of the failure of a number of nations, particularly Britain, to support collective security. Mussolini, the fascist leader in Italy, decided to wage a war of aggression against Abyssinia. The British and French governments equivocated. Their attitude, far from deterring Mussolini, served only to encourage him. The TUC, on the other hand, came out firmly in support of economic sanctions against the aggressor. The policy was strongly supported by the Boilermakers' Society.

In speaking on the resolution at the TUC pledging collective security against Italian aggression the General Secretary of the TUC, Sir Walter Citrine, underlined that aggression would not stop unless it was halted. He pointed out that Hitler was determined to plan an attack upon Russia:

Everybody who can read foreign policy knows that Russia's foreign policy is now based on the conviction that they will be attacked by Germany. I am going to put those delegates who so often declared themselves and pledged themselves to Soviet Russia to the touchstone of faith. Now is the time to defend Soviet Russia by defending Abyssinia.

Mussolini did not accept any proposal for conciliation from the League of Nations. He was well aware of the reluctance of many in the ruling circles in the West to take effective action against fascist

256

aggression. Economic sanctions were not effectively applied. Italian aggression succeeded and Abyssinia was defeated.

UNITED FRONT

In 1934 moves were made in a number of countries to bring about co-operation between socialist and communist parties to meet the menace of fascism and to help to arouse public opinion in favour of collective security against further aggression. In France an agreement on united action was reached by the socialist and communist parties.

In Britain the approach of the Communist Party for a 'united front' met with a hostile reception from the TUC and the Labour Party. In October 1934 a circular was sent to affiliated unions and to trades councils regarding what was described as the presence of disruptive elements within trades councils. The General Council said that it was determined that obstacles created by these disruptive elements should not be allowed to stand in the way of trades councils and loyal members rendering essential service to the trade union movement. Particular reference was made to the question of the 'united front'. In their letter to unions the General Council included the following paragraph:

> I have to ask that your Executive Committee will give consideration to the possibility of drawing up regulations or amending the rules of your organisation so as to empower them to reject nominations of members of disruptive bodies for any official position within your organisation, and the General Council hope that your committee assists them to the utmost of their ability in furthering the official policy of the movement as laid down by Congress from time to time.

The letter to trades councils said that the General Council had ruled that any trades council which admitted delegates who were associated with Communist or fascist organisations or their ancillary bodies should be removed from the list of trades councils recognised by Congress. Model rules for trades councils were revised and reissued which provided that councils should refuse to accept credentials from an affiliated branch if the delegate was a member of the Communist or Fascist parties or any subsidiary organisation of these parties or a member of an organisation proscribed by the General Council. The model rules said further that trades councils should not co-operate with or subscribe to the funds of the Communist or Fascist parties or any of their subsidiary organisations or of any industrial organisation proscribed by the General Council.

The reports of the boilermakers' delegation to the 1934 TUC and the 1935 TUC made no reference to the question of the 'united front', nor to the circulars issued by the General Council of the TUC on Communists within the trade union movement, nor on the debates which took place on these subjects. At the 1935 Congress there was a major debate on the General Council's circulars. The 'reference back' of the appropriate paragraph of the General Council's report was moved by the miners and supported by the AEU, the railwaymen and the furniture workers among others. The General Council were supported by the two general workers' unions and by the steel workers. The reference back was defeated by 1,869,000 votes to 1,427,000 votes.

In May 1935 the monthly journal of the Society published a statement from the Scottish TUC rejecting the united front. It said that the trade union, Labour and Co-operative movements represented a real and the only possible united front against injustice and oppression. The statement explained that in the view of the Scottish TUC the Communist Party did not accept the authority of the representative conferences within the trade union movement. It said that the Communist Party claimed the right to impose policies and tactics upon members and sections of unions in defiance of their national decisions. Its members were expected to adhere to a discipline not determined by the unions. Communist activities must therefore, it asserted, 'inevitably result in the undermining of the belief that trade unionists have in their organisations, in the weakening of the unions in their struggle against capitalism and . . . in making it more and more difficult to attract unorganised workers towards unions.' The so-called united front, it said, was sought for the purpose of providing an official platform for Communist speakers to discredit the official policy of the trade union and labour movement. This was an unreal united front which could only create confusion among the workers.

At the 1935 TUC there was a debate on a proposal for a united front against war and fascism and on a proposal from the Red

International of Labour Unions to the International Federation of Trade Unions suggesting an international conference to promote trade union unity. The British TUC was affiliated to the IFTU. The General Council reported that the IFTU had decided that no good purpose would be served by commencing discussions on the lines suggested by the RILU. In the view of the IFTU the desire for international unity expressed by the Red International of Labour Unions was devoid of any sincerity of purpose. The RILU, they said, consisted of unions which followed the policy of the Communist Party. Their changes in policy were the result not of decisions by the membership but of decisions by the Communist International.

A motion in favour of a united front was moved at the 1935 TUC by the furnishing trades and seconded by the building trade workers. The sponsors said that there were three main reasons why a united front should be established. The first was to establish a common policy of the working-class movement to preserve peace; the second was to obtain unity in the non-fascist countries against the advance of fascism; and the third was to press forward unitedly in all countries for improved conditions. The spokesman for the mineworkers pointed to the moves towards unity in France and urged that immediate steps should be taken to unite the working-class movement. Unity was needed to halt fascism, to avert war and to conduct the struggle against unemployment.

In his reply to the debate the General Secretary of the TUC, Sir Walter Citrine, said that no proof had been adduced that unity on the international plane would stop the advent of fascism. In his view if the Labour movement allied itself with groups and sects attached to the Communist Party the advance of fascism would not be retarded. On the contrary, such an attachment would tend to facilitate the advance of fascism. Sir Walter Citrine said that in any discussions with the Red International of Labour Unions it should be borne in mind that they took their instructions from the Communist Party in Russia. The policy of the General Council was upheld by the Congress.

There was no other reference to these developments in the journal of the Boilermakers' Society during 1934 and 1935. The policy of the Executive Council was nevertheless clear. Members who were Communists or associated with the Communist Party were regarded as ineligible to hold office or to act in any way as representatives of the

Society. This, in the view of the Executive Council, had been decided some years earlier by ballot vote of the membership.

During this period the journal of the Boilermakers' Society published a number of reports favourable to the Soviet Union. The General Secretary welcomed the USSR's constant efforts to promote collective security for resistance to fascist aggression. In February 1935 an article was published in the boilermakers' journal on the second five-year plan of the USSR. It was written by Herbert Tracey who was in charge of the publicity department of the TUC. The article was entitled 'From capitalist chaos to socialist order'. It spoke of the stupendous effort which had been put forth to energise, modernise and transform the national economy. The capitalist world in contrast, said the review, was sinking into chaotic ruin, torn asunder by its own monstrous self-contradiction. The review ended with the words 'Trade unionists and socialists should read this book and judge for themselves what the creative energies of mankind are capable of when the paralysing inhibitions of capitalism are thrown aside.'

CENTENARY

The year 1934 marked the centenary anniversary of the formation of the Boilermakers' Society. It coincided with the celebration by the British trade union movement of the hundredth anniversary of the Tolpuddle Martyrs, the Dorset labourers who were convicted and transported to Australia because they had joined a trade union in the village of Tolpuddle. The members of the Boilermakers' Society were asked by ballot whether they favoured national or district celebrations. They voted in favour of both propositions. They also voted in favour of a national celebration in Newcastle and a national celebration in Manchester. The majority for Manchester was, however, substantially higher than for Newcastle. The centenary celebration took the form of a march, a formal meal and a meeting in Manchester. Thousands of members participated in the march and about 8,000 sat down to the meal. The main speakers at the meeting were the General Secretary, John Hill, the chairman of the Executive Council, Mark Hodgson, and David Williams, MP.

Celebration events were also held in many other areas. The

branches in Hampshire and Dorset celebrated the anniversary with a day's outing to Tolpuddle. In the Humber district more than 300 members and their wives assembled in the banqueting chamber of the Hull Guildhall. More than eighty superannuated members from Hull and Beverley were special guests at the celebration. On the Clyde a special outing was arranged to Troon. Music was provided by pipe and brass bands.

ORGANISATIONAL CHANGES

One of the economy measures taken in 1934 was the reduction in the panel of parliamentary candidates from five to three. On a low vote this was confirmed in a ballot by 722 to 210. In a subsequent election for the panel M. H. Connolly and T. Irwin were successful, together with David Williams, MP.

In the summer of 1934 there was a sharp exchange between the Executive Council and the chairman of the General Council of the Society regarding proposals to retain certain full-time official positions in the Society. In 1933 the General Council had proposed, among a wide range of economy measures, that the number of permanent officers should be reduced, including a reduction from five to four in the membership of the Executive Council, the elimination of the post of Assistant General Secretary and a reduction in the number of district delegates.

Some of the other proposals of the General Council affecting subscriptions and benefits were not endorsed by the membership. The Executive Council then decided to submit further proposals to the membership, among which was the suggestion that some of the full-time officers should be retained. Some of the members of the General Council felt that the Executive Council were usurping their function. The Executive Council pointed out, however, that their own membership had been reduced in accordance with the proposals submitted by the General Council, and the number of district delegates had been reduced by two. The Executive Council said that any further reductions would prevent the Society from securing the full benefit of the improvement in trade which was now being recorded.

Early in 1935 the Executive Council issued a strong statement calling for no further reduction in the number of full-time officials and, in effect, for the reversal of the earlier decision to eliminate the post of Assistant General Secretary. The Executive Council pointed out that with the reduction of the Executive Council from five to four it was now difficult to carry on the work of the general office without an Assistant General Secretary. Any further reductions, they said, would result in delay in dealing with problems raised by the branches. This would be detrimental to the interests of the members. They also opposed any further reduction in the number of district delegates which, they said, would deprive the membership of essential services. The Executive Council pointed out that there had been a welcome change in trade and in their view it was now necessary to retain the post of Assistant General Secretary and to retain the existing number of district delegates.

This statement by the Executive Council aroused opposition from the chairman and a number of the members of the General Council. The General Council members published a letter saying that when six additional delegates were appointed in 1919 the membership was over 100,000. Membership in 1935 was only just over half that number. There was, therefore, a strong case to reduce the number of district delegates. The General Council members felt that the attitude of the Executive Council constituted a challenge not only to the General Council but also to the membership. The General Council members said that the Executive Council had acted in violation of the rules of the Society.

This sharp controversy came to an uncertain end when as a result of a ballot of the membership in May 1935 the post of Assistant General Secretary was retained by 2,525 votes to 2,161. There was a slightly larger majority for the retention of the existing number of district delegates. The question of the respective powers of the General Council and the Executive Council had not, however, been resolved.

One other indication of the change in the financial circumstances of the Society and of the attitude of the membership towards the economies introduced during the depression was the decision taken in autumn 1935 to increase the wages of the full-time officials. By 3,280 votes to 1,841 the members on a ballot vote agreed to restore the 10 per cent reduction which had been introduced in March 1932. In a statement published before the ballot was taken the Executive Council of the Society said that during the previous two years the finances of the Society had been slowly but steadily improving. The Society, it was pointed out, had actively engaged in negotiations for wage increases for many members. Not only had the salaries of the full-time officials been reduced in 1932 but in addition, there had been a reduction in the number of officials. The salaries of the full-time officials, it was argued, were altogether inadequate.

APPRENTICES

The revival in trade led to renewed interest in the organisation of apprentices. In the autumn of 1935 a special campaign was opened to recruit apprentices into membership of the Society. They were eligible for registration in the Society on a payment of 2s. In addition there was an optional payment of 3d per week which made an apprentice eligible for sickness, accident and death benefits and legal assistance.

In initiating this new campaign the Executive Council recalled that a similar effort had been made in 1912 and that it had been successful. Before that date the Society held agreements both with the Shipbuilding Employers' Federation and the Engineering Employers' Federation on apprenticeship. Both agreements lapsed, partly because of a decline in trade, partly because the employers, and the shipbuilding employers in particular, wanted to introduce arrangements to permit apprentices to end and begin their apprenticeship up to the age of 25 years, but above all because of the fall in the number of apprentices in the shipbuilding industry.

During the slump very few apprentices entered the boilermaking trades in shipbuilding and the organisation of apprentices inside the Society declined. Previously the Society had not only recruited apprentices into the adult branches but had also opened apprentice branches which were officered and managed by the apprentices themselves. One adult member was assigned to each apprentice branch to initiate the apprentices into the rules and methods of the Society. At the beginning of 1912 the Society had no more than seventy apprentice members. By 1920 apprentice branches existed in many parts of England, Ireland and Scotland and the total apprentice membership was nearly 15,000. By 1934 it had declined to 1,300.

In the new campaign it was left to the discretion of branch and district officers to consider the advisability of opening new branches for apprentices. The Executive Council recalled that in the previous campaign the apprentice branches were 'on the whole successful in keeping apprentices interested in the Society'. The most successful area for the new campaign proved to be the Tees district. Apprentice branches existed in Darlington, Hartlepool, Middlesbrough, Stockton and Thornaby.

RESIGNATION OF JOHN HILL

In 1935 John Hill indicated that he wished to resign as General Secretary at the end of his current term of office. He said he was retiring because for the previous two or three years the responsibilities of the job had affected his health and strength to such an extent that he could not continue to maintain the exacting standard of service required of the chief official of the Society.

In recalling his long period of service to the Society John Hill said that the membership had passed through the depths of depression. In thousands of homes there had been misery, hopelessness and broken hearts, all because skilled men were denied the opportunity to work and to earn wages. In those dark days, said John Hill, no organisation could have done more than the Boilermakers' Society to relieve brothers in need. Over £1 million was spent in benefits and grants and all other expenses were reduced. In the final paragraph of his letter of resignation John Hill said that he had been offered honours by past and present governments but his joy had been to serve the membership.

In one of his final contributions in the monthly report of the Society John Hill attacked the devastation in the shipbuilding industry caused by National Shipbuilders Security Ltd. He said that NSS was closing shipyards and laying them waste for forty years ahead. NSS Ltd, he said, was destroying the industry in which honest workers had invested their lives.

There were many tributes to the service of John Hill to the Boilermakers' Society. The Executive Council said that he had rendered yeoman service and that he had never shirked duty. He had always done his best to promote the interests of the Society and its members.

He presented and defended the claims of the Society with vigour and ability.

A warm tribute to John Hill was also paid by the former General Secretary, D. C. Cummings. For thirty-five and a half years, he said, John Hill had worked as a full-time official of the Society. He was a good trade unionist and a sound socialist. He was aware that under capitalism great depressions were inevitable. But he always encouraged others and renewed their faith in trade unionism.

Chapter 17

Trade Revival and the Anti-fascist Struggle

Ten members contested the election for General Secretary following the retirement of John Hill. Mark Hodgson, the chairman of the Executive Council, started as strong favourite. The main competitor was Ted Hill, the London district delegate. The committee sponsoring Mark Hodgson drew attention to his long experience in the Society, the respect in which he was held as chairman of the Executive Council and his strong interest in education. The Committee said that he had proved himself to be straightforward in his methods, modest in demeanour, resolute in action and inflexible in his adherence to the principles of honesty and equity.

Ted Hill, in his personal statement to the membership, said that he was standing as a militant trade unionist who strongly abhorred Mondism. He said that he was an advocate of the united front of all workers against fascism. He urged the strengthening of the shop steward system and said that quarterly shop stewards' meetings should be introduced into the Society. His sponsoring committee, of which Alf Whitney was secretary, included a number of well-known militants. The sponsoring committee said that Ted Hill was known for his sincerity and fearlessness. They urged support for him because, they said, it was necessary to introduce a new viewpoint 'representing the urge of the younger members'.

A NEW GENERAL SECRETARY

The result of the election was an easy victory for Mark Hodgson. He polled more votes than all other candidates combined. His vote was 3,355. His nearest rival, Ted Hill, secured 844 votes.

Mark Hodgson was a very different union official from his predecessor, John Hill. Hill was a militant who believed that the strike weapon was the most effective in the armoury of the membership. Mark Hodgson, on the other hand, placed his emphasis on negotiation and conciliation. Hill never missed an opportunity to draw attention to the failings and cruelties of the capitalist system. He was a constant propagandist for socialism. Mark Hodgson, though Labour in his sympathies, spoke less frequently of wider political issues. He attached particular importance to encouraging self-education among the membership. He was always interested in technical education and when he became General Secretary a new impetus was given to the association of the Boilermakers' Society with the Workers' Educational Association.

John Hill's last editorial in the monthly journal appeared in March 1936. He recalled that it was in 1900 that he had been elected as a district delegate. Some eight years later he had been elected General Secretary. He said that two reforms which had been secured during his period of service had given him special pleasure. The first was the publication of safety regulations for shipbuilding and shiprepairing. It had taken nearly thirty years of agitation to win this reform.

The second reform which had given him special pleasure was the change in the method of paying piece-work wages. Before 1910 piece-work wages for a whole squad, said John Hill, were 'handed out of a window like a dog's breakfast with no details of how the total sum was made up'. Mistakes were frequent, and members were sometimes defrauded from receiving the pay to which they were entitled. The employers fought against reform at every stage but eventually, after pressure from the membership, reform was achieved. John Hill concluded by stating that he was sure that Mark Hodgson would maintain and improve all that was best in the Boilermakers' Society He described Mark Hodgson as a capable and painstaking officer.

The journal also published a tribute to John Hill from the newly-elected General Secretary, Mark Hodgson. Hodgson paid a warm personal tribute to John Hill and said that he carried with him the esteem and respect of his fellow men. He added that the Society was emerging from a long period of serious depression and he looked forward not only to the preservation of all that was good in the Society but to improving the conditions of the membership.

Mark Hodgson was born in Hull in 1880. He was taken to Sunderland in his infancy. He joined the Sunderland No. 10 branch at the age of 20 in December 1900. During the next thirteen years he held a succession of branch posts and in 1913 he was elected a member of the Executive Council for the Tyne and Wear district. Ten years later he was elected chairman of the Executive Council. For a period of two years during the First World War Mark Hodgson was seconded for service with the Admiralty as a technical officer. He was appointed a magistrate in 1930. He was closely associated with technical education in the county of Northumberland.

At the time of John Hill's retirement there was still no provision for the payment of a pension to retired officials. John Hill had, therefore, no alternative but to publish an appeal to the membership for a retirement allowance. In his appeal, published in June 1936, John Hill said that for the last twenty-four years he had returned part of his salary every week to the general funds of the Society. He said that he had refused other full-time service at a higher salary and had retired without any kind of remunerative work. He asked for a pension of £2 per week.

The Executive Council supported the appeal of John Hill and pointed out that he had regularly handed back to the Society approximately two-thirds of the allowance given to him for his services to the Boilermakers' Approved Society. On a ballot vote the appeal for a retirement allowance was supported by 2,883 votes to 1,501.

At the 1936 TUC John Hill was presented with the gold badge of the Congress. In his speech of reply he said that he had no regrets for the work that he had done. There was still, he pointed out, very much more to do, and he referred to the resolutions passed at the 1936 Congress on the extension of social ownership, on low wages and on the need to strengthen trade union organisation. John Hill's place on the General Council was taken by Mark Hodgson. He was nominated for the shipbuilding trade group and was elected by a comfortable majority over Mr W. Westwood of the Shipwrights' Association. Mark Hodgson received 2,238,000 votes and W. Westwood 1,300,000 votes.

The election of Mark Hodgson as General Secretary left a vacancy for the chairman of the Executive Council. This resulted in a keenly contested election. It was won on a second ballot by Tom McKinney. He secured 1,565 votes against 1,333 for J. S. Holmes.

GENERAL ELECTION

The election of a new General Secretary of the Boilermakers' Society coincided with a General Election. The General Election took place on 14 November 1935. There were three Labour candidates from the Boilermakers' Society. David Williams was given an unopposed return for Swansea East. Tom Irwin was the candidate in Greenock and Alf Short in Doncaster.

The Conservatives and their allies in the national coalition won a clear majority. They won 432 seats against 154 for Labour, 21 for the Liberals, 4 for the Independent Labour Party, 1 for the Communist Party and 4 Independents. The Conservative vote was more than 11,800,000 whereas the Labour vote was 8,325,000.

Alfred Short was victorious at Doncaster. The voting was:

Alfred Short (Lab)	29,963
A. H. E. Molson (C)	22,011
Labour majority	7,952

He thus turned an anti-Labour majority of 4,842 into a Labour majority of 7,952.

At Greenock Thomas Irwin was unsuccessful though he reduced the majority of his opponent by a substantial amount. The voting was:

Rt Hon. Sir Godfrey Collins (L)	20,299
Thomas Irwin (Lab)	16,945
J. L. Kinlock (Ind)	1,286
	——
Liberal majority	3,354
	——

TRADE REVIVAL

Trade improved steadily in 1936 and by 1937 there was relative prosperity in the shipbuilding industry with unemployment at a lower level than at any time since 1920. In 1936 membership increased by more than 1000 to a total of more than 50,000. The number of members unemployed during the year fell from 15,285 to 9,062. The financial reserves increased by £32,627. In 1937 the upward trend became even more pronounced. Membership rose by more than 2,500 to a total of 53,320. Unemployment fell to just over 8,000 by the end of 1937 and the financial reserves of the Society increased during the year by more than £50,000.

The revival of the shipbuilding industry was a reflection of the general improvement in the economy. It was also stimulated by rearmament. In shipbuilding the revival was assisted by the scrap and build scheme introduced by the Government. Financial assistance was given conditional upon the scrapping of two tons of shipping for every ton built, and the scrapping of one ton for every ton brought up to date. In a period of less than two years advances totalling more than £3½ million were made under this scheme. The advances were to be repaid at low rates of interest over a long period.

In June 1937 the Society reported to the membership that some fifty new vessels of approximately 186,000 tons gross had been constructed under the scheme. Nearly half of them were built in Sunderland, but the other vessels were constructed in a wide number of shipbuilding areas from Aberdeen in the north to Bristol in the south. Surprisingly, the demand for shipping rose so quickly that part of the scrap and build scheme could not be fulfilled because of the scarcity of scrap tonnage. Some of the spokesmen of the big shipping interests were critical of the scheme. They regarded it as a form of interference with market forces. The

270

Boilermakers' Society remained committed to support for the scheme, and said that it was satisfied with the results.

Many of the district committee reports in this period spoke of the new activity in shipyards. The West of Scotland District Committee, for example, said that there had been a very notable reduction in the number of unemployed. Members who had been out of work for years had secured employment. When the men resumed work, said the district committee, they had 'aching bodies and painful hands'.

The district committee reports spoke of a new spirit among members in the defence of wages and conditions. The West of Scotland District Committee reported that aggregate meetings of shipyard caulkers and welders had taken place in different towns in the west of Scotland. At these meetings the members had unanimously decided to resist any attempt on the part of the employers to reduce wages by the revision of piece-work price lists.

The East of Scotland District Committee reported that few members were out of employment and that caulkers were resisting changes in piece-work price lists. The London District Committee said that the volume of work available to members was steadily improving and very few members were unemployed. The Manchester District Committee said that constructional engineering shops were busy but that new problems were arising over the training of welders. The Midlands District Committee reported a campaign to secure 100 per cent membership and the Barrow District Committee reported that nearly all members were in employment.

One effect of the revival in trade and the new confidence among the membership was a growth in the number of elected shop stewards. The London District Committee, for example, said that they were pleased to report that members in various shops were electing shop stewards but that the committee would not be satisfied until every member was covered by a shop steward.

In September 1936 Mark Hodgson spoke of the appearance of a 'silvery lining' which had provided an opportunity for the members of the Boilermakers' Society to make good the ravages of depression and unemployment. He pointed out that employers were now expressing concern about the shortage of skilled men. The Boilermakers' Society, he said, had in the past offered to co-operate with employers in the training of apprentices only to be told that it was

271

not the business of the Society. The employers had always held that they should retain exclusive responsibility for the training of apprentices. Shipbuilding employers had imposed onerous conditions on apprentices, including a requirement that they should not join a trade union. Employers had insisted upon their 'right' to suspend apprentices or put them on short time during periods of trade depression. It was not surprising, therefore, that lads were reluctant to enter the industry.

A NEW MOOD

At the beginning of 1937 the Society reported that shipyards which had been idle for years had secured orders. There was a growing mood of militancy among the membership. In February 1937 Mark Hodgson felt it necessary to warn that agreements should be loyally observed by the membership. To take advantage of circumstances, he said, when either side had 'the ball at their toe' was not playing the game. The Society, he said, was entitled to insist upon the terms of arrangements made with the employers being carried out by the members.

During the years 1936 and 1937 the Boilermakers' Society was engaged in a continuous round of negotiations on wages and conditions both at national and at local level. At the beginning of 1936 feeling was running high because of the delay in reaching a settlement in the shipbuilding industry on a claim which had been submitted during the previous year. The unions were on the point of taking a national strike ballot when the employers indicated their readiness to agree to a wage increase. The settlement provided for an increase of 2s per week bonus to time workers and 4 per cent on the gross piece-work earnings of piece-workers from the beginning of the first full pay week in April 1936. One of the clauses of the settlement was that no further step should be taken towards an alteration in wages until after a period of nine months from the beginning of April.

In the spring of 1936 another major dispute began in the London ship repair industry. The members claimed increased wages, a reduction in the working week and increased premium payments for overtime. They imposed a piece-work and overtime embargo which lasted for twelve months. Eventually in 1937 a settlement was secured under which wages were increased by amounts ranging from 11s 6d to 17s 6d per week; the working week was reduced from forty-five to forty-four hours without any reduction in pay; and the overtime premium was increased to double time. The London District Committee said that by their action and determination the London membership had added another chapter to trade union history. It was a notable victory.

SHIPBUILDING WAGES

Towards the end of 1936 the shipbuilding unions submitted a claim for another increase in wages. A preliminary conference to review the state of the industry was held on 18 December 1936. At the end of the conference the employers indicated that they were prepared to increase wages and agreed to the setting up of a joint committee with the unions to negotiate the terms of a settlement. This time the negotiations were conducted quickly, and in February 1937 a recommendation was made to increase to 6s per week the 2s bonus advance granted in April 1936 and to increase to 12 per cent the 4 per cent advance given to piece-workers. These increases were introduced in two equal instalments, the first from the beginning of February and the second from the beginning of July 1937. The employers and the unions undertook not to initiate any step towards a further alteration in wages for a period of six months.

Shortly afterwards the shipbuilding employers, in response to a claim from the Boilermakers' Society, agreed to increase the time rate for riveters and caulkers to that of other shipyard craftsmen. The pay of riveters and caulkers had been 2s 6d per week below other craftsmen. The effect of this increase for riveters was to widen the differential over holders-on. A further conference was held with the shipbuilding employers on 28 May 1937 when it was agreed that holders-on engaged on time rates would also receive an increase in pay of 2s 6d per week.

ENGINEERING WAGES

In the engineering industry the unions submitted a claim for wage increases and for the restoration of working conditions as they existed before the cuts of June 1931. A settlement was reached in the early summer of 1936. It provided for an increase of 3s per week in the war bonus paid to all adult male workers. The increase was to be paid in three stages, the first at the end of June, the second at the end of September and the third at the end of December. The settlement also provided for the maintenance of the 'status quo' in respect of local wage applications. The 'status quo' was to last for a period of six months after the payment of the first instalment of the increase. The settlement also provided an increase in the nightshift premium payment. The new rate was to be time-and-one-fifth. The first two hours of overtime on nightshift were to be paid at the rate of time-and-one-third and all hours worked thereafter at time-and-one-half.

The revival in trade led also to new local claims by engineering workers. Discussions took place between the engineering employers and the unions regarding the procedure for dealing with local wage applications. In November 1936 a memorandum was agreed which provided that a national committee of the employers would be created to deal with unresolved local wage applications submitted by a union or unions in respect of all classes of workpeople in an area or district. Claims to this national committee following a 'failure to agree' at a local conference would be presented by national representatives of the union or unions concerned. If it was not found possible to reach a settlement in these national negotiations the procedure was deemed to be terminated.

In April 1937 the engineering unions returned to the employers with a further claim. They asked for an increase in wages, the restoration of the 1931 cuts and the consolidation of war bonus into the basic rate. Agreement was reached to operate from 23 August 1937 for an increase of 3s per week in the national bonus. The increase was to be paid in two stages, the first from the pay period covering the week beginning 23 August and the second from the pay period covering the week beginning Monday 15 November 1937. The premium rate for overtime on dayshift working was increased from time-and-one-quarter to time-and-one-third for the first two hours. The agreement said that there should be no local wage applications for a period of three months after the second instalment of the increased war bonus had been paid. It stipulated that local wage applications 'may be promoted only in respect of areas or districts or specific classes of workpeople where wages are claimed to be unduly low'.

One of the most important provisions in the agreement was for the introduction of holidays with pay. It was agreed that an allowance in respect of holidays should be credited to a worker for each full week's work performed at a rate representing one fiftieth of the appropriate daytime rate plus the time worker's national bonus. A full week's work was defined as forty-seven hours. When less than forty-seven hours' work had been performed in any week the holiday credit was to be proportionately reduced.

The new more militant mood among the workers as a result of the revival in trade extended to the apprentices. In March 1937 a movement among the apprentices swept along the Clyde in support of claims for more pay, trade union recognition and a reasonable ratio of apprentices to journeymen. Nearly 13,000 apprentices took part in a strike which began on 18 March and lasted until early in May. At a later stage the strike extended to a number of other main engineering centres including Manchester and London. This movement among the rank and file of the apprentices had the desired effect. Negotiations took place between the employers and the unions and ultimately in October 1937 the Engineering Employers' Federation agreed to recognise the right of the unions to negotiate for apprentices, boys and youths.

RAILWAYS

On the railways the unions pressed for the restoration of the cuts made in the depression of the early 1930s. In the summer of 1936 the railway companies agreed that the existing deduction of $2\frac{1}{2}$ per cent of the gross earnings of all railway shopmen should be replaced by a deduction of $1\frac{1}{4}$ per cent. This agreement was to last for one year from 1 July 1936 to 1 July 1937.

At the end of September 1936 the Society called a conference of boilermakers' representatives from all railway workshops to consider the strengthening of trade union organisation, the campaign for the restoration of the wage cuts, and the possibility of joining the machinery established by other unions for dealing with shopmen's problems. This was the first conference of boilermakers' representatives from railway workshops to be held for about six years. The main debate was on the proposition that the Boilermakers' Society should join the national machinery for railway shopmen. Those who were in favour of the proposition urged that unity among all workers was essential. Those who were opposed argued that the Boilermakers' Society should retain its autonomy to deal with piece-work problems, and should not involve itself in machinery which provided for the representation not only of trade unionists but of non-unionists. Eventually the proposition that the Boilermakers' Society should become part of the national machinery for railway shopmen was carried by twenty-six votes to eleven.

In the summer of 1937 the unions covering railway shopmen put in a claim for the restoration of the last part of the pay deduction made during the depression. Agreement was reached that the deduction would be discontinued with effect from the first full pay period following 1 July 1937. Wage increases were also granted for some low-paid workers in railway workshops. An increase of 1s per week was granted to workers on a base rate of 43s 6d per week including war bonus. Workers on a base rate of 44s 6d per week including war bonus received an increase of 6d per week. A significant improvement was secured by the introduction of the principle of holidays with pay. The agreement provided for one week's holiday with pay after twelve months' continuous service.

ICI LIMITED

Towards the end of 1936 the Boilermakers' Society concluded an agreement with ICI Limited to provide that all questions of wages and conditions affecting members of the Society would be negotiated nationally. This gave the Society the right to company-wide as well as local negotiations. The agreement gave immediate increases in wages to all members of the different trades represented by the Boilermakers' Society including angle ironsmiths, platers, riveters, caulkers, welders and platers. They were all put on the same flat standard rate per hour. In September 1937 an agreement was signed with ICI on behalf of the Boilermakers' Society and a number of other engineering unions providing for the introduction

276

of a supplementary bonus of 6¼ per cent on gross weekly earnings. A retrospective payment of 25s was made to cover the period from the beginning of August 1937.

CSEU

At the beginning of 1936 agreement was reached between a number of engineering and shipbuilding unions, but excluding the AEU and some of the foundry unions, for the formation of a new confederation to promote their mutual interests. It was intended to replace the old Federation of Shipbuilding and Engineering Trades, from which the Boilermakers' Society had withdrawn in 1923. Draft rules were prepared and accepted at a meeting held in London in January 1936. The new organisation was to be called the Confederation of Shipbuilding and Engineering Unions.

The formation of this new body was of major significance for trade unionism in the engineering and shipbuilding industries. The objects of the new Confederation were specified in the rules. They were to organise all workers in shipbuilding and engineering and to secure their complete solidarity. The rules specified that the Confederation should negotiate general agreements covering wages and working conditions on behalf of shipbuilding and engineering workers. Affiliated unions agreed that the membership of each union would remain inviolate and that no excluded member of any of the affiliated unions would be admitted into membership of any other union until his former union had been consulted and all dues fully paid.

The rules of the CSEU provided for a general council, with representation from each affiliated union on the basis of one representative for every 10,000 members, with a maximum of six members from any one affiliated union. There were to be two group executive councils covering respectively shipbuilding and engineering. There was also to be an executive council appointed by the annual meeting of the CSEU. Provision was made for the appointment of a committee for railway shopmen. The basis for representation at the annual meeting was set out in the rules together with the arrangements for finance and for the election of a general secretary. Provision was also made for the election of district committees.

In reporting this important development to the membership the Executive Council of the Society recalled that their association with the previous Engineering and Shipbuilding Trades Federation had ceased at the time of the shipyard lockout in 1923. Since then other trade unions had seceded but the need for co-operation between the unions remained. The new organisation was welcomed by the Executive Council of the Society. It was decided to ballot the membership on a proposal that the Society should affiliate to the CSEU.

In a statement published to the membership in June 1936 in connection with the ballot the Executive Council said that experience had shown it to be necessary to maintain co-operation with a number of other unions in shipbuilding and in engineering. Members in many districts had also urged that new efforts should be made to promote trade union unity. The Executive Council urged members to vote in favour of affiliation to the new Confederation.

The result of the ballot was announced in August 1936. It showed a substantial majority in favour of affiliation. The voting was:

> In favour of affiliation   2,859
> Against affiliation   703

INTERNAL PROBLEMS

In February 1936 the Executive Council came to an understanding with the breakaway organisation which had been established in Belfast following the controversy in April 1934 about the finances of the Society and the publication of disruptive circulars. The understanding provided for the dissolution of the breakaway society and its reunification with the Boilermakers' Society. It was said that there were about 750 members in the breakaway organisation. Financial arrangements were outlined to facilitate the proposed changes. These proposals were commended to the membership by the Executive Council and were approved on a ballot vote by 3,480 votes to 665.

Unfortunately this development did not resolve all the problems

278

amongst the Belfast membership. In the following year there was a bitter controversy regarding the election of the district delegate. The controversy led to legal action in the High Court. A new district delegate was eventually elected but the issue was not finally resolved until much later.

Another problem which was finally resolved in 1936 concerned the funds brought to the Society by the Sheet Iron Workers' Society at the time of its amalgamation. This also led to litigation. In accordance with a court judgement the Boilermakers' Society allocated to each of the former members of the Sheet Iron Workers' Society a sum of £3 4s 6d.

OFFICIALS' WAGES

In March 1937 the full-time officials of the Society applied to the membership for an increase in wages of £1 per week. In their statement they recalled that since 1929 they had accepted reductions ranging from 20 to 25½ per cent. A 10 per cent restoration was made in 1935. Certain other payments for subsistence and attendance at meetings had been suspended. The officials pointed to the wage increases which had been secured by the membership. Despite this strong appeal the membership voted against increasing the wages of the full-time officials by 2,665 votes to 1,663.

This decision by the membership brought a vigorous protest from the London district delegate, Ted Hill. He said that he had been responsible for prompting the application by the full-time officials. He felt that the result of the ballot was a discredit to the Society, and he went on to say that he intended to resign at the end of his current term of office. Ted Hill pointed out that the branches in his own district had voted substantially in favour of the increase. He concluded by saying that it would be a sham if he did not maintain the same militancy in fighting for his own wages and conditions as he had displayed on behalf of the wages and conditions of the members. Fortunately this issue was resolved some months later. In January 1938 the full-time officials re-submitted their application for a £1 a week increase. On this occasion the members voted in favour of the increase by 2,615 votes to 1,848. Ted Hill did not resign.

PROGRESS

An allegation that was sometimes made against the Boilermakers' Society was that it was so concerned with the preservation of the jobs of its craft members that it resisted technical progress. There is no evidence, however, from its publications in the 1930s that the Society resisted the introduction of welding. This was the principal new technique for ship construction and was to have a dramatic effect on some of the trades represented by the Society. The Society's concern was always to insist that welding should be performed by competent men and that the new technique should not be used merely as a means of employing cheaper labour.

In November 1936 the Boilermakers' Society published an article in the monthly report which discussed at length the use of welding in the shipbuilding industry. It said that it was an indisputable fact that various people had used spurious and unreliable modes of welding and had brought welding into disrepute. Trainees had been introduced who lacked knowledge and experience. The article went on, however, to call for co-operation between employers and members to secure the development of high-class welding performed by competent welders in the industry. The article said

it is essential for all shipbuilding employers and all members of our Society to co-operate in a spirit of goodwill to bring about rapid development and successful expansion of the use of welding in shipbuilding.

The article called for the training of apprentices in welding techniques.

In 1937 Parliament passed a new Factories Act. The existing legislation dated from 1901. In the intervening years the trade union movement made repeated representations for improved factory legislation. The new Act introduced improved statutory minimum conditions affecting the health, safety and welfare of millions of employees in factories and workshops. It also established maximum hours of labour for women and young persons. It did not meet all the expectations of the trade union movement but it was undoubtedly a major step forward, and was welcomed by the

Boilermakers' Society. Mark Hodgson in commenting on the new Act said that there were not enough inspectors to visit all the factories at least once a year. It was the informed activity of workers that would do much to compel the enforcement of the law.

POLITICAL ACTION

Throughout this period the major political issues were the continuing advance of fascism and the struggle for collective security. The February 1936 issue of the monthly report of the Boilermakers' Society carried an article about mass trials in Germany. The article spoke of three monster trials of social democrats in Hamburg and the trial in the same city of 270 communists. In another trial at Wuppertal the number of persons charged with anti-fascist 'offences' numbered 628. Wuppertal, it was pointed out, had a long social democratic, communist and trade union tradition. Seven workers had been beaten to death and three had died of injuries after torture. The article referred also to another German worker whose mind had been unhinged by torture.

The London District Committee appealed to all branches to send resolutions direct to the German Government demanding the release of Ernst Thaelmann, the imprisoned leader of the German Communist Party. The London District Committee said that Thaelmann had now been in prison for more than three years. They appealed to trade unionists to support Thaelmann in the same way as they had supported Dimitrov at the time of the Reichstag fire trial. The Nazis had set fire to the German parliament building and then blamed it on the Communists. One of the accused was the exiled Bulgarian Communist leader, George Dimitrov, who was put on trial before a German court. He conducted his own defence and, heroically, despite threats, turned the proceedings into an indictment of his accusers. There was a wide protest movement in many countries and Dimitrov was acquitted.

The biggest campaign was waged around the demand for arms for Spain. The legally elected Government of Spain, consisting predominantly of liberals and socialists and with communist support, was attacked by the rebellion of some of its own generals together with assistance from Hitler and Mussolini. Troops were brought over from northern Africa by the insurrectionary generals, and large numbers of Italian troops were sent to Spain to fight against the Government. German airmen were also sent to Spain.

The London District Committee expressed their abhorrence of the attack made by the fascists on the Spanish Government and appealed to all members to support any agitation that had for its object the complete defeat of the fascists and the maintenance of democratic government in Spain.

At the 1936 TUC the President, Mr A. A. H. Findlay of the patternmakers, said that this was the fourth successive year that Congress had to take account of a deadly attack upon liberty, justice and human rights. In 1933, he said, their thoughts had been filled with the destruction of trade unionism and socialism in Germany. In 1934 there was a murderous assault upon the working class in Austria. In 1935 there was an unjust and rapacious attack by fascist Italy on Abyssinia. In 1936 the fascist aggression had shifted to Spain. Mr Findlay made a strong attack upon the misrepresentation of many British newspapers about the events in Spain. These newspapers, with their pro-fascist sympathies, were abusing the freedom of the press.

At the 1936 TUC there was a debate on Spain. A resolution was moved by Ernest Bevin on behalf of the General Council expressing profound sympathy with the Spanish Government but in effect supporting the policy of non-intervention to which the British Government had subscribed. The Furnishing Trades Association moved an amendment which deplored the attitude of the democratic governments of Europe in withholding supplies from the Spanish Government. The amendment said that this act of so-called neutrality could only make more difficult the defence of Spanish democracy and encouraged fascism to greater acts of aggression. It called upon the trade union and labour movement to campaign to abandon the deceptive policy of neutrality so as to enable the Spanish Government to exercise its right to obtain arms necessary for the defence of European peace and democracy. The amendment was defeated by 3,029,000 votes to 51,000.

The Boilermakers' Society supported the majority at the 1936 TUC. Subsequently Mark Hodgson in the monthly report said that 'in Spain the great powers have followed a policy intended to avoid a major war . . .' This, as events were to prove, was a misguided and short-sighted view. It underestimated the danger of fascist aggression, and misread the motives of the British Government. The British Government did not support effective collective security against fascist aggression.

By the following year the great majority of trade unionists had come to recognise the real nature of so-called non-intervention. It was little more than a screen to cover fascist insurrection and aggression. The Spanish Government was being denied the opportunity to buy arms for its own defence.

By the time of the 1937 Congress events had convinced the British trade union movement that non-intervention was utterly one-sided. A resolution was carried which was moved by the General Council and seconded by the Furnishing Trades Association who in the previous year had moved a critical amendment. The terms of the TUC resolution were as follows:

This Congress expresses its deep abhorrence of the murderous attacks on defenceless men, women and children in Spain by Franco's fascists, aided by German, Italian and Moorish forces. It further deplores the fact that the British and other governments continue to deny the legal government of Spain the right under international law to purchase necessary arms and equipment, thus affording support to the fascist rebels.

The Congress declares its complete solidarity with the Spanish Government in its new appeal to the League of Nations. The presence of a regular Italian army on Spanish soil is now officially and defiantly avowed by the head of the Italian Government. Acts of aggression against Spanish merchant ships and ships of other nations have been committed recently in different parts of the Mediterranean by ships of the Italian Navy. It should be obvious that armed foreign intervention in Spain, which now endangers the freedom of shipping in the Mediterranean, threatens to disturb international peace. It is therefore the duty of the Council of the League of Nations to examine this problem in all its aspects and to propose measures, including the withdrawal of foreign troops from Spain, which will effectively safeguard the peace of nations and enable the Spanish people to recover their political and territorial independence.

Many of those on the left of the movement who had been critical of the leadership of the TUC and Labour Party because of their initial support for the policy of non-intervention in Spain were also associated with a campaign to promote a united front of the Labour Party, the Independent Labour Party and the Communist Party. Some of them also supported a Popular Front, on the lines of the alliance which had been established in France and Spain, to embrace not only various trends within the working-class movement but also the Liberals. This issue came up for debate at the 1937 Labour Party Conference.

The boilermakers' delegation opposed the unity campaign. In their report they said that in the debate on the unity campaign Stafford Cripps and Harold Laski, two of the more prominent advocates of the united front campaign, were clever and sincere but unconvincing. The delegation said that Herbert Morrison, who opposed the unity campaign, handled the debate in brilliant fashion. The policy of the supporters of the united front was rejected by 2,116,000 votes to 331,000 votes. The boilermakers voted with the majority.

Although there was comparative prosperity in the years 1936 and 1937 there were still many workers who were unemployed. In the Boilermakers' Society unemployment rarely fell below about 17 per cent, though by no means all this number were long-term unemployed. Some were temporarily out of work because, for example, they were moving from job to job in ship repair. Some ship repair workers, for example, would work long hours on a succession of days to help in the quick turn-round of a ship in port and would then be without work for a further number of days.

The London District Committee of the Society took a leading part in 1936 in welcoming protest marchers to London against the means test and the unemployment assistance regulations. In December 1936 the report of the London District Committee expressed special appreciation of the work done by Ted Hill in helping to organise the reception for protest marchers to London. The report said that it was an inspiring sight to see the protest marchers in their approach to Hyde Park and Trafalgar Square. Hill was joint treasurer of the protest march fund and was very active as a member of the London reception committee.

284

POLLITT'S APPEAL

In 1937 Harry Pollitt, who by this time was the General Secretary of the Communist Party, was nominated by the Erith branch for the boilermakers' delegation to the TUC. The Executive Council refused to accept the nomination on the grounds that in 1928 the membership had decided by ballot vote that the Society should not be represented by Communists. The Executive Council said that since that time the principle had been consistently applied in relation to the boilermakers' delegation to the Labour Party and to the TUC. It had also been applied in connection with applicants for office in the Society.

Harry Pollitt appealed against the decision of the Executive Council, and the EC agreed to submit his appeal to a ballot of the membership. Pollitt had based his appeal on the interpretation of rule 52 of the Society:

All candidates for trades congress must have been in the Society not less than five years and be in benefit. All members in benefit except district delegates and executive councilmen are eligible for election who fulfil the above conditions.

Pollitt said that he fulfilled these conditions. He pointed out that the only qualifications for a candidate were that he should have five years' membership and should be in benefit. There was no provision that a candidate must work at the trade or must or must not belong to any particular political party.

In his appeal Pollitt said that the 1928 ballot was improperly conducted and that he had been refused the opportunity to prove his charge. This, however, he said, was not now important. The existing rules had been passed in 1935 and made no reference to the disqualification of Communists. Pollitt said that he was a member of the Communist Party and had never attempted to conceal it. He had joined the Society in 1912 and had paid the political levy at all times. He had never been out of benefit. He recalled that he represented the Society at the TUC from 1921 to 1927. He acknowledged that he had no mandate from the membership for his point of view but neither, he said, had his co-delegates, for the membership never had an opportunity to discuss the agenda of the TUC. Nor were they asked to contribute motions for the agenda.

Pollitt concluded his appeal by saying that if the members did not wish him to be one of their delegates to the TUC they would show this by their votes and he would accept their decision. He claimed, however, that the rule regarding the eligibility of candidates for the TUC delegation should be impartially administered and that he should be given the same rights as any other member of the Society.

The reply of the Executive Council recalled that in 1928 the members had decided by an overwhelming majority in a ballot that the Society should not be represented by Communists. The Executive Council said that they had looked up the correspondence regarding the alleged improperly conducted ballot but they were unable to trace any evidence to support the allegation that the ballot had been conducted improperly.

The Executive Council recalled that on the occasion of the previous appeal their predecessors had pointed to the demoralising effect of the Communist Party on other trade unions as well as on the Boilermakers' Society. Unconstitutional committees of Communist origin had been formed and circulars had been issued ridiculing officials and advising members to oppose decisions which had been constitutionally reached. Harry Pollitt, said the Executive Council, was the secretary of the Communist Party and he would have to take instructions from them. He would be expected to promote the policy of the Communist Party. The delegates of the Boilermakers' Society should be responsible to the Society and not to any outside organisation. The Executive Council concluded by stating that they had nothing against Harry Pollitt personally but the question which had been raised was of wider importance.

Pollitt's appeal was rejected by 2,173 votes to 1,663. Pollitt's appeal was supported by a majority of branches in the London area, on the Mersey and in Scotland. Majorities against the appeal were registered in most of the branches on the north east coast, the Tees, Wales and Ireland.

Chapter 18

On the Eve of War

The trade revival reached its peak in 1937. There was a downturn in 1938, but the principal industries in which the members of the Boilermakers' Society were employed, shipbuilding and engineering, remained buoyant because they were affected by rearmament. Nevertheless, at the beginning of 1939 there were more unemployed members of the Boilermakers' Society than there were one year previously. The General Secretary noted that the new depression in trade was being most keenly felt in districts which depended mainly on merchant shipbuilding.

In 1938 the membership of the Society rose by more than 2,600 to a total of almost 56,000. The funds of the Society increased by more than £42,000. At the beginning of 1938 just over 8,000 members of the Society were unemployed. By the end of the year the number had increased to nearly 9,500. During the summer months the number of members who were unemployed fell and the average number for the whole year was 7,635, representing approximately 15 per cent of the employable membership. The annual report of the Boilermakers' Society for 1938 pointed out that had it not been for the rearmament programme the situation would have been serious. Merchant shipbuilding had diminished substantially.

In 1939 the increase in membership accelerated. It rose by more than 4,000. For the first time for many years the total membership of the Society was more than 60,000. The funds of the Society increased during the year by more than £47,000. In the months before the outbreak of war unemployment gradually declined. The average number of unemployed from January to September 1939 was 8,563. From the beginning of the war unemployment declined much more rapidly and by the end of the year the number of unemployed members was 3,150.

The improvement in the finances of the Society prompted the Executive Council to put forward proposals for increases in certain benefit payments. This was submitted to the membership and approved overwhelmingly by ballot. The new benefits came into effect from 3 January 1938. For first class members the sickness benefit, for example, was increased from 7s 6d to 10s per week. Superannuation benefit was extended from five to eight years. The benefit after the fifth year was 2s per week. Bonus benefits for industrial injuries were also reintroduced.

During 1938 and the early part of 1939 the Society continued to make representations for Government assistance to merchant shipbuilding. It was central to the case made by the Society that subsidies were being granted to merchant shipbuilders in countries with whom British shipbuilders were competing.

In March 1939 the President of the Board of Trade announced that a sum of £2,750,000 a year was to be made available for a period of five years as a subsidy for tramp shipping, but excluding the coasting trade. War came, however, before the scheme had any real effect.

YOUNG WORKERS

From the beginning of 1938 a new procedure came into operation for dealing with issues concerning apprentices, boys and youths. The new arrangements gave to the Boilermakers' Society and other engineering unions the right to raise issues through the full-time district representatives. If no settlement was reached the unions had the right to refer the question to a local conference between the employers and the unions. If there was still no settlement the issue could be referred for central discussion between the Engineering Employers' Federation and the union concerned. The agreed memorandum said that the proportion of apprentices to journeymen, or boys to adults, should not be subject to specific determination. Nevertheless the unions had the right to raise questions concerning the proportion of apprentices to journeymen. The agreed memorandum also provided for wage increases to apprentices, boys and youths in proportion to the wage increases negotiated for adult workers. A similar agreement was concluded some months later between the Shipbuilding Employers' Federation and the CSEU. The shipbuilding agreement came into effect from 1 June 1938.

The struggle in the shipbuilding and engineering industries to secure the right of trade union representation for apprentices and young workers stimulated the trade union movement to a keener interest in the organisation of youth. As a result of a resolution carried at the 1937 Congress of the TUC the General Council drew up a youth charter calling for minimum wage rates negotiated by trade unions to be paid to all young workers; the introduction of a forty-hour working week for young workers; the abolition of overtime for all workers under 18 years of age; a fortnight's annual holiday with pay in addition to statutory holidays; the abolition of night work for all persons under 18 years of age; the abolition of the household means test for unemployed young workers; the payment of adequate unemployment insurance benefits; the raising of the school leaving age to 16 years with adequate maintenance allowances; the provision of technical training and control of entry of young people into industry with a view to preventing blind alley employment; and the abolition of premiums for apprenticeship and fee charging by employment agencies.

The TUC called a conference of representatives of executive committees of affiliated trade unions to consider the organisation of youth in trade unions. The conference was held on 28 January 1938. A series of regional conferences was then arranged. Publicity for the youth charter was secured by two special leaflets of which about 300,000 copies were circulated. These activities were fully supported by the Boilermakers' Society.

SHIPBUILDING WAGES

In February 1938 an agreement was concluded between the Shipbuilding Employers' Federation and the Confederation of Shipbuilding and Engineering Unions to provide for wage increases, holidays with pay, and the regulation of the pay of apprentices and youths. The wage increase was 2s per week for time workers and 4 per cent increase for piece-workers. A scale of increases, related proportionately to adult increases, was also agreed for apprentices and youths.

By the late summer of 1938 unemployment was again rising. In shipbuilding it was estimated that no fewer than 35,000 of the 173,000 insured persons in the industry were unemployed. This represented an unemployment ratio of more than 20 per cent. It strengthened the resistance of the employers to any new wage claim. It was not until after Britain's entry into the Second World War that the shipbuilding unions were able to secure another wage increase. On 28 September 1939 the employers agreed to an increase of 2s per week for time workers and 4 per cent on earnings for piece-workers. The increases were backdated to the beginning of the first full pay week in September 1939.

REARMAMENT AND THE UNIONS

In March 1938 the Prime Minister invited representatives of the General Council of the TUC to meet him to hear a statement on the need to accelerate the rearmament programme. The Prime Minister appealed for the goodwill of the trade unions but made it clear that he realised that any practical discussions on the subject would have to be conducted between the employers and the trade unions in the industries concerned. No pledges were asked for from the General Council and none were given.

The Minister for the Co-ordination of Defence, Sir Thomas Inskip, and the Minister of Labour, Mr Ernest Brown, then met the Confederation of Shipbuilding and Engineering Unions. At this meeting the ministers urged the unions to enter into discussions with the employers with the view to accelerating the rearmament programme. A special conference between the Engineering Employers' Federation and the engineering unions was held on 25 May 1938. At this conference the employers asked the unions to consider sympathetically limited proposals for the dilution of skilled labour. They did not suggest that there should be any change in working practice where the class of labour usually employed was available, but where there was a shortage of skilled labour the employers felt that the existing workforce might be supplemented temporarily by skilled labour from another trade or by the up-grading of semi-skilled workers. The employers also asked the unions to consider the possible part which women could play in jobs for which they were capable. A further suggestion was that there should be some relaxation of the overtime agreement.

In reply the unions said that priority should be given to the employment of all available skilled labour. It was pointed out that there were still thousands of workers who were unemployed. The unions also recalled that after the First World War promises to restore conditions which had been changed during the war had been broken and pledges had gone unredeemed.

The General Council of the TUC held a further meeting with the Prime Minister at which they expressed their concern at aspects of the Government's policy. They said that suspicion existed among trade unionists that arms which were being produced might ulti-mately be employed in support of fascist powers. The General Council expressed very grave concern at the policy of the Govern-ment particularly in regard to the Spanish war. It pointed also to an agreement which Britain had concluded with the Italian Govern-ment. The unions drew attention to the high profits that were being made out of rearmament at the same time as the unions were asked to agree to dilution.

In 1939 the Government introduced compulsory military service. This, and other developments affecting the employment of labour, were considered at a special conference of trade union executives held on 19 May. A resolution was carried which protested against the introduction of compulsory military service and said that it was in violation of a pledge given by the Prime Minister when co-operation was sought in the organisation of voluntary national service. The resolution spoke of the resolute determination of trade unionists to resist aggressors and strengthen the defence of democ-racy. It urged the immediate conclusion of an agreement with the USSR in order that a genuine peace front could be created which, with the co-operation of the USA, would make it possible to re-establish international confidence. The resolution reaffirmed the opposition of trade unions to conscription, and demanded that the Government pass without delay the necessary measures to control prices, limit profits and conscript wealth. The resolution was carried by 3,678,000 votes to 450,000 votes.

LONDON DISPUTES

In the winter of 1938–9 the Society was engaged in a number of strikes in the London district. On 5 November 1938 members employed at Messrs Redpath, Brown and Company Limited, Greenwich, came out on strike to enforce 100 per cent membership, recognition of shop stewards, the regulation of the number of apprentices and the restoration of a bonus scheme which had operated before the depression. The strike was endorsed by the London District Committee and the Executive Council. An appeal was launched for financial assistance and approximately £350 was received. The strike lasted for a number of weeks and, although all the claims were not achieved, the settlement was regarded as a victory. The strike was an indication of the determination of the Society in engineering and in construction sites to achieve 100 per cent membership and the full recognition of shop stewards.

A little later in the winter there were three other strikes in the London district. One was at the Steel Barrel Company, Uxbridge, another on the construction of the Waterloo Bridge and the third at Neill and Son, Purfleet. The first two strikes were successful but the third failed. One of the issues in the strike at the Steel Barrel Company was 100 per cent trade unionism. One of the issues on the construction of the Waterloo Bridge was the victimisation of two leading members of the Society.

NEGOTIATIONS

In September 1938 the engineering unions presented a claim to the Engineering Employers' Federation for an increase in wages and improvements in working conditions. The first reply of the employers was to the effect that the claims were not opportune. The unions decided to persist in their claim and met the employers again towards the end of February 1939. At this further conference the employers said that the industry was now facing a decline. The unions continued to press their claim. Finally in May 1939 recommendations for a wage increase were made. These were considered at a conference of representatives of the CSEU on 9 June 1939 and were accepted. They provided for an increase of 2s per week in the national bonus to be paid to all adult male workers. The wages of apprentices, boys and youths were to be increased proportionately. The increase was to apply from the beginning of the pay period at the beginning of June 1939.

Improvements were secured in a number of other industries in which members of the Boilermakers' Society were employed. At the end of 1937 a number of claims had been submitted to ICI Limited affecting overtime rates, shift arrangements, holiday arrangements, employment under obnoxious conditions and the recognition of shop stewards. Agreement was reached for significant improvements in working conditions but the issue of recognition of shop stewards was deferred for further consideration. The company argued that it was an issue which affected all unions with employees in ICI.

At the beginning of 1938 the Boilermakers' Society secured representation on the railway shopmen's council of the CSEU. Branches with members in railway workshops were advised that it was now the policy of the Society to submit nominations for workshop committees. The CSEU was entitled to four seats on the railway shopmen's council together with representatives of the NUR. One of these CSEU seats was allocated to the Boilermakers' Society. Mark Hodgson was elected to fill this seat.

At the beginning of February 1938 the Society called a conference of representatives of members employed in railway workshops. At this conference it was emphasised that by joining the railway shopmen's council the Society had not surrendered its responsibility for negotiations on the piece-work prices of its members. The representatives agreed to join with other unions in submitting a wage claim to the railway companies. Various problems were discussed in connection with the introduction of the principle of holidays with pay. The delegates agreed to press for a welders' rate and their demand was for a 50s minimum wage. The conference agreed to elect a co-ordination committee of five members, one each from the LNER, the LMS, the Southern Railway, the GWR and the Carriage and Wagon Departments.

In September 1938 a further conference was convened of representatives of the Society's membership in railway workshops. The main item on the agenda was the formulation of a claim to the railway companies for improved wages and conditions. It was agreed to ask that the base rate and the war wage should be consolidated, that rates of pay should be increased by 2d per hour with a minimum base rate of not less than 50s per week, that the standard working week should be forty hours and that each employee who was available for work should be guaranteed a standard week's pay. It was also decided to ask for an increase in the holiday with pay entitlement to twelve working days per year.

At the shopmen's conference the General Secretary reported that the NUR had indicated their intention to withdraw from the national negotiating machinery for railway shopmen. The conference delegates received this information with some concern but felt that in future the representation of workers on all committees under the railway shopmen machinery should be limited to members of unions signatory to the joint negotiating agreement. This, presumably, would have excluded members of the NUR.

The railway companies rejected the claim of the unions for improvements in wages and conditions. The shopmen's unions then decided to submit three of the disputed issues, namely rates of pay, the claim for a guaranteed day and week, and the claim for an improvement in holidays with pay, to the Industrial Court.

The Industrial Court heard the claims in June 1939. Each of the claims was rejected. In their award the Industrial Court said that the number of railway shopmen affected by the claim was about 93,200. The Court was influenced by the submission of the railway companies that wage increases had been conceded in August 1937 and a week's holiday with pay had been granted to all employees. This, it was suggested, was not out of line with changes in other industries.

The National Union of Railwaymen did not withdraw their notice to withdraw from the railway shopmen's council. The constitution of the council required that twelve months' notice should be given. This notice was submitted on 23 November 1938. The notice took effect, therefore, on 23 November 1939.

HOLIDAYS WITH PAY

Early in 1938 the principle of holidays with pay was introduced in the iron and steel industry. The agreement stated that each year between May and September inclusive, or by arrangement with the management, workers should have a maximum of six consecutive days' holiday with pay.

In April 1938 a report was published of a committee on holidays with pay. The committee under the chairmanship of Lord Amulree had been appointed by the Government and had been asked in its terms of reference 'to investigate the extent to which holidays with pay are given to workpeople and the possibility of extending the provision of such holidays by statutory enactment, or otherwise, and to make recommendations'. The committee reported that about 19½ million people in Britain were gainfully occupied not on their own account, and of this number about 18½ million were manual workers and non-manual workers not in receipt of more than £250 per year. It was estimated that of this total fewer than 8 million were already provided with annual consecutive days' holidays with pay. Of those who received holidays with pay the majority were non-manual workers. The committee recommended that an annual holiday with pay, consisting of at least as many days as there were in the working week, should be established without undue delay. The committee made the specific recommendation that during the parliamentary session of 1940–1 (ie two to three years ahead) legislation should be passed making provision for holidays with pay in industry.

In its annual report for 1938 the Society said that for the first time the majority of members had enjoyed holidays with pay. This was a significant step forward in the improvement of working arrangements.

FASCIST ADVANCE

The period 1938 and 1939 was a time of accelerated fascist advance in Europe. In Spain the majority of the population continued heroically to defend their democratically-elected government against the uprising of General Franco and the intervention of Italy and Germany. But the so-called civil war was grossly uneven. The Spanish Government was denied the right to purchase arms, its only supplies coming from the USSR and Mexico. In contrast troops and weapons were put into Spain by the fascist dictators, Hitler and Mussolini. Volunteers from many countries, including Britain, came to the assistance of the Spanish people. The International Brigade, as it was called, was often badly armed and hastily trained, but it served with bravery.

The role of the British Government in relation to the war in Spain came under strong criticism from the British trade union movement. A statement issued by the TUC General Council, the National Executive of the Labour Party and the Executive of the Parliamentary Labour Party on 8 September 1938 said that the whole world stood upon the brink of war. It placed on record that a heavy responsibility for this situation rested upon the misdirected policy of the British Government. The weakness of the British Government in the face of the aggression of the fascist powers had served as an incentive to the fascists to pin their faith in force. The statement emphasised that the authority and prestige of the League of Nations had been undermined and the right of the Spanish Government to purchase arms necessary for its own defence had been denied.

In September 1938 a fatal step was taken towards the Second World War. By agreement between the German Government and the British Government, concluded at Munich, Czechoslovakia was dismembered and the Sudeten part of the country was handed over to Germany. Germany had conducted an intense propaganda campaign calling for the incorporation of the Sudeten territories into the German state and had threatened Czechoslovakia with invasion. France and the Soviet Union were bound by treaty to support Czechoslovakia if it were attacked. They announced that they would honour their obligation. On the pretext of saving peace in our time, however, the British Government stepped in and concluded the Munich agreement, the practical effect of which was to achieve Hitler's demands. The USSR pressed strongly for collective security against German aggression but among the dominant ruling circles in France there were many, as in Britain, who were only too pleased to withdraw from the obligation which they had previously accepted. The Soviet Government later warned that they had no intention of being left alone to 'pull the chestnuts out of the fire' for the Western Powers.

In its statement on 8 September 1938 the British labour movement said that every consideration of democracy 'forbids the dismemberment of the Czechoslovakian state by the subjection of the Sudeten German regions to Nazi Government control. British Labour emphatically repudiates the right of the British or any other government to use diplomatic or other pressure to compel an acceptance of such a humiliation'. These protests were in vain.

The subjection of Czechoslovakia was completed in the spring of 1939. Hitler's troops marched in and occupied the whole country. The way was now clear for the Second World War. The USSR, whose efforts to build collective security with the Western Powers had been spurned, now looked to its own defences. In the late summer of 1939 it concluded a treaty of non-aggression with Nazi Germany. Shortly afterwards Hitler attacked Poland. Britain then declared war on Germany.

The anti-fascist campaign was conducted vigorously inside Britain during 1938 and 1939. Instances were reported of dockers and ship repair workers refusing to work on Japanese ships and on ships associated with the rebel forces in Spain. The London District Committee of the Boilermakers' Society reported, for example, in January 1938 that they had written to all branches regarding a possible embargo on repairs to Japanese and rebel Spanish ships. In March 1938 the Society gave publicity to a call from the National Council of Labour to co-operate in organising mass protests against Japanese aggression in China. Citizens were urged to boycott Japanese goods.

In June 1938 the Society published an article from the retired General Secretary, John Hill, drawing attention to the dangers of fascism. He explained the origin of fascism in Italy and Germany in these words:

Trade unionism was strong and the ruling classes saw power slipping from their hands. They could not stop this by fair means and they turned to force. Capitalists and financiers, with their long tail of luxurious idlers and gamblers, organised for revolution. Trade union funds and officers were seized. Leaders were

297

shot or put into concentration camps, and all workers were terrorised into subjection.

John Hill went on to indict Government supporters in Britain for their support of the fascist cause. He asked members of the Society whether they had read of the cheers from Government benches in the House of Commons for fascist dictators and their successes. He asked whether members had read the Prime Minister's 'song of praise to Mussolini'. He then went on:

make no mistake about it, capitalists in this country realise the financial advantages of a fascist system of industry and government, and they are already thinking and planning. They also realise that time is short as labour is on the brink of political power.

The Society's delegates to the 1938 TUC reported at length on the discussions on the international situation. They said that the Congress had upheld the Spanish people in their determination to achieve their democratic rights and that resolutions had been carried in favour of arms for Spain and a further appeal for funds to alleviate distress among the Spanish people. It was agreed also that a campaign should be conducted to persuade the British Government to remove the ban on the supply of arms to the Spanish Government.

In the October issue of the monthly journal of the Society the General Secretary, Mark Hodgson, referred to the Munich agreement in these words:

Sane men and women everywhere have had an anxious time during the past fortnight. The shadow of imminent war darkens the hearts of all, and it was an hour of intense relief when it became known that the tragedy had been averted at least for the time being. In the excitement of the moment everyone cheered and it was only when the terms of the Munich agreement became known and understood that people began to experience an uneasy feeling within themselves, and now there are multitudes who think that the price paid for peace is too high.

Mark Hodgson asked who was the victor. He said that up to the last moment the Czech nation were led to believe that they would be supported 'and then suddenly that hope was dashed'.

The response of Mark Hodgson to the Munich agreement was characteristic of some sections of the British labour movement but by no means all. Some were inclined to welcome the Munich agreement as having saved peace. But their sense of relief was very short-lived. Others in the labour movement saw the Munich agreement from the outset as a betrayal of Czechoslovakia and as a symbol of the British Government's refusal to engage in collective security against the threat of fascist aggression. In the annual report for 1938 the General Secretary, Mark Hodgson, said that 'fascist powers are loose, pursuing a policy of aggression. They are bent upon a new capitalist imperialist division of the territories and spoils of the earth.'

In January 1939 the Society published an appeal from the TUC for help for Spain. The appeal said that the Spanish people were starving, that scabies was spreading rapidly because there was no soap for the population and that Spanish towns were being bombed. Nevertheless, said the appeal, the morale of the Spanish people, despite their punishing privations, was as splendid as ever. The people of Spain, it said, were putting up the greatest fight history had ever known in the cause of democracy.

Unfortunately it was now too late. The Spanish Government, denied by the Western powers the arms needed to defend itself, was not able to withstand the growing strength of Franco with the heavy support he was receiving from the fascist powers of Germany and Italy. The Spanish republic was finally defeated early in 1939. Tens of thousands were subsequently persecuted and there was a huge stream of Spanish refugees into other parts of the world.

A UNITED FRONT

Controversy about the manner in which the anti-fascist struggle should be conducted was reflected in debates within the labour movement about proposals for a united front and a popular front. One of the principal advocates within the Labour Party of a united front and a popular front was Sir Stafford Cripps. In 1939 he was expelled from the Labour Party.

The ostensible cause of the expulsion was the circulation to affiliated organisations by Sir Stafford Cripps of a memorandum of support for a proposed popular front. By a fairly narrow majority on a card vote Cripps was permitted to speak in his own defence at the 1939 Labour Party Conference but his expulsion was endorsed by 2,100,000 votes to 402,000. Later in the conference resolutions in support of a proposed popular front were defeated by even larger majorities.

These political controversies were also reflected in debates in the international trade union movement. Those who were in favour of a united front and a popular front were also usually sympathetic to joint action between the International Federation of Trade Unions, which united most of the trade union centres in western Europe, and the Russian trade unions. Proposals for such united action had been discussed at length at the TUC.

A delegation from the International Federation of Trade Unions visited Moscow in November 1937 when, according to the 1938 TUC report, certain conditions were presented on behalf of the Soviet trade unions. The TUC report described these conditions in the following terms:

> Briefly these proposed: the intensification of the fight against fascism and war; working class sanctions against Germany, Italy and Japan; refusal to transport goods to those countries and strikes in undertakings manufacturing arms and war material for them; effective aid to Spain and China; the bringing about of trade union unity in countries such as the United States, Canada, Czechoslovakia, etc and support of the united front and the people's front where they exist.

The Soviet trade unions also proposed certain organisational changes. They suggested that the IFTU should have three presidents, one of whom would be Russian and two or more general secretaries, one of whom would be a Russian. They sought an assurance, according to the TUC report, that no part of the financial contribution made by the Soviet trade unions would be used for propaganda against the USSR and the Soviet trade union movement. They also asked that a special congress be called to strengthen the unity of the international trade union movement.

300

These conditions and proposals led to a great deal of discussion within the IFTU. Eventually they were rejected by a majority of the affiliated trade union centres.

Some of those who were opposed to the affiliation of the Russian trade unions argued that it was necessary for the IFTU to fight all forms of dictatorship, whether communist or fascist. It was also disputed whether the affiliation of the Russian trade unions would result in any intensification of anti-fascist activity.. The Soviet Union, it was said, had trading relations with fascist countries and Russian workers were employed on fulfilling fascist trade orders. The Soviet trade unions were reproached for demanding action of trade unions in other countries which they could not themselves put into effect.

The reference back of the General Council's report was moved at the 1938 Congress of the TUC but was defeated. The boilermakers' delegation in their report said that the matter need never have been forced to a vote if the advice of the TUC General Secretary had been accepted. He had urged those responsible for the critical resolution not to press it but to leave the issue with the General Council to use their persuasive influence in favour of international trade union co-operation. The reference back was defeated by 2,619,000 votes to 1,493,000.

PERSONALITIES

At the beginning of 1938 the previous controversy within the Boilermakers' Society concerning disruption among certain of the Belfast and Merseyside branches took a new turn. The Executive Council issued a statement indicating that they had received information about numerous letters written by one of their number, J. S. Holmes, designed to disrupt the Society. These letters, they said, had been written from 1935 onwards. J. S. Holmes was a member of the Executive Council from January 1932 until the end of December 1937 when his term of office expired.

In its statement the Executive Council said that passages in the letters were libellous, and showed that, contrary to the rules, J. S. Holmes was divulging Executive Council business to others, was advising members to refuse to carry out the Executive Council's decisions and had been breeding discontent and disruption over a period of years. In October 1937 J. S. Holmes left the Executive Council because of illness. The Executive Council offered to provide the services of a medical specialist but this was refused. Mr Holmes then engaged in a bitter exchange of correspondence with the Executive Council.

The Executive Council proceeded cautiously and early in January 1938 Mr Holmes signed a declaration apologising for the statements which he had made relating to members of the Executive Council. He undertook to hand over immediately all correspondence, letters and papers relating in any way to the affairs of the Society and promised that he would not repeat any statement contrary to the interests of the Society or divulge any business of the Society. Mr Holmes said that he was not able to follow his trade as a riveter and he asked for employment in the office of the Boilermakers' Society. This was considered by the Executive Council but they replied that there was no suitable position in which his services could be useful. It marked the conclusion of an unhappy chapter in the history of the Boilermakers' Society.

On 24 August 1938 the Boilermakers' Society lost its first Member of Parliament, Alf Short. He died in the Royal Free Hospital in London. He had a long and distinguished service in the interests of the labour movement. He was a branch secretary of the Sheffield branch of the Society for about twenty-five years, and he served as secretary of the Sheffield Trades and Labour Council for approximately ten years. He was a member of the Sheffield City Council from 1913–19. After his election as a Member of Parliament he qualified for the Bar and passed his final examination in 1922. He was called at Gray's Inn in January 1923. In the Labour Government of 1929–31 he was the Parliamentary Under-Secretary for Home Affairs.

Towards the end of 1938 Mark Hodgson was re-elected unopposed as General Secretary. Mark Hodgson was nominated by more than 100 branches. This was a remarkable tribute to him. He had brought a high standard of efficiency and diligence to the conduct of the business of the Society. A number of other candidates were nominated by branches but all declined. The only exception was J. S. Holmes. He was nominated by three branches but his nomination was not accepted in view of his previous conduct. In the meanwhile J. S. Holmes's seat on the Executive Council had been won by R. Allcroft who, in a second ballot, was elected by 733 votes against 719 for A. Green.

In December 1938 David Williams, MP for Swansea East, wrote to the General Secretary to state that he would not be a candidate at the next General Election. He pointed out that he was 73 years of age and suffered from recurring attacks of bronchial asthma. He thanked the Society for their support during the time he had been their official candidate. David Williams at that time had been a member of the Society for forty-six years and had been active in public life for more than forty years.

John Sanderson, the longest serving full-time official of the Society, died on 24 June 1939. He was a district delegate in the West of Scotland. He had been elected district delegate in 1901 and had served in that capacity for more than thirty-eight years. He was born in 1865. He died whilst carrying out his duties as a district delegate. He was interviewing the manager in Lithgow's shipyard, Port Glasgow, when he collapsed. He was taken to the Greenock Royal Infirmary but never recovered.

CHANGES

In the spring of 1939 the Executive Council reported that they had received numerous requests from branches for a revision of the rules. On a ballot vote the membership decided by 3,123 votes to 762 that the General Council should be called together for this purpose. However, before an election could be held for the district representatives on the General Council, the Second World War began. The Executive Council decided in the circumstances not to proceed with convening the General Council. They said that those likely to be elected were engaged on work of national importance and it would not be advisable to require them to seek leave of absence.

At the beginning of 1939 the Society announced that as a result of discussions with the Inland Revenue new flat-rate income tax allowances were being introduced. Platers, angle ironsmiths, welders and burners were to receive a flat-rate allowance of £11 per year. Riveters, drillers, caulkers and holders-up were to receive a flat rate allowance of £10. The Inland Revenue authorities also agreed that part of the subscriptions of members of the Society was to be treated as payment for superannuation and funeral benefits. This portion amounted to £2 per year.

In 1938 and 1939 the Society became increasingly aware of the need to strengthen trade union organisation among welders and other workers on constructional steel work. This kind of work was expanding in various parts of Britain. Some of the workers were unorganised and others were in the Constructional Engineering Union. At the request of a number of branches the Executive Council decided to convene a national conference of representatives engaged in constructional steel work. The conference took place in August 1939. The main conclusion to emerge from the conference was that a campaign should be launched to strengthen trade union organisation. It was reported that a number of branches had refused to recruit constructional steel workers. It was resolved to urge all district committees, branches and full-time officials to extend membership among constructional steel workers.

Chapter 19

Some Concluding Observations

The history of the Boilermakers' Society between 1906 and 1939 is rich in incident. The narrative is fast moving and there is a succession of colourful events. In recounting it in the preceding chapters the problem has not been to search for issues of drama but rather to choose those which are relevant to a number of main evolutionary themes.

The recording of trade union history has its own justification. It is right that trade unionists of each generation should know something of the struggles, the hopes and disappointments of their forebears. Even those who do not wish to attempt to draw lessons for future conduct will find in trade union history a fascinating story of human endeavour. Moreover, it is a story which rests on the actions and aspirations of ordinary working people. Trade union history has its martyrs and its heroes yet in an important sense it is history without heroes. The individual leader is as nothing without the support of those whom he represents. It is the rank and file who write the most stirring pages.

So it is with boilermakers. Their history shows them to have had certain weaknesses of strategic conception, limitations of craft outlook and an occasional lack of generosity to their own representatives, but no one who reads through their records can be in any doubt that they have contributed much to the traditions of the British labour movement. When all the weaknesses and strengths have been put in the balance the only possible judgement is that they have a grand and glorious history. There is no better reason for the story to be told to the present generation of members.

The study of trade union history has, however, another justification. It can offer lessons for guidance in the future. Trade union activity is nearly always a combination of spontaneity of action, leadership, and membership response to the objectives put forward by the leadership. Leadership provides the vital link between the spontaneous reaction of the membership to conditions as they find them and the manner in which they translate this reaction into purposeful activity. In the course of this translation the views of the membership, their consciousness of their grievances and of their strength when they act in a united and organised manner can be very significantly influenced. Thus the role of leadership in trade unionism should never be underestimated.

CONFLICTING INTERESTS

The first and the most obvious conclusion to be drawn from the period 1906–39 is of the existence of conflicting interests between employers and employees. The period was one of struggle in which first the employers and then the union made advances, dependent primarily on the state of trade in the shipbuilding and engineering industries. This is not to suggest, of course, that the entire content of the relationship between employer and employee was one of conflict and struggle. Both had an interest in prosperity, though even on issues vitally affecting the state of trade the employers and the Boilermakers' Society often had very different remedial measures to suggest. The union, for example, was strongly committed to a state-sponsored scrap and build scheme to stimulate investment in the British shipbuilding industry. The employers generally, and certainly the Conservative Party, were at the outset less enthusiastic because they regarded such a scheme as an interference with the free operation of market forces. Ultimately, when the depression in shipbuilding had persisted for years and showed few signs of recovery, the employers and the Government came round to the acceptance and, indeed, sponsorship of a scrap and build scheme.

Another example of the differences of view between the employers and the Boilermakers' Society, even on an issue vitally affecting the future of the shipbuilding industry, was in relation to the activities of National Shipbuilders' Security Ltd which in the mid–1930s bought and then eliminated as productive units so many shipyards. The employers claimed that this was no more than the rationalisation of resources in an industry with vastly surplus capacity. Unless, they said, there was a reduction in capacity with an accompanying concentration on fewer units there was no likelihood of anyone surviving. In the scramble for the few orders available to the industry prices were being quoted which made no allowance for long-term investment or even for the recovery of certain fixed costs. Such a situation, said the employers, could lead only to the ruination of all.

The Boilermakers' Society charged that the motivation of NSS Ltd was not primarily the employers' concern with shipbuilding efficiency but with profits, and that the two were not necessarily identical. The yards which were eliminated were not always the least efficient. They were those which were financially most vulnerable, and this vulnerability was in some cases caused by business arrangements which had nothing to do with the efficient utilisation of production resources. In this connection the words of Ellen Wilkinson, MP, in describing the circumstances of the closure of Palmer's Yard at Jarrow, confirmed in detail the suspicions voiced and charges previously made by the Boilermakers' Society about NSS Ltd.

Thus even on issues such as the need for prosperity, where employers and employees had certain common interests, they expressed them in different and in some respects opposing directions. But it was in the direct relationship between employer and employee – above all regarding pay and the control of working arrangements – that the conflict and struggle were most evident.

CONFLICTS ABOUT PAY

In the trade depression of 1908 wage reductions were enforced by the employers both in shipbuilding and engineering. When trade revived in 1911 the pendulum swung quickly in the other direction. There was widespread unrest and wage increases were secured. This unrest continued up to the beginning of the First World War. It was part of a mass movement which embraced millions of British workers and was an attempt to win improvements after some years of decline in real standards. It was also fuelled by strong agitation in favour of workshop solidarity and militancy which was partially a reaction to disillusionment with the lack of achievement of political action after the election of the first substantial group of Labour MPs in 1906.

The highlights of this period of rank-and-file activity of the Boilermakers' Society were the winning by local action of wage increases throughout the shipbuilding industry, the movement for a shorter working week, the winning of a forty-seven-hour week by Merseyside boilermakers, the reluctance of the membership early in 1912 to be party to a negotiating procedure agreement in shipbuilding, and and overwhelming ten-to-one majority in a ballot on proposed strike action in support of a wage claim in shipbuilding in 1913.

During these years the militancy of the membership found articulate expression in the person of the new General Secretary, John Hill. His election at the end of 1908 following the resignation of D. C. Cummings was itself partially a consequence of the humiliation felt by many of the Society's members at the defeats which they had suffered at the hands of the Shipbuilding Employers' Federation in 1907 and 1908. John Hill's election address was an uncompromising call for militancy. The call was made at an opportune time.

The outbreak of the First World War brought the earlier period of unrest to an end. The majority of workers, including members of the Boilermakers' Society, supported the stated war aim of defending the independence of Belgium against German aggression. This new calm did not last long. In 1915, even though the shipbuilding and engineering unions had accepted the suspension of the right to strike, there was a new wave of unrest on the Clyde. This was one of the areas where the Boilermakers' Society was strongly represented. Many of the leaders of the 'unofficial' Clyde Workers' Committee did not support the war and said, in the fashion of the earlier declarations of the Socialist (Second) International, that it was the outcome of rivalry between British and German imperialism. The workers, they said, were being made to suffer and to die for capitalism. Significantly, in 1915 Clydeside

308

boilermakers elected a new full-time district delegate, William Mackie, a militant and a leader of the Clyde workers' movement.

Engineering and shipbuilding workers were by now much more ready to protect their interests by action, particularly on the Clyde, and the unrest continued in 1916. In the following year another militant, J. M. Airlie, was elected as a full-time district delegate on the Clyde and thus joined his colleague, William Mackie. This too was an indication of the then attitude of many Clydeside boiler-makers.

After the ending of the First World War in November 1918 there was a strong feeling throughout the membership of the Boiler-makers' Society that the initiative had to be taken to press for improvements in conditions. The reduction in working hours was felt to be overdue. Official propaganda had promised 'a land fit for heroes'. Prices were still rising and the existing arbitration pro-cedures were felt to be unsatisfactory. Finally, there was the example of the Russian revolution which had brought into existence the beginnings of a new kind of social system and had stimulated workers' demands in every industrial country.

In 1919 there were again many local disputes as members took matters into their own hands when pressing wage claims. Over £100,000 was paid in dispute benefit. Members of the Boilermakers' Society voted by a majority of more than two to one to reject the proposed forty-seven-hour working week agreement in shipbuilding and engineering but they were outvoted by other unions. On the Clyde many boilermakers participated in a large-scale 'unofficial' strike for a forty-hour week. Early in 1920 the unions brought the war-time arbitration arrangements to an end.

The beginning of the first post-war slump in 1921 quickly brought demands from the employers for wage reductions. The members of the Boilermakers' Society again demonstrated that they were more willing than the members of the other engineering and shipbuilding unions to resist the employers. They voted on three occasions to reject proposed wage reductions but they were outvoted on two occasions by an aggregate vote of all the unions. In 1921, when at one period some 40,000 members of the Boilermakers' Society were out of work, there were successive wage reductions. The 'land fit for heroes' had become the land where there was the harsh reality of capitalist depression.

In 1922 the members of the Boilermakers' Society voted yet again by a large majority to oppose proposed wage reductions in shipbuilding, enforced this time by a national lockout. The aggregated vote of the other unions revealed, however, more divided opinions amongst the total workforce. The Engineering and Shipbuilding Trades Federation held that, although there was a majority against a recommendation for two further wage reductions, a two-thirds majority, required under the rules, had not been obtained. The unions accepted the employers' terms. Wages had already been reduced on 10 March 1922. They were reduced again on 17 May 1922 and 7 June 1922. In addition to the wage cuts introduced at national level there were also many reductions made at local level.

In 1923 the struggle between the shipbuilding employers and the boilermakers reached a new intensity, with a national lockout lasting from 30 April to 16 November. The cause of the dispute was the insistence of the employers that the boilermakers should accept a new overtime agreement already concluded with other unions but which the Boilermakers' Society said would worsen overtime pay for their piece-working members. The members of the Society employed in shipbuilding were overwhelmingly piece-workers. The Society conducted a magnificent struggle in which the best traditions of solidarity were demonstrated. The circumstances, with mass unemployment, the existence of the new overtime agreement with other unions and the financial plight of the Society, were all unfavourable for the boilermakers. Nevertheless they were not defeated. The final settlement went some way in the direction of the boilermakers' demand. In 1923 the Society paid out in dispute benefit more than its total income from contributions.

In 1924 there was a short-lived recovery in trade. In many shipyards and engineering factories the membership put in new claims to recover some of the loss in wages sustained during the height of the depression. Many members secured wage increases. By 1925 unemployment was again rising and boilermakers found themselves once more on the defensive.

This defensive position on wages and conditions was to remain through the period to the General Strike of 1926. After the defeat of the General Strike many employers took revenge on the trade union movement. There was widespread victimisation of active trade unionists and the workshop organisation of many unions was

310

attacked. On the railways the principal unions felt that they had no alternative but to accept humiliating terms of settlement. The Boilermakers' Society reported that conditions in many firms had worsened.

In 1927 there was some recovery in trade and the engineering and shipbuilding unions pressed for wage increases. When the engineering employers offered a wage increase the boilermakers by ballot rejected it as insufficient. They were outvoted by the other unions. In 1928 wage increases were secured in shipbuilding but on the railways there were wage reductions.

In the great depression of the early 1930s shipbuilding and engineering workers suffered a succession of wage cuts and had to accept a worsening of overtime and shift pay arrangements. The new wave of reductions started towards the end of 1930. In 1931 the engineering unions were forced to accept a number of measures designed to reduce manufacturing costs, including lower premium rates for overtime and shiftwork and a reduction in the normal piece-work premium for a worker of average ability. In shipbuilding the employers imposed a two-stage reduction in pay. Although the unions did not accept the employers' ultimatum they lacked the strength to resist. More than half the workers in the industry were unemployed. Wage reductions were also made on the railways, including railway workshops.

In London shiprepairing firms, boilermakers resisted the employers' demands for substantial wage cuts in 1931. A seven-week-long dispute did not end in victory for the boilermakers but it partially repulsed the full onslaught of the employers. The strike also had important repercussions within the Society. One of its leaders, Ted Hill, was later to challenge and to defeat in an election the incumbent district delegate. Ted Hill much later was to become the General Secretary of the Society.

The year 1932 was even worse than 1931. Wages were reduced in engineering very early in the year. In shipbuilding, due largely to the resistance of the Boilermakers' Society, negotiations on the employers' request for pay cuts and changed conditions continued for many months without agreement. The employers then turned their attack to the level of the individual shipyard. Reports of wage reductions were received by the Society during every month of the year.

It was not until 1934 that the members of the Boilermakers' Society were able, very hesitantly at first, to try to recover some of the wage cuts they had suffered in the depths of the depression. A scrap and build scheme helped trade in the shipbuilding industry. The first significant break-through came on the railways where an agreement was concluded in September 1934 to recover partially in two stages the pay reduction of $4\frac{1}{6}$ per cent imposed in 1931. Even after the second stage, beginning 1 January 1935, the reduction was still to be $2\frac{1}{2}$ per cent.

In the spring of 1935 the engineering unions were able to negotiate their first national wage increase for many years. An increase of 2s per week, to be given in two stages of 1s each, was accepted by the unions. The Boilermakers' Society would have preferred to have submitted the offer to a ballot of the membership but the majority of the unions felt that the offer should be accepted without a ballot. In shipbuilding the employers continued to refuse a negotiated increase throughout 1935. By the beginning of 1936 the unions in the industry, particularly the Boilermakers' Society, were preparing to take a ballot on strike action. Further negotiations then took place and an agreement was concluded for wage increases similar to those conceded in the engineering industry some months previously.

During the slow recovery in trade in 1934 the London shiprepair industry was again the scene of a prolonged and bitter dispute. A seven-week strike in 1934 was successful. At the end of the dispute the employers withdrew proposals which their workers said would have reduced wages. Two years later, in 1936, a piece-work and overtime embargo was imposed in ship repair by the London District Committe and it lasted for a year. The outcome was a very significant settlement which included the introduction of a basic forty-four-hour working week.

The trade recovery of 1937 brought the biggest rank-and-file movement for wage increases since the brief period of prosperity following the ending of the First World War. District committees reported claims, action or threatened action, and settlements in yards and workshops in every part of Britain. National increases and improved conditions were negotiated in engineering and shipbuilding. The movement for holidays with pay began to make progress, and apprentices on the Clyde and in one or two other areas

312

took up the struggle for trade union recognition and wage increases. In all, it was a period of significant trade union advance and showed once again that when immediate fears about unemployment had diminished there was no lack of readiness on the part of ship-building and engineering workers to press for improvements in their conditions of life.

In 1938 and in the months of 1939 up to the outbreak of the Second World War the initiative remained with the unions though trade, apart from rearmament, declined from its peak level in 1937. Workshop organisation and the election of shop stewards was extended to more and more firms and wage increases were nego-tiated both nationally and locally. The unions were not, however, able to secure any national reduction in basic hours of work. On the other hand, most boilermakers enjoyed for the first time one week's annual holiday with pay.

CONFLICTS ABOUT CONTROL

It was not only on wages that the conflict of interest between the employers and boilermakers constantly revealed itself. Equally significant, and perhaps even more significant for the long term, were the conflicts about the control of working arrangements. There were four main areas where there were major differences of approach, though all these areas were related to each other and concerned the location of the frontier of managerial control. The first was on negotiating procedure, the second on changes affecting piece-work earnings, the third on so-called managerial functions, particularly the control of overtime, and the fourth on the arrange-ments for the introduction of new techniques, particularly welding.

The history of the Boilermakers' Society demonstrates very clearly that negotiating procedure agreements carry with them both rights and obligations or, as some would argue, both advan-tages and disadvantages. A procedure agreement is the symbol of trade union recognition. Its existence is testimony to the fact that the employer accepts the presence of the union and has agreed that his employees who are members of the union have the right of collective representation. A procedure agreement which provides for the determination of pay and conditions by negotiation also implies that the employer has accepted that the terms of employment are no longer to be settled by his unilateral decision. Thus, in the history of trade unionism, the signing of a new procedure agreement where previously a union has not been recognised by the employer has been seen as a decisive step forward.

An employer does not, however, usually sign a procedure agreement as an act of benevolence towards trade unionism. He may do it because of the strength of feeling among his workers and his recognition that his own interests will be served by coming to terms with reality. But he may also become conscious that a negotiating procedure agreement can be of considerable advantage for his own purposes. In the first place it provides a formal channel for collective representation. When the employer has agreed, either because he feels it right or by necessity, to negotiate about pay and conditions, he clearly wants to be assured that those who conduct the negotiations are representative of the workforce and have a mandate to conclude agreements. Secondly, he wants the agreed procedure to be followed and the agreements to be observed. In other words, as he sees it, a negotiating procedure agreement provides a framework for voluntary discipline to supplement the more normal disciplines of management. Thirdly, a negotiating procedure agreement provides a means whereby grievances can be ventilated, discussed and resolved expeditiously without stoppages of work. It is not in the interest of good management that grievances should remain suppressed and unresolved. If there are no adequate means of discussion and representation grievances may undermine the motivation to work. Finally, the employer may recognise that a negotiating procedure agreement provides an important form of worker participation. If an employer wishes to explain and to discuss his objectives and his problems with his workforce in an attempt to secure their co-operation and understanding, the machinery of consultation and negotiation established by a procedure agreement offers a vital means of communication. Thus a procedure agreement has many advantages to management.

The period covered by this second volume of the history of the Boilermakers' Society opened with a dramatic example of a difference between the shipbuilding employers and boilermakers about negotiating rights. In 1907 in the Walker yard of Armstrong Whit-

314

worth the management instructed apprentice platers to do the work of caulkers. The caulkers objected, the district delegate tried unsuccessfully to persuade the management to suspend action pending negotiations, and the caulkers then went on strike.

The Shipbuilding Employers' Federation threatened the Society with a national lockout unless the strike was ended at the Walker yard. In the outcome (the events are described in more detail in Chapter 1 of this volume) the Society capitulated. Because of financial weakness the Society's leaders felt that they were not in a position to take up the challenge. The SEF insisted upon the Society accepting a provisional procedure which guaranteed management the 'right to manage'. The agreement could be interpreted as meaning that the Society's members were under obligation to remain at work even when their conditions were changed by unilateral decision of the employer. If the members objected the only course open to them, apart from ending their employment, was to take their grievance through every stage of the negotiating procedure from yard, to district, and then to national level. The Society regarded this provisional arrangement, pending the conclusion of a new more permanent national procedure agreement, as a humiliation. The employers had demonstrated vividly that a procedural obligation could be an onerous form of discipline to supplement managerial control.

This, however, was not the conclusion of the episode. When the provisional agreement was submitted to a ballot vote of the membership it was rejected by a substantial majority. The employers then threatened a national lockout unless the agreement was accepted. The Executive Council of the Society decided to conduct a campaign to explain that because of financial weakness the Society was in no position to resist. The campaign achieved its purpose. On a second ballot the agreement was accepted though not by an overwhelming majority.

The indignity suffered by the Society had its repercussions. There was a dissident movement on the Clyde and the criticisms voiced of the leadership of the Society helped to bring about the election of John Hill as General Secretary. When a new procedure agreement was negotiated in 1909 the mood had changed. Trade was recovering, the boilermakers had shown a new determination in wages disputes, and the new General Secretary, John Hill, was determined that the provisional procedure agreement was going to be changed.

In the event, the new agreement was substantially more favourable to the workers' interests than the provisional agreement, eliminating a number of objectionable features (see Chapter 2). Even so, many members of the Society were by now sceptical about the value of any kind of procedure agreement which limited their right to take immediate strike action on piece-work disputes. The new agreement was accepted on a ballot by a majority of about three to two.

The issue, however, was still not resolved. In the following year the employers and the Society differed in their interpretation of the new agreement. The employers argued that there was an obligation on the men to remain at work whilst grievances were negotiated. The boilermakers argued that the employers should not introduce changes which affected earnings or conditions without first negotiating about them. As a result of disputes on the Tyne and Clyde the Shipbuilding Employers' Federation began a national lockout of boilermakers to try to enforce their interpretation of the agreement. Moreover, they proposed that fines should be imposed on men who stopped work in breach of procedure.

Surprisingly, the Executive Council of the Society, influenced no doubt by the drain on the funds caused by the dispute, were inclined to accept terms of settlement which embodied the employers' demands, providing that negotiations on piece-work disputes could be speeded up. The membership, however, by a very narrow majority rejected the proposed agreement. Eventually, after more than fourteen weeks' dispute, the employers withdrew their proposal. They accepted instead that any disagreement about whether a stoppage of work was in breach of procedure should be examined by a joint committee of employers and union representatives. The outcome could be regarded as a victory for the boilermakers. It did not give them all they wanted but they had successfully challenged the 'right' of the employers to introduce without negotiations changes affecting earnings or conditions.

This experience strengthened the conviction of many boilermakers that a procedure agreement was, on balance, disadvantageous. It was a view shared at that time by John Hill. Why, asked the critics, did the boilermakers need what was in effect no more than a 'certificate of recognition' from the employers when, in return, the boilermakers had to accept obligations which could be interpreted as limiting their right to strike whenever they had an unresolved grievance. Boilermakers, they added, did not need a 'certificate of recognition'. Their strength compelled recognition. These views were held sufficiently widely in the Society in 1912 to result in the rejection by ballot of any proposal for the renewal or revision of a procedure agreement.

The Executive Council of the Society, against the advice of John Hill, were more sympathetic to the idea of an agreed procedure for dealing with national issues. Representatives from the shipbuilding areas were consulted late in 1912 and gave their support to the Executive Council but on the understanding that local issues would be dealt with locally and that they would not be covered by or included in the national procedure. These proposals were unacceptable to the employers.

It was not until 1918 that the shipbuilding employers and the Boilermakers' Society again turned their attention to negotiating a procedure agreement. They agreed to open discussions for a new procedure. This formed part of a package which included also the restoration of pre-war practices and the maintenance of a 'closed shop'. In the meantime the emphasis of the existing informal arrangement was on the settlement of local issues at local level. By this time the Society had also secured the full and effective recognition of shop stewards. National claims continued to be dealt with under war-time arrangements. The discussions for a new procedure made very slow progress and were overtaken by other events.

In 1927 there were further discussions on negotiating procedure. By this time the unions had been defeated in the General Strike, the war-time arrangements for dealing with national claims had been brought to an end, the Federation of Engineering and Shipbuilding Trades had concluded a new procedure with the shipbuilding employers and the Boilermakers' Society were no longer members of the Federation. In February 1927 the Executive Council, with the support this time of John Hill, recommended that the Society should sign the procedure agreement concluded between the Shipbuilding Employers' Federation and the Federation of Engineering and Shipbuilding Trades. In two separate ballots the membership rejected this advice. The tradition that the membership

317

should retain freedom of action in local disputes, particularly on piece-work issues, was still strong. Many members also objected to any other union having any part to play in resolving problems affecting boilermakers.

In 1929 the Shipbuilding Employers' Federation again pressed the Society to sign the procedure agreement which existed with other unions. They agreed on this occasion to introduce two supplementary clauses to meet the criticism that the existing agreement did not deal satisfactorily with disputes on local piece-work issues. The amended proposals were supported by the Executive Council but again, in two separate ballots, they were rejected by the membership though by narrow majorities. At this stage the Federation said that they would regard the procedure, together with the supplementary clauses, as applying to members of the Boilermakers' Society. They did not succeed, however, in persuading the Society to sign the agreement. The members yet again rejected it; this time by a majority of more than two to one. No further steps were taken by either side to provoke a confrontation.

The difference of approach between the Shipbuilding Employers' Federation and the Boilermakers' Society concerning negotiating procedures – a difference which spanned the entire period recorded in this volume – centred primarily on the control of changes affecting piece-work earnings. The members of the Society were insistent on their right to regulate jointly with the employers their piece-work arrangements. Only in the aftermath of the defeat in the industrial dispute of 1907 did they temporarily depart from this very firm stand. Even then it is clear from subsequent events that many members never really accepted the settlement which followed the defeat but waited indignantly for an early opportunity to change it. This they achieved when the provisional agreement was replaced by a more permanent agreement.

The right of working people to join in the regulation of working conditions is at the very heart of trade unionism. The instinct of the boilermakers that changes in piece-work arrangements should not be made without first discussing and, if necessary, negotiating about their effect on earnings and working conditions, is a commendable one. It had its counterpart in the engineering industry in the tradition of what became known as 'mutuality'. Both employer and worker have a mutual interest in piece-work arrangements,

318

including the effect on earnings of any proposed changes in the means of production (i.e. the machine tools and equipment), the method of production (i.e. the particular operation or process and the tooling for the operation) and the material (i.e. its specification). Changes which affect earnings should be introduced after negotiations on piece-work prices or times.

The other issue on which there was constant underlying friction was on the control of overtime. Employers in shipbuilding and engineering saw this as the issue on which, perhaps more than any other, they felt it necessary to maintain managerial control. Their wish to control overtime was an assertion of the discretion which they felt rightly belonged to them because of their ownership of the industry and their obligation to manage resources to meet production targets and delivery dates. Because of the strength of the unions, particularly in periods of prosperity when the need for overtime was likely to be more pressing, the employers were prepared to accept that there should be some limitation on overtime providing that the limitation took account of numerous possible exceptional circumstances. The employers also wanted these exceptional circumstances to be defined as widely as possible in any overtime agreement.

The official attitude of the Boilermakers' Society was consistently in favour of the strict limitation of overtime. Such a policy was seen to have a number of advantages. In the first place, it could effectively limit the hours which a member could be called upon to work in any one week or month. To this extent it was a necessary safeguard against labour exploitation. Secondly, it was seen as part of trade union efforts to secure a satisfactory wage. Workers, it was felt, should not have to depend on overtime earnings to bring their pay up to an adequate level. Workers who become dependent on habitual overtime tended to become more concerned about the opportunity to work overtime than to seek a higher basic rate. Thus, the dependency of workers on overtime undermined the efforts of the Society to secure higher basic rates. Finally, the elimination of overtime was seen by the Society as a means of reducing unemployment. Why, it was asked, should some men work overtime whilst others with equal skill were out of a job.

The struggle about the control of overtime and the periodic efforts by the Society to reduce the length of the basic working week extended over the entire period 1906–39. The defeat sustained by the Society in the shipbuilding dispute of 1907 led to an undertaking by the Society not to interfere with the working of 'necessary overtime'. In the very same year, however, that the Society accepted this understanding they had been urging the engineering and shipbuilding unions to press for the control of overtime. Some two years later the Society was able in the new more permanent procedure agreement to secure the elimination of the objectionable clause on overtime.

The efforts of the Society to eliminate overtime formed part of a wider campaign to secure a shorter working week. In the prosperous period immediately before the outbreak of the First World War the movement among boilermakers for an eight-hour day was gaining momentum and John Hill called for militant action to enforce the claim. The winning of a forty-seven-hour week by Merseyside boilermakers in 1913 was an outstanding achievement.

During the First World War the Society focused attention at the TUC on the need to win a shorter working week as an objective of British trade unionism. When the war ended the Society pressed strongly for a forty-hour week, with a forty-four-hour week as a temporary compromise, and would have been prepared to reject the proposal for a forty-seven-hour week made by the engineering and shipbuilding employers. Indeed, the Society's membership voted by a two to one majority to reject the employers' offer but the total vote of the other unions went in favour of accepting the offer.

In the national engineering lockout of 1922, where the central issue was the claim of the employers to exercise their 'managerial function' to control overtime, the Boilermakers' Society offered determined resistance. The Society shared the strongly held view of the AEU that when tens of thousands of engineering workers were unemployed it was totally unreasonable that an individual employer could require his employees to work long hours of overtime on the plea that he was exercising a 'management function'. The Society resisted the employers to the very end and only asked the members to return to work when the other unions had been defeated and the boilermakers were left in isolation.

Similarly, the 1923 national shipbuilding lockout, though concerned primarily with overtime premium payments, also had as one of its implications the issue of the control of overtime. The outcome of this dispute strengthened the tradition of the Boiler-makers' Society that it would not surrender to managerial claims its right jointly to regulate by negotiation and agreement the working of overtime and the premium payments for overtime.

In the late 1920s the Society continued to press for the stricter control of overtime. In 1929 the Shipbuilding Employers' Federation was asked to strengthen the existing arrangements for the control of overtime. They refused. In 1933, when millions of workers were unemployed, the Society sponsored a motion at the TUC calling for the strict control of overtime. A circular was also sent to all branches urging members voluntarily to limit overtime to the amount strictly necessary. At local level the representations of the Society were sometimes more successful than they were in national negotiations.

The year 1933 saw the beginning of a long dispute in the Mersey shipbuilding and shiprepairing industry concerning overtime and nightshift working. An attempt was made by the employers to persuade the boilermakers to accept an agreement which had been signed with other unions. The boilermakers said that the new agreement would worsen some of their existing arrangements. An overtime and nightshift embargo was introduced as a result of decisions taken at mass meetings of the members. The embargo lasted for sixteen months and was lifted only after improvements had been secured in the terms of the agreement concluded with the other unions and after an explicit instruction for the resumption of normal working had been issued by the Executive Council. The feeling among the Merseyside boilermakers was such that many of them were prepared to continue the dispute to establish even better terms for overtime and nightshift working.

In the mid–1930s the Society continued to press at the TUC and in its own publicity for a forty-hour week. John Hill took a leading part in the representations made by the TUC to the Government. Inside the Society he made no secret of his view that, with the recovery of trade and the consequently greater strength of the Society, the existing arrangements for overtime should be ended. The employers would then be obliged either to negotiate a new national agreement or to face unilateral action by the Society. The constant campaigning on hours of work helped to strengthen the resolve of London shiprepair workers in their dispute in 1937 when they secured a major breakthrough with the introduction of a basic forty-four-hour week.

When, in the second half of the 1930s, the Government pressed the unions for a relaxation of overtime controls in the interests of rearmament they received, not surprisingly, a sharp rejoinder about the number of men still unemployed. The Boilermakers' Society were also concerned about the looseness of the existing arrangements for the control of overtime and were unsympathetic to any suggestions for its further relaxation.

The conflict between engineering and shipbuilding employers and the Society on the control of overtime during the period 1906–39 provides an interesting background to and commentary on the tradition established in many sectors of British industry since the Second World War for habitual overtime working. Overtime seems to continue in a considerable number of firms and areas of employment despite the peaks and troughs of trade. In very few other industrial countries in Europe is the control of overtime so ineffective as it is in Britain. Habitual overtime in circumstances of varying industrial activity is a symptom of inefficiency and is conducive to further inefficiency.

Undoubtedly there are many workers who have come to regard overtime earnings as part of their normal income and overtime working as part of the pattern of their working lives. Employers have often claimed, with some justification, that in periods when there was a relatively high level of employment they were unable to attract sufficient numbers of workers into their employment unless overtime was offered as an inducement. It is worth recalling that even as long ago as 1933 the Boilermakers' Society in a circular to branches pointed to the existence of a minority of workers who were always anxious 'to grab' overtime.

It is one thing to complain of this phenomenon in Britain since the Second World War; it is another to understand how it arose and how the opportunity in earlier years to develop a tradition of firm overtime control was thrown away. For this the responsibility rests principally with the employers. They refused in engineering and shipbuilding to join with the unions in establishing effective joint machinery for the control of overtime. Instead they demonstrated an ideological commitment to what they believed was a right of

322

management. In many cases it proved to be no more than a facade behind which there was managerial inefficiency.

Another issue on which there was a sharp conflict between the shipbuilding employers and the Society was on the effect on employment and earnings of the introduction of new techniques, particularly welding. The evidence points clearly to the readiness of the Society to co-operate in the use of new techniques but to resist any attempt to use the techniques as a means of employing cheaper labour. Conversely, the evidence of the early and middle 1930s points equally to the intention of most employers to develop a new category of employee, a 'ship welder', whose earnings would be lower than the employee using more traditional methods whom he displaced.

The employers, after long and abortive negotiations, decided to introduce their proposed new arrangements and posted notices to this effect. The Society, acting on this issue in full co-operation with the other unions in the industry, said in reply that if and when any trainees or wage reductions were introduced their members would refuse to touch the work in dispute. The unions decided that the issue should be fought yard by yard but that, providing any new welding work was done by displaced labour, suitably trained for the purpose, work would continue as normal. Thus the responsibility for precipitating any dispute was put firmly on the employers. In the outcome, the unions succeeded in their objective. Welding was widely introduced and existing labour was trained to use the new techniques without wage reductions.

NEED FOR SOLIDARITY

Another main conclusion to be drawn from the history of the boilermakers in the period 1906–39 is the need for co-operation and solidarity between all workers in the engineering and ship-building industries. The boilermakers by themselves were able on occasions to protect their interests in their relations with employers, but there were also other occasions when the lack of unity among various trades and occupations damaged the interests of all. In the national lockouts in 1922 and 1923 both in engineering and ship-building the unions were not united. The friction between them

323

and their differences on important issues of policy undermined their effectiveness.

The low point in trade union co-operation was registered when the Boilermakers' Society was expelled from the Federation of Engineering and Shipbuilding Trades in May 1923. This was an expulsion which was not resisted by the Society. Indeed the Society had already notified the Federation of its intention to withdraw. The Society had a real grievance against a new overtime and night-shift agreement concluded by the FEST with the shipbuilding employers. The Society contended that the new agreement reduced the overtime earnings of boilermakers who were piece-workers. Most other tradesmen were time workers. Nevertheless, whatever case could be made for or against the new agreement, the disunity of the unions did not help the workers. Only after a very long national lockout were the boilermakers able to secure a settlement which went some way towards resolving their grievance. Unfortunately this experience permanently soured relations between the Society and the Federation of Engineering and Shipbuilding Trades.

The need for unity, however, remained. In 1936 the formation of the Confederation of Shipbuilding and Engineering Unions opened up the possibility of a new era of co-operation between the unions. The leadership of the Boilermakers' Society responded sympathetically and they were supported in a ballot vote of the membership. The Society became part of the new CSEU.

At a more immediate and intimate level the Society came very near to an amalgamation with the shipwrights and blacksmiths in 1920. An Amalgamated Union of Shipbuilding, Engineering and Construction Workers was actually established but the proposed integration did not take place. It fell apart in the post-war slump which began in 1921. Many members then became more concerned about benefit entitlements and the financial reserves of each union rather than the longer-term advantages of greater industrial solidarity.

Moreover, the initiative for the proposed amalgamated union had received something of an impetus from the moves culminating in the formation of the Amalgamated Engineering Union. The Boilermakers' Society did not respond favourably to the unity moves which led to the bringing together of a large number of engineering unions for the creation of the AEU. There were two

324

main reasons for the reluctance of the Society to get involved in this development. The first was that the Boilermakers' Society regarded itself as a union with a primary base in shipbuilding rather than engineering. The second was that the Society could not see itself playing what it felt might be a subordinate role to any other group of craftsmen. Numbers were not the key factor. The decisive point was that the boilermakers regarded themselves as the premier group in the shipbuilding industry. It was intended that the amalgamation between the boilermakers, shipwrights and blacksmiths should be extended to the formation of a wider federal body, based primarily on shipbuilding, to be known as the General Combination of Ship Constructional and Engineering Workers.

On a less ambitious level some progress towards trade union unity was made by the acceptance into the Society in 1912 of the membership of a Liverpool Shipwrights' Association, by the creation of a membership section for drillers in 1916, and by the amalgamation of the Sheet Iron Workers' and Light Platers' Society in 1919. None of these developments took place smoothly. The drillers were accepted into membership only on condition that they did not compete for employment in other branches of the boilermaking trade. The amalgamation with the Sheet Iron Workers' and Light Platers' Society led later to prolonged litigation in which it was held that the amalgamation, inadvertently, had not been carried out according to the requirements of the existing law.

The need for trade union co-operation not only between engineering and shipbuilding workers but between all unions was underlined repeatedly in the period 1906–39. It was not until after the First World War, however, that the TUC began to act more as a centre of leadership for the trade union movement rather than as an organisation which existed primarily to formulate trade union views at an annual congress on issues which might be the subject of legislation and then to make representations about them to the government of the day. Even so, the authority of the TUC was very limited except in circumstances where the unions were prepared voluntarily to give their support to a common policy. On the other hand, the tradition was maintained and strengthened that there should be one and one only national trade union centre in Britain. Other trade union federations existed based primarily on common industrial interests but they were not regarded, nor did they see themselves, as rivals to the TUC. There were still some white-collar unions outside the TUC during their period but they did not challenge the central representative role of the TUC. This tradition of the existence of a single national trade union centre in Britain, irrespective of religious, industrial or occupational differences, has been of great advantage to the trade union movement.

The First World War did much to demonstrate the need for a stronger trade union national centre. There was a range of issues including, for example, regulations relating to labour mobility, provisions for arbitration, dilution, rent control, rationing, conscription and reserved occupations, on which the Government sought the views and assistance of the unions. Conversely, union members wanted their views to be made known to the Government because decisions were being taken which affected their working conditions and living standards.

At the end of the war the need for the collective representation of trade union views was even greater. All kinds of promises had been made during the war to win the co-operation of workers. The unions had to press that these promises were not forgotten. Millions of men and women who had gone into the armed forces, nursing and the arms industries had to be rehabilitated in other occupations.

Following the end of the First World War the unions managed to secure a significant reduction in working hours in most industries. Yet it is at least open to speculation that even more might have been achieved had there been a stronger central co-ordination of the campaign for a shorter working week. The fact was, however, that even the sections of the working class that were prepared to do more, including the members of the Boilermakers' Society, did not at that stage see the TUC as having a significant role in the campaign.

Another issue in the period immediately following the ending of the First World War which underlined the need for a united trade union campaign was that of foreign intervention against the Russian revolution and the creation of a Soviet Republic. The British Government was deeply involved in the armed intervention. It was stopped in its intervention by the action of British trade unionists, among whom boilermakers played a significant part, in preventing the despatch of supplies to assist the armed forces of counter revolution. The campaign to stop the war was organised nationally with both official and 'unofficial' participation, but it would have been impossible for one union alone to have achieved the objective which the campaign had set itself.

In the 1920s it was the sequence of events surrounding the mining industry that emphasised as never before the central role of the TUC. Millions of workers in Britain, including the membership of the Boilermakers' Society, grasped the simple but profound truth that the miners were constantly in the front line of the struggle about wages, hours of work and employment. They saw that to assist the miners was not only an act of compassion for a group of workers whose lives were spent in arduous conditions but was also an act of self-interest. Every victory secured by the miners deterred the employers in other industries; every defeat became the signal to many employers to attempt to reduce wages elsewhere.

This is not the place to discuss at length the reasons for the defeat of the General Strike. It can, however, be asserted with certainty that it was not defeated because of any lack of rank-and-file solidarity with the miners or any failure of workers to respond to the call for strike action. The working class of Britain, including boilermakers, accepted for the moment that the leadership of the movement was in the hands of the TUC. It represented an immense expression of power. For various reasons this was later to give way to widespread disillusionment, but nothing can diminish the historic significance of the readiness of workers in 1926 to express their solidarity with the miners.

In 1931 the TUC took the lead in dissociating the labour movement from the policies advocated and pursued by the three Labour Party leaders, MacDonald, Snowden and Thomas, who joined with Conservative MPs to form a new government. The TUC pointed out that the proposed policy of cutting unemployment pay, reducing wages and salaries in areas of public employment and reducing the level of public expenditure, far from helping to solve the economic crisis would only make it worse. This warning proved to be right. In the grim days of 1931, when so many in the labour movement felt they had been betrayed by some of the most prominent of their political leaders, the TUC took the decisive stand which helped to preserve the integrity of the movement.

Similarly, in the campaign in the 1930s against unemployment and the means test there could be no substitute for the role of the

TUC. Certainly the campaign was helped and at times stimulated by political activists and, in particular, by the efforts of the 'unofficial' National Unemployed Workers' Movement which organised some of the hunger marches and some of the big demonstrations against unemployment and the means test. The NUWM also sought to build a bridge between the unemployed and the trade union organisation of employed workers, and to combat any attempt to exploit the unemployed either for anti-trade union purposes – as for example in strike-breaking – or for reactionary political purposes. The NUWM was sometimes treated with hostility by the TUC because it was regarded as a self-appointed body under Communist leadership. It was the TUC which provided the main forum for the trade union movement to express its opposition to unemployment and the means test and to work out the details of an alternative policy.

THE LIMITATIONS OF COLLECTIVE BARGAINING

Another lesson to be drawn from the period 1906–39 concerns the limitations of collective bargaining. This is not intended in any way as a denigratory observation. No one who reads the pages of this volume will be left with any doubt of the value of collective bargaining. Nevertheless, great as its contribution is, it also has its limitations. Collective bargaining may help on occasions to mitigate the worst effects of an economic depression on workers' standards but it does not by itself prevent unemployment. Through the 1920s and 1930s unemployment was the greatest scourge affecting boilermakers.

The long and bitter experience of unemployment points to the necessity for trade unionism to have a wider vision, extending beyond the boundaries of collective bargaining. The very existence of the TUC and its developing role in British trade unionism indicates how unions have come to recognise that their policies, their representations and their pressures must extend over a wide field of economic issues if the interests of trade unionists are to be effectively prosecuted. The depression in the shipbuilding industry, the effect of unemployment, the campaign for a 'scrap and build' scheme, the pressure for shipbuilding safety regulations and the campaign conducted at various levels to win holidays with pay, all served to emphasise to boilermakers that collective bargaining with employers needs to be supplemented by other efforts on various industrial, economic, social and political issues.

During his period as General Secretary John Hill never failed to point to the political lessons of his experience as a trade unionist. His purpose, as he saw it, was not only to obtain better terms and conditions of employment for the men he represented in collective bargaining, but to bring to an end the system of capitalism and to replace it with socialism. Capitalism, based on the private ownership of the principal industries, enables a favoured few to accumulate wealth and to enjoy privileges derived from the labour of those whom they employ. Moreover, capitalism leads inevitably to periodic booms and slumps which bring unnecessary suffering to millions of workers. The system is unplanned and lurches into crisis because of many kinds of uneven development and because of the contrast between the potential of production and the limited purchasing power of workers. John Hill on numerous occasions drew attention to the connection between the search for private profits, cheap raw materials, markets and war.

John Hill also drew the attention of the membership to the use made by the employers, and the political representatives whom they supported, of legislation to restrict trade union rights. He was, for example, a critic of the Osborne judgement of the House of Lords in relation to the use of trade union funds for political purposes, and of the subsequent Trade Union Act 1913. Trade unions, he argued, were entitled to help to secure political representation if this was the wish of the membership. Why then should a minority be entitled by law to contract out of a majority decision? The purpose, said John Hill, was none other than to weaken trade union representation.

John Hill was even more critical of the Trade Union and Trade Disputes Act 1927. He saw this Act as a vindictive measure designed to weaken trade unionism by curtailing the right of workers to act in solidarity, by widening the area of legal liability of pickets, by denying the right of civil service trade unionists to associate with other trade unionists, by protecting non-unionism in public employment and by changing 'contracting out' to 'contracting in' for the

329

payment of contributions for political purposes. In his comments on the Act John Hill emphasised that its sponsors were motivated by considerations of class interest. The Act represented, he argued, a legislative attack by the employers on the rights of workers. The Executive Council of the Boilermakers' Society fully supported the campaign against the 1927 Act and urged branches to hold special meetings for the purpose of expressing opposition.

In the 1930s the dominant international political issue was the advance of fascism in a number of European countries. From the outset John Hill was alert to the threat to trade unionism represented by fascism. He recognised that fascism was a form of capitalist rule which denied the most elementary democratic rights to citizens and, in particular, suppressed and waged a campaign of terror against the trade union and labour movement. The menace of fascism demonstrated as never before that trade unionists could not remain indifferent to politics. In Italy, Germany and Austria the trade union movement was temporarily destroyed. When Hitler took control in Czechoslovakia and when in Spain the Fascists came to power, due to the military intervention of Hitler and Mussolini, the trade union movement was similarly crushed.

John Hill did not hesitate in his articles in the monthly report of the Boilermakers' Society to draw attention to the sympathy for fascism shown in Britain by many Conservative leaders and Members of Parliament. He was more aware than most trade union leaders of his time that Britain's failure to join in effective collective security against the advance and aggression of fascism in Europe was due not so much to weakness as to political motivation. Given the choice between fascism, with the preservation of the capitalist system, or a strong labour movement with the possibility of social change, the preference of many Conservative Party leaders was for fascism. To this was added the attraction, as they saw it, that the fascist powers were totally hostile to the USSR and that their aggression might ultimately be diverted in that direction. Winston Churchill was one of the few Conservative leaders at that time who took a different view of the danger to Britain represented by Hitler.

With the change in General Secretary from John Hill to Mark Hodgson there was a change in political tone. Mark Hodgson's views were closer to the views of most of the prominent trade union leaders of his day. They were certainly opposed to fascism and they supported collective security against fascist aggression. On the other hand, in the decisive period of the opening months of the Spanish war when the Franco rebellion was launched with the backing of Hitler and Mussolini, they supported the policy of 'non-intervention'. The only practical effect of this policy was to give an enormous advantage to Franco. Hitler and Mussolini totally disregarded the request for non-intervention, whilst Britain and France denied the legitimate Spanish Government its undoubted legal right to buy arms for its own defence against insurrection and foreign intervention. This failure to save democracy in Spain served as the overture to the Second World War. The British trade union movement fairly quickly reversed its policy on the farce of 'non-intervention' but by then the British Government was well set on its course.

Similarly, on the tragic events leading to the total subjection of Czechoslovakia by Hitler in 1938 and 1939 the reaction of Mark Hodgson and many of his colleagues in the leadership of the Boilermakers' Society was similar to that of most, though by no means all, of the more prominent leaders of the British trade union and labour movement. There was no question of their hostility to fascism, to Hitler's threatened aggression or their support in principle for Czechoslovakia and collective security. But at the vital moment of the flight of the British Prime Minister, Neville Chamberlain, to Munich to meet Hitler they wavered. Temporarily, they were more inclined to join in the false euphoria that peace had been saved than to condemn the betrayal of Czechoslovakia. Within days their fears were aroused and their consciousness grew of the real nature of the surrender.

In the 1930s the London District Committee of the Boilermakers' Society demonstrated a sharp awareness of the implications for trade unionism of the political events of the day. Their representatives were always to the fore in the campaigns against unemployment and the means test, for a shorter working week and against fascism and war. No doubt there were many individual members who were involved but a number of them, Ted Hill, Alf Whitney and Ted Williams, were in later years to play a prominent part in the national leadership of the Society.

THE MINORITY MOVEMENT

Of special interest in the history of the Boilermakers' Society in the 1920s was the role of the Minority Movement, and in particular of Harry Pollitt. Pollitt's own estimation of the contribution of the Minority Movement has already been quoted: '. . . despite mistakes and weaknesses it did a great deal of good work inside the trade unions'. In contrast, the opinion of the Executive Council of the Society at the time of the ballot on Aitken Ferguson's appeal against the decision not to accept his nomination for election as a TUC delegate, was that the effect on trade unions of the activity of the Minority Movement and of the Communist Party was demoralising. They said:

> Attention was also drawn to the unconstitutional committees of Communist origin which had been formed, and circulars which had been issued ridiculing officials, and advising members to oppose decisions constitutionally reached, dealing with trade questions.

How far were these very different estimations of the Minority Movement justified? On the one hand, the Minority Movement sought to alert the trade union movement to the preparations being made by the employers, with the support of the Conservative Party leadership, for a major assault on working-class standards and on trade union organisation. The assault took place in 1926 in the events which led to the General Strike. The TUC leadership did not demonstrate the same alertness to the many signs of an impending battle.

On the conduct of the General Strike the Minority Movement was fiercely critical. It argued that the workers, who responded so magnificently to the call for strike action, were let down by the General Council. The TUC leadership, it was said, became frightened by the power which they had released. They ended the strike not because of its weakness but because of its strength. They seized upon the hint of a compromise settlement as justification for ending the strike when, indeed, a compromise had not been conceded by the Government. They took this decisive step not because they were easily deceived but because they were eagerly looking for any grounds to end the strike.

The defence put up by the General Council of the TUC was that in exercising their leadership, and in order to retain the confidence of the millions of trade unionists who were supporting them, they had to demonstrate that they were responsive to suggestions for a conciliated settlement. They did not reject the overtures made to them and accepted at their face value the discussions and suggestions initiated by Samuel. These suggestions were subsequently repudiated by the right-wing forces in the Government, led by Winston Churchill.

The General Council also pointed out that constitutionally the unions had placed the conduct of the strike in the hands of the TUC. This was inevitable following the appeal of the miners for assistance. Once other unions were involved the miners could no longer claim autonomy in the conduct of their dispute. Similarly, the General Council insisted throughout that the strike was an industrial dispute and that it had never been part of their strategy to challenge the political authority of the Government. Once they had been given an indication that, as they believed, a compromise between the mine-owners and the miners was possible, the strike had achieved its purpose.

Some union leaders were probably of the view that, in the light of experience, the trade union movement should have avoided the confrontation of a General Strike in an economic situation in which eventual defeat for the miners was almost inevitable. They may have felt that a retreat by the miners would not necessarily have led to a worsening of conditions for workers in some other more prosperous industries.

At this distance from the events the balance of argument is on the side of the critics rather than with the defenders of the role of the General Council of the TUC in the conduct – and more particularly in the ending – of the General Strike. Many trade unionists felt they had been let down. The General Strike failed, but it was a vivid example of a failure of leadership. The leadership was without doubt much more representative of the general opinions of the rank and file than the Minority Movement, but in the historic days of the General Strike the mood of the workers moved strongly in favour of solidarity with the miners. When the strike was called off the views of the TUC leadership had moved out of step with the mood of the strikers.

A more serious point is to question whether the General Strike, despite the support given to it by workers, was not doomed from the very outset. The mining industry was already in serious decline and the problems of the economy could not be resolved by trade union action. Trade unionism is not a substitute for political action and economic change. The British working class were not ready for radical political change and, perhaps, the trade union leadership grasped by instinct that they were involved in a fight for which they, the leaders, had no real appetite and which they did not believe they could win.

In relation to the Mond–Turner discussions which followed the General Strike the predominant leadership of the TUC and the Minority Movement were again in sharp conflict. The General Council's view that in the aftermath of the General Strike no opportunity should be lost to maintain and develop collective bargaining arrangements and to try to bring to an end the victimisation of many trade unionists was surely valid. There had to be discussions with the employers and obviously in those discussions the employers could be expected to put forward their own suggestions. Moreover, some of the employers associated with Sir Alfred Mond represented the more far-sighted and prosperous sections of British industrial leadership. Some of the statements adopted as a result of the Mond–Turner discussions – notably on trade union recognition – were helpful.

The TUC was, of course, well aware that the group of employers associated with Sir Alfred Mond did not carry authority from the representative British employers' organisations. Nevertheless, they were an influential group and they were prepared to discuss issues with the trade union leadership on the basis of an acceptance of trade unionism and not of declared hostility to it. As the TUC leadership pointed out, the readiness of trade unionists to talk with employers about problems was in conformity with the very reason for trade union existence.

The criticisms made by Minority Movement supporters were directed primarily at the purpose of the Mond–Turner discussions. Illusions were being created, they said, that a policy of class collaboration to bring about what was described as industrial rationalisation would offer a way forward towards the recovery of capitalism. The reality, argued the Minority Movement, was very different. The storm clouds were gathering for an economic slump. The unions were being led into a blind alley. Despite the Mond–Turner discussions many employers, according to the Minority Movement, continued to attack trade unionism and to victimise trade unionists. Industrial rationalisation usually meant, it was said, nothing more than the speed-up of work and the reduction of the size of the workforce.

In retrospect, neither the views of the TUC leadership nor the Minority Movement can be dismissed as wrong. In the circumstances following the General Strike the TUC was right to enter into discussions with a group of influential employers who indicated that they accepted that the trade union movement had a part to play in dealing with industrial problems. But it is also true that some of the TUC leaders gave the impression that they saw these discussions as opening a new era of co-operation. This was, for example, reflected in statements made at the time in the Boilermakers' Society. The Minority Movement, on the other hand, was wrong in opposing the Mond–Turner discussions but justified in their warnings about the illusions created by leaders whose commitment to the Mond–Turner discussions was matched by their failure to recognise that, at best, the suggestions to emerge might be marginally helpful but would not offer radical measures to deal with the failings of British capitalism and the impending slump.

Another main area of conflict between the predominant trade union leadership and the Minority Movement concerned the creation of self-styled alternative centres of leadership. One of the most valuable weapons of a trade union is its organisational unity. The various centres of authority are determined by the constitutions of the unions. In the Boilermakers' Society, for example, the Executive Council, the General Council, the General Secretary, the district committees, the district delegates and the branches all had their respective powers. These were supplemented by the tradition, confirmed in the rules, of the holding of ballots on various questions.

This is not to suggest that trade union constitutions and practices are always the last word in democracy. Hence, great care has to be exercised when operating the constitution of a union and upholding the constitutional rights of the duly elected or appointed committees and officials, not to suppress the voice of dissent. Unity in action is not the same thing as unanimity in discussion. Moreover, within trade unions it is unlikely that significant changes will be made in policy or rules unless members of like mind discuss together how they can most effectively put forward their point of view. How to combine, on the one hand, proper respect for constitutional authority within unions and unity of action, and, on the other, the effective functioning of the democratic process, is one of the most difficult problems of trade union leadership.

The problem with the Minority Movement was that it saw itself for a number of years as a continuing centre of alternative leadership with organised groups and publications in each union. These groups did not hesitate on occasions to call on members to defy the policy decisions of the constitutional authorities of the unions. This was a situation which could not last.

The Minority Movement was itself the creation of a deeper split in the working-class movement. There is no doubt that the Minority Movement came into existence on the initiative of supporters of the Communist International. This International had been created following the Russian revolution. It was the conviction of Lenin and his colleagues that a sharp break had to be made from those in the labour movement whom they regarded as having betrayed the working class by siding with their respective governments in the First World War. Lenin believed that these leaders had failed to give militant leadership for social change at the end of the war.

This is not the place to discuss the circumstances of this split. It is sufficient to say that in relation to Britain – though there were plenty of grounds for criticism of many trade union and labour leaders – the putting forward of a programme for the discrediting of parliamentary democracy and its replacement by a Soviet society based on the dictatorship of the proletariat was dramatically unrealistic. As part of this policy most of the existing trade union leaders were attacked as the 'agents of the employing class within the labour movement'. Those who used 'left-wing phrases', as, for example, John Hill, were often regarded by the Minority Movement as the worst enemies because, it was alleged, their deception of the workers was all the greater.

At some stage this policy had to be brought to an end. Fortunately, it was, when after the coming to power of Hitler, there was a new realisation that the workers' movement could not afford such internecine war. It is fair to record that in Britain Pollitt himself, who had earlier led the Minority Movement faction in the Boilermakers' Society, played an important role in bringing about the change in policy. The Minority Movement was brought to an end. But by then much damage had been done. The majority of active trade unionists saw the Minority Movement as a disruptive force, owing no loyalty to the democratic machinery and centres of elected authority of British trade unionism but instead serving the interests of the Communist International and ultimately of a foreign power, the USSR.

The provocation and challenge of the Minority Movement to the constitutional authority of unions, though involving sometimes legitimate criticisms of policy, formed part of the background to the decision of the Boilermakers' Society to exclude Communists and Minority Movement supporters from eligibility for office. It was not a decision which even in the circumstances was justified. The membership was entitled, if it so wished, not to be represented by Communists and Minority Movement supporters, but the democratic way to exercise this choice was through the electoral processes of the Society. In fact, the exclusion from eligibility for office was introduced because Pollitt, in particular, had proved on successive occasions his popularity in the elections for the TUC and Labour Party delegations. This did not mean that Pollitt was successful in every election for which he stood. He was not, but as a rank-and-file representative for the TUC and Labour Party delegations he had shown that he was always a very strong candidate.

The manner in which Aitken Ferguson's appeal against exclusion from office was submitted to the membership was unfair. The real issue was whether a member who was qualified under the rules had the right to stand for office. Clearly he was. His personal opinions, whether of the left, right or centre, were irrelevant for the purpose of his eligibility for office. At no stage was it suggested that there was any provision in the rules which permitted the Executive Council to declare a qualified member ineligible for office on the grounds of his political opinions or support for a particular political party.

The issue, when presented to a ballot of the membership, was posed as for or against Communist representation. This was a deliberate confusion of the issue designed to secure a majority to deny Ferguson the right to stand for office. Pollitt was probably right when he declared that if the question had been taken to court the whole exercise would have been declared invalid. Members' rights under the rules cannot be over-ridden.

This is not to suggest that the Executive Council had no authority at all to declare candidates ineligible for office. If the rules specify, for example, that candidates for a particular post must be working at the trade, or unemployed and registered as such with the Society, or already occupying a full-time position with the Society, then the Executive Council are not only entitled to declare ineligible for office a member who fails to satisfy these conditions but they are under an obligation to do so. They were entitled, for example, to declare Pollitt ineligible in an election for membership of the Executive Council precisely because he did not satisfy the conditions set out under the rules.

Similarly, providing the rules specify that a member can be suspended from office, or declared ineligible for office, as a disciplinary measure against an offence, and providing that 'natural justice' has been observed in reaching the decision that an offence has been committed and that disciplinary action should be taken, the Executive Council are entitled to declare a particular member ineligible for office, at least for the period set out in the rules. There was, however, no suggestion of disciplinary charges against Ferguson or Pollitt. The sole ground for their exclusion was that they were Communists. There had been no change of rule to exclude Communists from any of the normal rights of membership.

In 1937 Pollitt appealed against his continued exclusion from eligibility to stand in the election for the TUC delegation. His appeal was rejected on a ballot of the membership. Again, it is unlikely that the decision to exclude Pollitt was valid under the then existing rules. No doubt, however, some of the members who voted in the ballot considered that a member who had not worked at the trade for many years should not represent the Society at the TUC. This was a reasonable view to put into the scales of the discussion and it was sensible that it should be expressed. The proper course, however, was either to have changed the rules to exclude out-of-trade members from eligibility for office and delegations, or alternatively for those members who did not want to be represented by an out-of-trade member to have expressed their preference in their vote.

TRADE UNION DEMOCRACY

These episodes in the 1920s and 1930s concerning eligibility for office and, similarly, the decisions made by ballot votes from time to time on changes in benefits and subscriptions which later proved to be inoperable, pointed to a weakness in the constitution of the Boilermakers' Society which persisted throughout the period 1906–39. There was no provision for a regular rank-and-file delegate assembly which could discuss at length policy questions and the administrative arrangements of the Society. The nearest to such an assembly was the General Council but it did not meet regularly and was brought together only after the members had decided by ballot that it should be convened. Moreover, the very occasional meetings of the General Council were confined almost entirely to discussions on possible changes in rules, benefits and subscriptions.

The holding of ballots on a variety of issues provided the membership with an opportunity to influence certain aspects of policy. The strongest area of influence was in the acceptance or rejection of proposed agreements with the employers, where the arguments were familiar to the membership. There was, incidentally, nothing in this experience to suggest that the membership was usually less militant than the leadership. Nevertheless, the holding of ballot votes as the primary means of members' influence was a truncated form of democracy, better than nothing but not a substitute for arrangements through which there could be a thorough discussion and exchange of opinion on disputed issues.

Balloting on issues, as distinct from balloting in elections, raises a number of preliminary questions which need to be answered. First, who determines which issue shall be submitted to a ballot? Secondly, who decides in what form the issue shall be presented? What, for example, will be the wording on the ballot paper, and will more than two options be offered for choice? Thirdly, who determines, and in what circumstances, whether the result of the ballot will be regarded as decisive or consultative? Fourthly, who determines whether statements or other material will be published concerning the ballot? Will statements expressing different views be permitted? Fifthly, what arrangements, if any, will be made to stimulate discussion and to provide for the exchange of opinions within branches and workplaces before the ballot takes place? Finally, what should be the relationship between the normal process of decision-making, whether at workplace level or through the branches, district committees, General Council and the Executive Council and, on the other hand, ballots?

In the concluding chapter of the first volume of this history it was suggested that the holding of referenda within the Society, with the simultaneous absence of regular delegate conferences and controversy within the journal, provided to a considerable extent a facade of democracy behind which there was authoritarian control exercised by the then General Secretary, Robert Knight, and a number of district delegates. The real requirements of democratic trade unionism, including the ventilation and conflict of views at all levels through regular meetings and conferences and a lively journal, were missing. It was only on workplace trade union issues that the bureaucracy, personified by Robert Knight, was unable to stifle the discussion of the membership. In the end, changes were forced on a reluctant leadership and a full-time Executive Council was introduced to provide a new and alternative source of authority.

John Hill, who occupied the post of General Secretary for the greater part of the period covered by this volume, was a very different person from Robert Knight. He was not a bureaucrat by temperament, whereas Robert Knight's great contribution to the development of the Society was his insistence on strict and meticulous control of the records, finances and administration at head office, district level and in the branches. John Hill was by inclination a militant who was suspicious of authority. He did not try to dominate the Society administratively in anything like the same way as Robert Knight. He was more concerned with ideas and with trade union action. In any case, because of the existence of a full-time Executive Council, it would have been very much more difficult for John Hill, even if he had had the inclination, which he had not, to restore the authoritarian control characteristic of Robert Knight's final years.

Nevertheless, it would have been better from every point of view in the turbulent years of the 1920s if the Society had developed means of determining major issues of policy by debate and resolution at annual delegate conferences. It would have avoided the situation where at the TUC and Labour Party conferences no one could be sure whether Harry Pollitt, in expressing very vigorously the point of view of the Minority Movement, was speaking with the full backing of the Boilermakers' Society. As John Hill observed, Pollitt had been elected by the membership and he could not be accused of hiding his views when he stood for election. On the other hand, Pollitt's point of view was not necessarily shared by other members of the delegation, but there were very few policy decisions taken by the Society to which the delegation could refer for guidance. It was an unsatisfactory situation.

TRADE UNION FINANCE

The period covered by this second volume marked a very important change in the finances of the Society and the part they played in the functioning of trade unionism. During the period covered by the first volume the Society was able to accumulate substantial reserves. Robert Knight's standard of management was of the highest order. The members looked to the Society for financial assistance in times of unemployment, sickness, accident and retirement:

> The emergence of a professional central administration in the Boilermakers' Society had much more to do with the need to accumulate and safeguard the funds of the Society and to distribute them fairly to members in need than with the creation of a solid front of members for purposes of collective bargaining and industrial struggle with employers. (Volume 1, History of the Boilermakers' Society)

In the period covered by the second volume of the history the circumstances changed radically. With the introduction of state social benefits the membership looked primarily to public funds for assistance during unemployment, sickness, absence through industrial accidents, and old age. Financial help from the Society was still regarded as important but the high level of unemployment for the greater part of the 1920s and the first half of the 1930s meant inevitably that benefits had either to be reduced or suspended.

In the 1920s the financial reserves of the Society took on a greater burden and assumed a new significance. The greater burden came from the payment of dispute benefit, particularly in national strikes or lockouts. The new significance was that the assets of the Society were now more of an industrial fighting fund than a reserve for provident benefits. In turn, the Executive Council and the General Secretary were strategists in trade union struggle and collective bargaining rather than administrators of a voluntary organisation which collected funds and distributed provident benefits but left the local membership, with the assistance of district delegates, to conduct their own negotiations. It was a change which was to be carried even further in later years.

Events in the History of the Boilermakers' Society 1906–1939

1906   Liberal Government elected.
       Period of social reform.
       Trade Disputes Act passed by Parliament.

1907   Boilermakers' Society decide by ballot to establish a panel of parliamentary candidates.
       Society threatened with national shipbuilding lockout arising from a local dispute at Walker shipyard.
       Shipbuilding Employers' Federation insist on a 'right to manage' provisional national procedure agreement. Boilermakers' Society humiliated.

1908   Wage reductions.
       Special committee established to make recommendations to overcome financial crisis in the Society.
       D. C. Cummings resigns as General Secretary.
       John Hill elected General Secretary on an election appeal for militancy.

1909   Members vote narrowly for reduced benefits and increased contributions.
       Executive Council reduced from seven to five members.
       Membership drops below 50,000.
       New procedure agreement in shipbuilding eliminates some of the objectionable features of the provisional agreement of 1907.
       Society decides by ballot to establish a drillers' section but proposed rule changes encounter opposition.

1910   Proposed rule changes to establish a drillers' section rejected.
       National shipbuilding lockout lasts for three and a half months and ends in victory for the Society. Employers withdraw proposal to fine strikers.
       Following the Osborne judgement of the House of Lords the Society votes by ballot for the use of funds for political purposes.

1911   Trade revives and wage increases secured.
       Widespread industrial unrest.
       Death of Robert Knight, General Secretary 1870–99.
       Daily Herald established and supported by Boilermakers' Society.

1912   Members vote not to have a procedure agreement in shipbuilding.
       Approved Society established for purposes of National Insurance Act.
       Miners' strike – more than 1 million workers involved. Substantial donation made by Society to miners.
       Executive Council favour new procedure agreement in shipbuilding. General Secretary disagrees. Members vote in favour of EC proposals providing local issues are settled locally.
       Liverpool Shipwrights' Association federate with Boilermakers' Society.
       Unsuccessful negotiations on amalgamation with Shipwrights' Association.

1913   Movement for eight-hour day. John Hill calls for rank and file action.
       Merseyside boilermakers win forty-seven-hour working week.
       Members vote by ballot in support of political objects under Trade Union Act, 1913.
       Dublin lockout. John Hill visits Dublin as part of TUC delegation and

expresses strong support for Dublin workers. Society gives substantial financial assistance.

Ten to one majority for strike action in support of national wage claim in shipbuilding. Further negotiations lead to settlement.

1914 Outbreak of First World War.

John Hill at first equivocal but eventually expresses support for war effort against German aggression.

1915 Unrest on the Clyde. Formation of the Clyde Workers' Committee.

Unions accept suspension of the right to strike. John Hill signs an appeal condemning any restriction on output on war work.

Proposal to grant a retirement allowance to James Conley (twenty-eight years a full-time official) defeated in a ballot vote. New proposal for a donation to Conley carried by narrow majority after Conley had been defeated in seeking re-election as district delegate.

New district delegate, William Mackie, is more militant. He was a leader of the 1915 unrest on the Clyde.

Narrow majority to admit drillers into membership, but drillers must not 'progress to any other section of the trade'.

South African Council of the Society brought to an end.

Scheme approved for closer working between engineering and shipbuilding unions.

1916 Wave of strikes on Clydeside.

1917 New arrangements by an official Committee on Production for a review of wages every four months.

Another militant, J. M. Airlie, elected as district delegate on the Clyde.

Joint working agreement with the Shipwrights' Association. Later extended to the Blacksmiths' Society.

Two revolutions in Russia. Strong support expressed by John Hill who, following the October revolution, becomes very critical of the continued conduct of the First World War. Boilermakers' Society join with other unions to discuss war aims and oppose any expeditions of conquest.

1918 Moves towards amalgamation between the boilermakers, shipwrights and blacksmiths fail.

John Hill's views about the war and the Russian revolution stimulate controversy within the Society.

Agreement with shipbuilding employers for restoration of pre-war trade practices.

Discussions begin for a new shipbuilding procedure agreement but progress is slow.

Society presses strongly for a shorter working week at end of war. Society prepared to fight for a forty-four-hour week but majority of unions in shipbuilding and engineering favour compromise on forty-seven-hour week.

Membership exceeds 90,000.

Alfred Short elected as the first boilermakers' MP; successful at Wednesbury in General Election, December 1918.

1919 Forty-seven-hour week introduced in engineering and shipbuilding. Society votes by a majority of more than two to one to reject the employers' offer but the combined vote of the other unions shows a majority for acceptance.

Harry Pollitt attracts attention as secretary of the London District Committee of the Society and his leadership of the 'Hands off Russia' movement.

Membership exceeds 100,000.

Many local disputes. Society expenditure on dispute benefit exceeds £100,000 in one year.

344

Rank-and-file strike action on Clydeside for forty-hour week.

Agreement with engineering employers for recognition of shop stewards.

Sheet Iron Workers' and Light Platers' Society amalgamate with Boilermakers' Society.

1920   Unions dissatisfied with war-time arbitration arrangements. Agreement brought to an end.

Society does not participate in amalgamation discussions leading to formation of Amalgamated Engineering Union.

Amalgamated Union of Shipbuilding, Engineering and Construction Workers established as a federal union for boilermakers, shipwrights and blacksmiths.

Wider federal union proposed to be known as the General Combination of Ship Constructional and Engineering Workers to include also carpenters and sheet-metal workers, together with boilermakers, shipwrights and blacksmiths.

Industrial action brings to an end war of intervention against Russia. Boilermakers play significant part in campaign.

1921   Trade depression brings amalgamation moves to an end.

Boilermakers vote by large majority to reject wage reductions demanded by shipbuilding employers but are outvoted by other unions.

Society makes substantial donation to miners involved in national strike.

40,000 members out of work.

Successive wage reductions both in engineering and shipbuilding.

1922   Defeat for unions in an engineering national lockout. Boilermakers' Society the last to concede defeat.

Members decide narrowly by ballot to remain affiliated to the Engineering and Shipbuilding Trades Federation.

National shipbuilding lockout to enforce wage reductions. Society's members vote heavily to resist but the aggregated vote of the other unions reveals more divided opinions.

More wage cuts.

David Williams, a member of the Society but not a sponsored candidate, elected as Labour MP for Swansea.

1923   Boilermakers' Society refuse to accept a new overtime agreement concluded between the Shipbuilding Employers' Federation and the Federation of Engineering and Shipbuilding Trades. Society expelled from FEST.

National shipbuilding lockout of boilermakers lasts from 30 April to 16 November. Dispute finally ended with a compromise.

Expenditure far exceeds income of the Society. £155,000 paid in dispute benefit, £96,000 in unemployment benefit, £70,000 in superannuation benefit and £50,000 in sickness benefit. Contributions amounted to only £135,000.

General Election results in a minority Labour Government. Three boilermakers elected as Labour MPs.

1924   Industrial Court award on shipbuilding overtime vindicates the stand taken by the Society in the shipbuilding lockout but does not grant the full claim.

Special measures to deal with financial problems of the Society. First class membership subscriptions increased to 2s per week.

Two Communists, Aitken Ferguson and Harry Pollitt, elected to the parliamentary panel of the Society.

Labour Party Conference decides that no member of the Communist Party shall be eligible for membership of the Labour Party or for endorsement as a Labour candidate.

Another boilermaker, J. Gibbins, elected in a by-election as a Labour MP.

Fall of minority Labour Government.

345

In General Election four boilermakers elected as Labour MPs.

Short-lived revival in trade. Many members secure wage increases.

Legal action by three members of the former Sheet Iron Workers' and Light Platers' Society to recover some of the funds absorbed into the Boilermakers' Society at the time of the amalgamation.

1925 More than 25,000 members unemployed. Society urge need for 'scrap and rebuild' scheme to help recovery in shipbuilding industry.

Joint inquiry by shipbuilding employers and unions into foreign competition and working conditions.

Membership falls to 74,287.

Mine-owners demand lower wages and longer hours from miners. Solidarity from railway and other transport workers helps miners to avert defeat. 'Red Friday'. Government prepare for industrial struggle.

1926 General Strike. Boilermakers' Society vote to give General Council authority to organise the strike. 10,441 members on strike in coal, railways and steel.

Strike called off by General Council on assurances – which proved worthless – of a compromise settlement. Many workers victimised and conditions worsened in many firms. Humiliating terms for resumption of work on railways. John Hill defends the action of the General Council.

Society in financial difficulty. Many economies made.

Society's members in railway workshops reject by ballot proposed new negotiating procedure with railway companies.

Society's members in shipbuilding reject by ballot proposed new joint working arrangements with other unions and a new negotiating procedure with the Shipbuilding Employers' Federation.

1927 Society no longer eligible to administer state unemployment benefit because it cannot afford to pay unemployment benefit from its own funds.

Press conduct campaign against the Society and its financial difficulties.

Trade Disputes and Trade Unions Act passed by Parliament. Society participate in campaign of opposition.

Unemployment among members falls from nearly 30,000 to 11,000.

Membership continues to decline.

Members reject by ballot vote wages offer by Engineering Employers' Federation but aggregated vote of all engineering unions is in favour of acceptance.

Members reject by ballot EC proposal to reduce number of district delegates.

Sharp controversy in the Society regarding Pollitt's role as a delegate of the Society at the Labour Party conference and at the TUC.

Mond–Turner discussions initiated.

1928 EC decide to exclude Communists from nomination for TUC and Labour Party delegations. An appeal by Aitken Ferguson against this decision is rejected on a ballot vote of the members.

Communists and Minority Movement supporters banned from all representative positions within the Society.

John Hill supports Mond–Turner discussions. Society support continuation of the discussions.

The Minority Movement, of which Pollitt is now the secretary, attacks the Mond–Turner discussions as 'class collaboration'.

Wage reductions in railway industry.

National wage increase in shipbuilding.

1929 TUC report on disruptive activities. Unions urged to take action against Communists and Minority Movement supporters.

Members again reject by ballot proposed shipbuilding procedure agreement.

Shipbuilding employers reject request by Society to strengthen agreement for control of overtime.

Society's bank overdraft reaches £150,000. Further reduction in benefits.

Second minority Labour Government takes office.

Four boilermakers elected as Labour MPs.

Society urge Government to encourage building of new ships.

1930 30 per cent of shipbuilding workers unemployed.

Society in competition with Constructional Engineering Union for the organisation of structural steel workers.

1931 Wage reductions and worsened conditions for many members.

Seven weeks bitter dispute in London ship repair. Ted Hill secretary of dispute committee.

Ted Hill defeats sitting district delegate in election.

Scale of benefits again cut. Superannuation benefit payments exceed the total annual income of the Society.

World economic crisis.

Fall of Labour Government. A number of Labour leaders join in a coalition 'National' Government. Opposition from the TUC and the labour movement.

General Election results in big defeat for Labour. Only one boilermaker elected to Parliament.

'National' Government cut unemployment benefit and introduce means test for longer-term unemployed.

1932 More than 50 per cent of members unemployed.

Superannuation benefit again reduced.

Further wage cuts and worsening of conditions. Despite financial difficulty Society collects money to assist cotton workers engaged in an industrial dispute.

1933 Society express concern at activities of National Shipbuilders Security Ltd in closing down shipyards.

Shipbuilding employers seek to introduce new category of 'ship welder'. Society and other unions do not resist welding but oppose any scheme to introduce cheap labour.

Demonstrations against unemployment and the means test.

Society sponsor successful motion at TUC calling for legislation for the control of overtime. Society conduct campaign to limit overtime.

Society warmly welcome President Roosevelt's measures in the USA to stimulate employment.

Hitler comes to power in Germany. Repression against German labour movement. Support for Hitler from big business.

Further economies made by Society to reduce expenditure.

Action taken by EC against a group of disruptive members in Belfast and Birkenhead who allege irregularities in the finances of the Society. No evidence to support allegations.

Special section established to assist recruitment in HM Dockyards.

Beginning of long dispute on the Mersey concerning overtime.

1934 Breakaway branches established in Belfast.

Membership falls to just under 50,000 of whom more than 5,000 are retired.

Slow improvement in trade.

Finances of the Society show a surplus of annual income over expenditure of about £15,000. 'Scrap and rebuild' scheme for shipping introduced by British Government.

Wage increases negotiated for members employed on railways.

Seven weeks' strike in London ship repair. Employers eventually withdraw proposals for wage reductions.

Contingent from Society join in greeting hunger marchers in Hyde Park, London.

Fascist attack on workers in Austria.

Peace ballot. British people support collective security. Campaign for 'united front' against fascism and war.

TUC circulars for the exclusion of Communists from trade union positions.

Centenary celebrations of the Society.

1935 Wage increases in engineering.

Italian attack on Abyssinia.

EC oppose any further reduction in number of full-time officials. Members vote to retain office of Assistant General Secretary.

Special campaign to organise apprentices.

Resignation of John Hill as General Secretary.

General Election – substantial victory for Conservatives and their allies. Two boilermakers elected as Labour MPs.

1936 Mark Hodgson elected General Secretary. John Hill presented with the gold badge of the TUC on his retirement.

Trade revives and membership rises to more than 50,000.

Wage increases negotiated in shipbuilding and on the railways.

Piece work and overtime embargo in London ship repair. Embargo lasts for twelve months and leads to settlement for wage increases and reduced hours.

Wage increases and improved nightshift conditions negotiated in engineering.

Formation of Confederation of Shipbuilding and Engineering Unions. Boilermakers vote by ballot to affiliate.

Breakaway Belfast branches rejoin the Society.

London District Committee active in the campaign against fascism.

1937 Wage increases negotiated in shipbuilding. Riveters and caulkers secure craftsman's time rate in shipbuilding.

Wage increases and improved overtime conditions negotiated in engineering.

Introduction of holidays with pay.

Apprentices strike. Engineering unions win right to negotiate for apprentices, boys and youths.

Pollitt's appeal against exclusion from eligibility to stand for TUC delegation rejected on a ballot vote of the members.

TUC youth charter launched.

1938 Financial benefits improved.

Negotiating rights secured for apprentices, boys and youths in shipbuilding.

Wage increases and holidays with pay secured in shipbuilding.

Society secures representation on Railway Shopmen's Council.

Munich agreement between Hitler and British Government for dismemberment of Czechoslovakia. Protest by labour movement.

Controversy on 'united front' and 'popular front'.

Death of Alfred Short, the boilermakers' first MP.

Mark Hodgson nominated by more than 100 branches for re-election as General Secretary. Re-elected unopposed.

1939 Membership exceeds 60,000.

Wage increases in engineering and shipbuilding.

TUC appeal for help for Spanish Government against Franco rebellion.

Industrial Court rejects claim for railway shopmen.

Germany occupies the whole of Czechoslovakia.

USSR and Germany conclude treaty of non-aggression.